REREADING FREDERICK JACKSON TURNER

REREADING

FREDERICK JACKSON TURNER

*"The Significance of the Frontier in
American History" and Other Essays*

WITH COMMENTARY BY

JOHN MACK FARAGHER

YALE UNIVERSITY PRESS   NEW HAVEN & LONDON

Published by Henry Holt and Company in 1994.
Published by Yale University Press in 1998.

Printed in the United States of America.

Library of Congress Cataloging-in-Publication Data
Turner, Frederick Jackson, 1861–1932.
Rereading Frederick Jackson Turner : "The significance of the frontier in
American history", and other essays / with commentary by John Mack Faragher.
p.   cm.
Originally published : New York : H. Holt and Co., 1994.
Includes bibliographical references.
ISBN 0-300-07593-6 (pbk. : alk. paper)
1. Frontier thesis. 2. Frontier and pioneer life—United States. 3. Sectionalism
(United States) 4. West (U.S.)—History. 5. United States—History—Philosophy.
6. United States—Territorial expansion. I. Faragher, John Mack, 1945–. II. Title.
[E179.5.T9577 1998]
973—dc21
98–12872
CIP

A catalogue record for this book is available from the British Library.

The paper in this book meets the guidelines for permanence and durability of
the Committee on Production Guidelines for Book Longevity of the Council on
Library Resources.

10 9 8 7 6 5 4 3 2 1

To Alvin Robert Faragher

C O N T E N T S

"The existence of an area of free land,
its continuous recession, and the advance
of American settlement westward
explain American development."

—FREDERICK JACKSON TURNER, 1893

REREADING
FREDERICK JACKSON TURNER

"A NATION THROWN BACK UPON ITSELF"

FREDERICK JACKSON TURNER
AND THE FRONTIER

It has been more than a century since Frederick Jackson Turner first read his paper "The Significance of the Frontier in American History" before an audience of some two hundred historians assembled in Chicago for the "World's Columbian Exposition," the celebration of the four hundredth anniversary of Europeans' discovery of the Americas. Yet Turner's essay remains the classic expression of the "frontier thesis": that "the existence of an area of free land, its continuous recession, and the advance of American settlement westward, explain American development"; that this frontier accounted for American democracy and character; and that at the end of the nineteenth century the continental frontier finally closed forever, with uncertain consequences for the American future.

Turner's essay is the single most influential piece of writing in the history of American history. According to the late historian William Appleman Williams, "His thesis rolled through the universities and into popular literature as a tidal wave." By 1910, the year Turner assumed a chair at Harvard University and the presidency of the American Historical Association, his observation had become the commanding view of the American past, a position it held for more than half a century. The frontier thesis became the most familiar model of American history, the one learned in school, extolled by politicians, and screened each Saturday afternoon at the Bijou. A few years after his death in 1932, Turner was awarded a posthumous Pulitzer Prize, and in the early 1950s a survey of American historians placed his book of essays *The Frontier in American History* (published by Henry Holt in 1920) second on their list of favorites, sandwiched between Vernon Parrington's *Main Currents in American History* and Charles and Mary Beard's *The Rise of American Civilization*. As late as 1964, another survey of historians found Turner's ideas "still dominant."[1]

But nothing about the proceedings in Chicago a century ago forecast such remarkable success. By the time Turner took his turn at the podium on the evening of July 12, 1893, it was already rather late. The last of five historical addresses, his followed a turgid exposition entitled "Early Lead Mining in Illinois and Wisconsin." Most of his audience had spent the day touring the "White City"—the exposition grounds on Chicago's South Side—and many had accepted Buffalo Bill Cody's invitation to a special performance of his Wild West show. Turner had remained behind, "in the final agonies," he wrote a friend, "of getting out a belated paper." It was understandable if the assistant professor from the University of Wisconsin could barely contain his enthusiasm for the freshly minted ideas in his address, but it was equally unsurprising if a number of the exhausted historians had already begun to nod off. "The audience reacted with the bored indifference normally shown a young instructor from a backwater college reading his first professional paper," one of those present later remembered. When Turner finished there was not a single question from the audience, and he must have returned to his room in bitter disappointment. Over the next few days and weeks a number of newspapers reported on the gathering, but Turner and his paper barely rated a mention.[2]

Of course, Turner did not long suffer midwestern isolation. His brilliance was to speak directly to the sense of crisis enveloping the intellectual discourse of the nation in 1893. The stock market had crashed shortly before the Chicago meeting, and that year some six hundred banks closed, more than fifteen thousand commercial houses failed, and seventy-four railroad corporations went into the hands of receivers. Unemployment rose to levels greater than any time in living memory. The Turner thesis about the closing of the continental frontier offered an explanation for the crisis—the United States had reached a critical watershed in its history—and to many it also seemed to suggest a way out. Just as the frontier had been essential to Americans' becoming who we were as a people, so it would require "new frontiers" to insure our continued development.

Turner was no ivory-tower historian; he was intimately involved with his times. But this explanation of his eventual success is too passive, for it discounts Turner's own role in the rise of his thesis. As Ray Allen Billington made clear in his fine biography, the man was a tireless promoter of his own cause. Faced with the difficulty of getting a hearing for his "new viewpoints," Turner later wrote, "I found it necessary to hammer pretty hard and pretty steadily on the frontier idea to 'get it in.'" When his essay appeared in print in 1894, he purchased hundreds of offprints and distributed them widely, not only to colleagues and associates but also to prominent members of the national intellectual elite—a practice he followed with all his publications. When not teaching or researching, he was usually on the lecture circuit, speaking to alumni audiences, teachers' groups, Chautauqua institutes, and civic societies. From the time he won an undergraduate oratorical medal, public speaking had been one of his greatest gifts. He had a deep, melodious voice that commanded attention—an admirer wrote of sitting "in quiet rapture under the spell of [his] words, as harmonious as poetry"—and the oratorical impress is clear in nearly all his published essays. Over the years he worked his lectures into articles that he placed in publications such as the *Atlantic Monthly*, *World's Work*, or *Review of Reviews*, the most influential national magazines of the day.[3]

Turner honed his ideas in the public forum and presented them as part of the public debate—his history was part of fin-de-siècle discourse. Thus conceived as part of a contemporary political debate, it should come as no surprise that his version of western history has lost much of its explanatory power and punch. What endures is Turner's commitment to history as contemporary knowledge, his understanding that debates about the past are always simultaneously debates about the present. It marks him as America's first truly modern historian.

"Each age writes the history of the past anew with reference to the conditions uppermost in its own time," Turner declared in his first published essay, "The Significance of History," written in 1891, the year of his professorial appointment at Wisconsin. Appearing in an obscure local journal, the piece had little immediate influence, but it denoted one of the earliest expressions of a presentist sensibility that would become the hallmark of the "new history" of the Progressive generation of historians such as James Harvey Robinson, Carl Becker, and Charles Beard. Nearly twenty years later in 1910, when Turner read his presidential address, "Social Forces in American History," to the meeting of the American Historical Association, he could refer to the "familiar doctrine that each age studies its history anew and with interests determined by the spirit of the time." To be sure, Turner's political temperament was that of a small-town, midwestern Republican, and his Progressivism was rather timid, certainly when compared to the rebelliousness of Beard. "I am determined not to get so interested actively," Turner wrote to a friend in 1911, "that I shall not be able to tell my story without prejudice." Nevertheless, he made it clear that his historical writing was shaped by a contemporary agenda.[4]

❧

The "conditions uppermost" for Turner were those associated with the great transformations of American life as the nation moved from a rural and agrarian past to an urban and industrial future. He opened his famous frontier essay by quoting a federal report that concluded, on the basis of maps prepared from the results of the 1890 census, that the unsettled land of the West was so rapidly disappearing that the "frontier line" had finally disappeared. This observation, Turner declared, marked "the closing of a great historic movement."

> Since the days when the fleet of Columbus sailed into the waters of the New World, America has been another name for opportunity, and the people of the United States have taken their tone from the incessant expansion which has not only been open but has even been forced upon them. He would be a rash prophet who should assert that the expansive character of American life has now entirely ceased. Movement has been its dominant fact, and, unless this training has no effect upon a people, the American energy will continually demand a wider field for its exercise. But never again will such gifts of free land offer themselves.

Turner's focus as a historian would remain on that frontier past, but it was the discontinuity of that past with the present that provided his inquiry its moral momentum. The concluding line in this most famous of American historical essays spoke directly to the looming sense of national crisis: "And now, four centuries from the discovery of America, at the end of a hundred years of life under the Constitution, the frontier has gone, and with its going has closed the first period of American history."

Turner's argument for the closing of the frontier has not held up well. His critics have long pointed out that far more public land in the trans-Mississippi West was taken up in the years after 1890 than in the years before. Western settlements continued to expand in the decades after the 1890s, yet on the census maps of 1900 and 1910 the "frontier line" made a mysterious reappearance. Frank and Deborah Popper recently pointed out that using Turner's own definition of "unsettled," there are in the late twentieth century 149 "frontier" counties in the West, and that many areas of the western Great Plains are steadily *losing* population. The cartography that so inspired Turner, it turns out, was less a work of science than of the imagination. A century later, the West has yet to fill up.[5]

A fair reading of Turner's essays, however, indicates in using the word "closing" he had something more complex in mind. He acknowledged that "great crowds gather at the land lotteries of the government as the remaining fragments of the public domain are flung to hungry settlers," but he argued that these lands "constitute the mountain and arid regions, only a small fraction of them capable of conquest, and then only by the application of capital and combined effort. The free lands that made the American pioneer have gone." He consistently talked of the fundamental distinction between the former era of the "solitary backwoodsman wielding his axe," and the present one of "companies capitalized at millions, operating railroads, sawmills, and all the enginery [*sic*] of modern machinery to harvest the remaining trees." But these more careful statements (from "Contributions of the West to American Democracy" and "Pioneer Ideals and the State University") did not have the impact of the original. It was the frontier essay—which Turner was proud to have reprinted widely in the thirty years after its delivery—that continued to shape the thinking of both his admirers and his critics. What got Turner into trouble was his oratorical attraction to hyperbole, his declaration that the frontier was *gone*. Later in his life, as his critics began to gather steam, he reacted in exasperation. "Of course the frontier did not come to an end 'with a

bang' in 1890," he wrote to a colleague; still, he insisted, "the importance of the frontier movement as a large factor in American history
did reach its close about that time."[6]

A strong case can be made in support of Turner's argument for
discontinuity. The decade of the 1890s closed a long period of economic
expansion kicked off in 1849 by the California Gold Rush and propelled
forward by the construction of rail lines across the Great West. The
crash and the resulting depression of 1893 ended this "entrepre-
neurial" phase of American capitalism and inaugurated the great
movement toward merger and consolidation that resulted in what
Turner described as "such a concentration of capital in the control of
fundamental industries as to make a new epoch." Moreover, although
the West was in no danger of "filling up," the last decade of the century
culminated a century of continental expansion. In 1889 and 1890 six
new western states entered the union, and over the next dozen years
the admission of the final four—Utah, Oklahoma, Arizona, and New
Mexico—finally completed the process of statemaking in the contig-
uous territory of the continent that Thomas Jefferson had inaugurated
with his Land Ordinance of 1784. There was real substance to Turner's
sense of "closure"—the West and the nation entered a new historical
phase around the turn of the century.

If the history of expansion was the key to understanding the American past, to many it offered the solution to contemporary problems as
well. After reading Turner's essay, Stuyvesant Fish, the president of
the Illinois Central Railroad, called Asia and the Pacific America's
"new West." Woodrow Wilson—who declared that all his ideas about
expansion originated in conversations with Turner when they were
both graduate students at Johns Hopkins—wrote that with the continent occupied "and reduced to the uses of civilization," the nation
must inevitably turn to "new frontiers in the Indies and in the
Far Pacific." President Theodore Roosevelt argued that American

colonies in the Pacific were the logical and necessary extension of continental westering, and in his typically bellicose manner likened Filipinos to Apaches and anti-imperialists to "Indian lovers." In the 1950s, Nelson Rockefeller wrote, "With the closing of our own frontier, there is hope that other frontiers still exist in the world."[7]

Turner understood the connection that Americans made between the West and the world. "This extension of power [was] the logical outcome of the nation's march to the Pacific," he wrote in 1910. "Having completed the conquest of the wilderness, and having consolidated our interests, we are beginning to consider the relations of democracy and empire." But even as Roosevelt urged his countrymen into a battle for imperial possessions, Turner lamented the "wreckage of the Spanish War." He, too, saw the necessity for new American frontiers, but he made a case for what amounted to the moral equivalent to westering.

Roosevelt envisioned a kind of American *reconquista*—the strenuous challenge of extending the nation's power against a savage enemy. But as historian Richard Slotkin has put it, Turner's project for the nation was "recuperative." The frontier indeed had operated as "a gate of escape" in the past, but as Turner argued in "The Problem of the West," with the close of the era of continental expansion the nation was now "thrown back upon itself." Social reorganization must replace "imperious will and force," he wrote in "The West and American Ideals." Turner placed much of his hope for the future in an expanded system of educational opportunity that would substitute for the social mobility of the frontier West. "The test tube and the microscope are needed rather than ax and rifle," he wrote; "in place of old frontiers of wilderness, there are new frontiers of unwon fields of science." In Turner's vision the American university system would be redesigned, keeping pioneer ideals alive by training new generations of leaders who would seek to "reconcile popular government and culture with the huge industrial society of the modern world."[8]

In the essays he wrote during and after World War I, Turner began to argue that the new era also called for a new spirit. In his original frontier essay, he had celebrated the spirit of individualism that he believed had driven the pioneers across the continent. A quarter century later, however, in "Middle Western Pioneer Democracy," he lamented "these slashers of the forest, these self-sufficing pioneers, raising the corn and live stock for their own need, living scattered and apart." Today, he wrote, "we are looking with a shock upon a changed world. The national problem is no longer how to cut and burn away the vast screen of the dense and daunting forest; it is how to save and wisely use the remaining timber." Struggling to resurrect a "usable past" from the pioneer legacy, he ended his essay by calling for a "revival of the old pioneer conception of the obligations and opportunities of neighborliness.... In the spirit of the pioneer's 'house raising' lies the salvation of the Republic."

This was the tone Turner brought to his final essays on sections in American history. These were, in part, calls for American historians to study *place* as well as *process*; in part, historical expositions on the importance of regions and sections in American history. But like all his essays, they were also linked to the contemporary debate about American culture, and Turner took the opportunity to emphasize the important role regional attachments would need to play in overcoming the atomistic tendencies born on the frontier. Mobility, he hoped, would in the new era give way to stability, and communities would grow stronger. "The world needs now more than ever before the vigorous development of a highly organized provincial life," he wrote in "The Significance of the Section in American History," "to serve as a check upon mob psychology on a national scale, and to furnish that variety which is essential to vital growth and originality."

Writing in the 1960s, historian Richard Hofstadter criticized what he called the "blandness" of Turner's proposals and was struck by "the imbalance between the major problem he [Turner] perceived and the minor means he proposed to solve it." Certainly Turner's were not the most radical of proposals, but after several successive presidential terms filled with empty frontier rhetoric about the nation "standing tall," I am inclined to feel more generous toward Turner's argument for rechanneling American expansionist impulses and encouraging the growth of community. One of the underlying themes in the essays of Frederick Jackson Turner is the necessity of confronting what William Appleman Williams called "empire as a way of life."[9]

ONE

THE SIGNIFICANCE
OF HISTORY

(1891)

The conceptions of history have been almost as numerous as
the men who have written history. To Augustine Birrell
history is a pageant; it is for the purpose of satisfying our
curiosity. Under the touch of a literary artist the past is to
become living again. Like another Prospero the historian
waves his wand, and the deserted streets of Palmyra sound to
the tread of artisan and officer, warrior gives battle to warrior,
ruined towers rise by magic, and the whole busy life of generations that have long ago gone down to dust comes to life again
in the pages of a book. The artistic prose narration of past
events—this is the ideal of those who view history as literature. To this class belong romantic literary artists who strive
to give to history the coloring and dramatic action of fiction,
who do not hesitate to paint a character blacker or whiter than
he really was, in order that the interest of the page may be
increased, who force dull facts into vivacity, who create impressive situations, who, in short, strive to realize as an ideal

Reprinted from *Wisconsin Journal of Education* 21 (October-November 1891).

the success of Walter Scott. It is of the historian Froude that Freeman says: "The most winning style, the choicest metaphors, the neatest phrases from foreign tongues would all be thrown away if they were devoted to proving that any two sides of a triangle are not always greater than the third side. When they are devoted to proving that a man cut off his wife's head one day and married her maid the next morning out of sheer love for his country, they win believers for the paradox." It is of the reader of this kind of history that Seeley writes: "To him, by some magic, parliamentary debates shall be always lively, officials always men of strongly marked, interesting character. There shall be nothing to remind him of the bluebook or the law book, nothing common or prosaic; but he shall sit as in a theater and gaze at splendid scenery and costume. He shall never be called upon to study or to judge, but only to imagine and enjoy. His reflections, as he reads, shall be precisely those of the novel reader; he shall ask: Is this character well drawn? is it really amusing? is the interest of the story well sustained, and does it rise properly toward the close?"

But after all these criticisms we may gladly admit that in itself an interesting style, even a picturesque manner of presentation, is not to be condemned, provided that truthfulness of substance rather than vivacity of style be the end sought. But granting that a man may be the possessor of a good style which he does not allow to run away with him, either in the interest of the artistic impulse or in the cause of party, still there remain differences as to the aim and method of history. To a whole school of writers, among whom we find some of the great historians of our time, history is the study of politics, that is, politics in the high signification given the word by Aristotle, as meaning all that concerns the activity of the state itself. "History is past politics and politics present history," says the great author of the *Norman Conquest*. Maurenbrecher of Leipzig speaks in no less certain tones: "The bloom of historical studies is the history of politics"; and Lorenz of Jena asserts: "The proper field of historical investigation, in the closer sense of the word, is politics." Says Seeley: "The modern historian works at the same task as Aristotle in his Politics." "To study history is to study not merely a narrative but at the same time certain theoretical studies." "To study history is to study problems." And thus a great circle of profound investigators, with true scientific method, have expounded the evolution of political institutions, studying their growth as the biologist might study seed, bud, blossom, and fruit. The results of these labors may be seen in such monumental works as those of Waitz on German institutions, Stubbs on English constitutional history, and Maine on early institutions.

There is another and an increasing class of historians to whom history is the study of the economic growth of the people, who aim to show that property, the distribution of wealth, the social conditions of the people, are the underlying and determining factors to be studied. This school, whose advance guard was led by Roscher, having already transformed orthodox political economy by its historical method, is now going on to rewrite history from the economic point of view. Perhaps the best English expression of the ideas of the school is to be found in Thorold Rogers' *Economic Interpretation of History*.[1] He asserts truly that "very often the cause of great political events and great social movements is economical and has hitherto been undetected." So important does the fundamental principle of this school appear to me that I desire to quote from Mr. Rogers a specific illustration of this new historical method. *Example*

In the twelfth and thirteenth centuries there were numerous and well frequented routes from the markets of Hindustan to the Western world, and for the conveyance of that Eastern produce which was so greatly desired as a seasoning to the coarse and often unwholesome diet of our forefathers. The principal ports to which this produce was conveyed were Seleucia (latterly called Licia) in the Levant, Trebizond, on the Black Sea, and Alexandria. From these ports this Eastern produce was collected mainly by the Venetian and Genoese traders, and conveyed over the passes of the Alps to the upper Danube and the Rhine. Here it was a source of great wealth to

the cities which were planted on these waterways, from Rat-
isbon and Nuremberg to Bruges and Antwerp. The stream of
commerce was not deep nor broad, but it was singularly fertil-
izing, and every one who has any knowledge of the only history
worth knowing knows how important these cities were in the
later Middle Ages.

In the course of time, all but one of these routes had been
blocked by the savages who desolated central Asia, and still
desolate it. It was therefore the object of the most enterprising
of the Western nations to get, if possible, in the rear of these
destructive brigands, by discovering a long sea passage to
Hindustan. All Eastern trade depended on the Egyptian road
being kept open, and this remaining road was already threatened. The beginning of this discovery was the work of a Por-
tuguese prince. The expedition of Columbus was an attempt to
discover a passage to India over the Western sea. By a curious
coincidence the Cape passage was doubled, and the new world
discovered almost simultaneously.

The discoveries were made none too soon. Selim I (1512–20),
the sultan of Turkey, conquered Mesopotamia and the holy
towns of Arabia, and annexed Egypt during his brief reign.
This conquest blocked the only remaining road which the Old
World knew. The thriving manufactures of Alexandria were at
once destroyed. Egypt ceased to be the highway from Hindustan. I discovered that some cause must be at work which
had hitherto been unsuspected in the sudden and enormous
rise of prices in all Eastern products, at the close of the first
quarter of the sixteenth century, and found that it must have
come from the conquest of Egypt. The river of commerce was
speedily dried up. The cities which had thriven on it were
gradually ruined, at least so far as this source of their wealth
was concerned, and the trade of the Danube and Rhine ceased.
The Italian cities fell into rapid decay. The German nobles, who

had got themselves incorporated among the burghers of the free cities, were impoverished, and betook themselves to the obvious expedient of reimbursing their losses by the pillage of their tenants. Then came the Peasants' War, its ferocious incidents, its cruel suppression, and the development of those wild sects which disfigured and arrested the German Reformation. The battle of the Pyramids, in which Selim gained the sultanate of Egypt for the Osmanli Turks, brought loss and misery into thousands of homes where the event had never been heard of. It is such facts as these which the economic interpretation of history illustrates and expounds.

Comment

Viewed from this position, the past is filled with new meaning. The focal point of modern interest is the fourth estate, the great mass of the people. History has been a romance and a tragedy. In it we read the brilliant annals of the few. The intrigues of courts, knightly valor, palaces and pyramids, the loves of ladies, the songs of minstrels, and the chants from cathedrals pass like a pageant, or linger like a strain of music as we turn the pages. But history has its tragedy as well, which tells of the degraded tillers of the soil, toiling that others might dream, the slavery that rendered possible the "glory that was Greece," the serfdom into which decayed the "grandeur that was Rome"—these as well demand their annals. Far oftener than has yet been shown have these underlying economic facts affecting the breadwinners of the nation been the secret of the nation's rise or fall, by the side of which much that has passed as history is the merest frippery.

But I must not attempt to exhaust the list of the conceptions of history. To a large class of writers, represented by Hume, the field of historical writing is an arena whereon are to be fought out present partisan debates. Whig is to struggle against Tory, and the party of the writer's choice is to be victorious at whatever cost to the truth. We do not lack these partisan historians in America. To Carlyle, the hero-worshipper, history is the stage on which a few great men play their

Depends on Author [handwritten annotation]

parts. To Max Müller history is the exposition of the growth of religious ideas. To the moralist history is the text whereby to teach a lesson. To the metaphysician history is the fulfillment of a few primary laws.

Plainly we may make choice from among many ideals. If, now, we strive to reduce them to some kind of order, we find that in each age a different ideal of history has prevailed. To the savage history is the painted scalp, with its symbolic representations of the victims of his valor; or it is the legend of the gods and heroes of his race—attempts to explain the origin of things. Hence the vast body of mythologies, folklore, and legends, in which science, history, fiction, are all blended together, judgment and imagination inextricably confused. As time passes the artistic instinct comes in, and historical writing takes the form of the Iliad, or the Nibelungenlied. Still we have in these writings the reflection of the imaginative, credulous age that believed in the divinity of its heroes and wrote down what it believed. Artistic and critical faculty find expression in Herodotus, father of Greek history, and in Thucydides, the ideal Greek historian. Both write from the standpoint of an advanced civilization and strive to present a real picture of the events and an explanation of the causes of the events. But Thucydides is a Greek; literature is to him an art, and history a part of literature; and so it seems to him no violation of historical truth to make his generals pronounce long orations that were composed for them by the historian. Moreover, early men and Greeks alike believed their own tribe or state to be the favored of the gods: the rest of humanity was for the most part outside the range of history.

To the medieval historian history was the annals of the monastery, or the chronicle of court and camp.

In the nineteenth century a new ideal and method of history arose. Philosophy prepared the way for it. Schelling taught the doctrine "that the state is not in reality governed by laws of man's devising, but is a part of the moral order of the universe, ruled by cosmic forces from above." Herder proclaimed the doctrine of growth in human institutions. He saw in history the development of given germs; religions were to be studied by comparison and by tracing their origins from superstitions up toward rational conceptions of God. Language, too, was no sudden creation, but a growth, and was to be studied as such; and so with political institutions. Thus he paved the way for the study of comparative philology, of mythology, and of political evolution. Wolf, applying Herder's suggestions to the Iliad, found no single Homer as its author, but many. This led to the critical study of the texts. Niebuhr applied this mode of study to the Roman historians and proved their incorrectness. Livy's history of early Rome became legend. Then Niebuhr tried to find the real facts. He believed that, although the Romans had forgotten their own history, still it was possible by starting with institutions of known reality to construct their predecessors, as the botanist may infer bud from flower. He would trace causes from effects. In other words, so strongly did he believe in the growth of an institution according to fixed laws that he believed he could reconstruct the past, reaching the real facts even by means of the incorrect accounts of the Roman writers.

Although he carried his method too far, still it was the foundation of the modern historical school. He strove to reconstruct old Rome as it really was out of the original authorities that remained. By critical analysis and interpretation he attempted so to use these texts that the buried truth should come to light. To skill as an antiquary he added great political insight—for Niebuhr was a practical statesman. It was his aim to unite critical study of the materials with the interpretative skill of the political expert, and this has been the aim of the new school of historians. Leopold von Ranke applied this critical method to the study of modern history. To him a document surviving from the past itself was of far greater value than any amount of tradition regarding the past. To him the contemporary account, rightly used, was of far higher authority than the second-hand relation. And so he searched diligently in the musty archives of European courts, and the result of his labors and those of his scholars has been the rewriting of modern diplomatic and political history. Charters, correspondence, contemporary chronicles, inscriptions, these are the materials on which he and his disciples worked. To "tell things as they really were" was Ranke's ideal. But to him, also, history was primarily past politics.

Superficial and hasty as this review has been, I think you see that the historical study of the first half of the nineteenth century reflected the thought of that age. It was an age of political agitation and inquiry, as our own age still so largely is. It was an age of science. That inductive study of phenomena which has worked a revolution in our knowledge of the external world was applied to history. In a word, the study of history became scientific and political.

Today the questions that are uppermost, and that will become increasingly important, are not so much political as economic questions. The age of machinery, of the factory system, is also the age of socialistic inquiry.

It is not strange that the predominant historical study is coming to be the study of past social conditions, inquiry as to landholding, distribution of wealth, and the economic basis of society in general. Our conclusion, therefore, is that there is much truth in all these conceptions of history: history is past literature, it is past politics, it is past religion, it is past economics.

Each age tries to form its own conception of the past. *Each age writes the history of the past anew with reference to the conditions uppermost in its own time.* Historians have accepted the doctrine of Herder. Society grows. They have accepted the doctrine of Comte. Society is an organism. History is the biography of society in all its departments. There is objective history and subjective history. Objective history applies to the events themselves; subjective history is man's conception of these events. "The whole mode and manner of looking at things alters with every age," but this does not mean that the real events of a given age change; it means that our comprehension of these facts changes.

History, both objective and subjective, is ever *becoming,* never completed. The centuries unfold to us more and more the meaning of past times. Today we understand Roman history better than did Livy or Tacitus, not only because we know how to use the sources better but also because the significance of events develops with time, because today is so much a product of yesterday that yesterday can only be understood as it is explained by today. The aim of history, then, is to know the elements of the present by understanding what came into the present from the past. For the present is simply the developing past, the past the undeveloped present. As well try to understand the egg without a knowledge of its developed form, the chick, as to try to understand the past without bringing to it the explanation of the present; and equally well try to understand an animal without study of its embryology as to try to understand one time without study of the events that went before. The antiquarian strives to bring back the past for the sake of the past; the historian strives to show the present to itself by revealing its origin from the past. The goal of the antiquarian is the dead past; the goal of the historian is the living present. Droysen has put this true conception into the statement, "History is the 'Know Thyself' of humanity—the self-consciousness of mankind."

If, now, you accept with me the statement of this great master of historical science, the rest of our way is clear. If history be, in truth, the self-consciousness of humanity, the "self-consciousness of the living age, acquired by understanding its development from the past," all the rest follows.

First we recognize why all the spheres of man's activity must be considered. Not only is this the only way in which we can get a complete view of the society, but no one department of social life can be understood in isolation from the others. The economic life and the political life touch, modify, and condition one another. Even the religious life needs to be studied in conjunction with the political and economic life, and vice versa. Therefore all kinds of history are essential—history as politics, history as art, history as economics, history as religion—all are truly parts of society's endeavor to understand itself by understanding its past.

Next we see that history is not shut up in a book—not in many books. The first lesson the student of history has to learn is to discard his conception that there are standard ultimate histories. In the nature of the case this is impossible. *History is all the remains that have come down to us from the past, studied with all the critical and interpretative power that the present can bring to the task.* From time to time great masters bring their investigations to fruit in books. To us these serve as the latest words, the best results of the most recent efforts of society to understand itself—but they are not the final words. To the historian the materials for his work are found in all that remains from the ages gone by—in papers, roads, mounds, customs, languages; in monuments, coins, medals, names, titles, inscriptions, charters; in contemporary annals and chronicles; and, finally, in the secondary sources, or histories in the common acceptance of the term. Wherever there remains a chipped flint, a spearhead, a piece of pottery, a pyramid, a picture, a poem, a coliseum, or a coin, there is history.

Says Taine: "What is your first remark on turning over the great stiff leaves of a folio, the yellow sheets of a manuscript, a poem, a code of laws, a declaration of faith? This, you say, was not created alone. It is but a mold, like a fossil shell, an imprint like one of those shapes embossed in stone by an animal which lived and perished. Under the shell there was an animal, and behind the document there was a man. Why do you study the shell except to represent to yourself the animal? So do you study the document only in order to know the man. The shell and the document are lifeless wrecks, valuable only as a clue to the entire and living existence. We must reach back to this existence, endeavor to recreate it."

But observe that when a man writes a narration of the past he writes with all his limitations as regards ability to test the real value of his sources, and ability rightly to interpret them. Does he make use of a chronicle? First he must determine whether it is genuine; then whether it was contemporary, or at what period it was written; then what opportunities its author had to know the truth; then what were his personal traits; was he likely to see clearly, to relate impartially? If not, what was his bias, what his limitations? Next comes the harder task—to interpret the significance of events; causes must be understood, results seen. Local affairs must be described in relation to affairs of the world—all must be told with just selection, emphasis, perspective; with that historical imagination and sympathy that does not judge the past by the canons of the present, nor read into it the ideas of the present. Above all the historian must have a passion for truth above that for any party or idea. Such are some of the difficulties that lie in the way of our science. When, moreover, we consider that each man is conditioned by the age in which he lives and must perforce write with limitations and prepossessions, I think we shall all agree that no historian can say the ultimate word.

Another thought that follows as a corollary from our definition is that in history there is a unity and a continuity. Strictly speaking, there is no gap between ancient, medieval, and modern history. Strictly speaking, there are no such divisions. Baron Bunsen dates modern history from the migration of Abraham. Bluntschli makes it begin with Frederick the Great. The truth is, as Freeman has shown, that the age of Pericles or the age of Augustus has more in common with modern times than has the age of Alfred or of Charlemagne. There is another test than that of chronology; namely, stages of growth. In the past of the European world peoples have grown from families into states, from peasantry into the complexity of great city life, from animism into monotheism, from mythology into philosophy; and have yielded place again to primitive peoples who in turn have passed through stages like these and yielded to new nations. Each nation has bequeathed something to its successor; no age has suffered the highest content of the past to be lost entirely. By unconscious inheritance, and by conscious striving after the past as part of the present, history has acquired continuity. Freeman's statement that into Rome flowed all the ancient world and out of Rome came the modern world is as true as it is impressive. In a strict sense imperial Rome never died. You may find the eternal city still living in the Kaiser and the Czar, in the language of the Romance peoples, in the codes of

European states, in the eagles of their coats of arms, in every college where the classics are read, in a thousand political institutions.

Even here in young America old Rome still lives. When the inaugural procession passes toward the Senate chamber, and the president's address outlines the policy he proposes to pursue, there is Rome! You may find her in the code of Louisiana, in the French and Spanish portions of our history, in the idea of checks and balances in our constitution. Clearest of all, Rome may be seen in the titles, government, and ceremonials of the Roman Catholic church; for when the Caesar passed away, his scepter fell to that new Pontifex Maximus, the Pope, and to that new Augustus, the Holy Roman Emperor of the Middle Ages, an empire which in name at least continued till those heroic times when a new Imperator recalled the days of the great Julius, and sent the eagles of France to proclaim that Napoleon was king over kings.

So it is true in fact, as we should presume a priori, that in history there are only artificial divisions. Society is an organism, ever growing. History is the self-consciousness of this organism. "The roots of the present lie deep in the past." There is no break. But not only is it true that no country can be understood without taking account of all the past; it is also true that we cannot select a stretch of land and say we will limit our study to this land; for local history can only be understood in the light of the history of the world. There is unity as well as continuity. To know the history of contemporary Italy we must know the history of contemporary France, of contemporary Germany. Each acts on each. Ideas, commodities even, refuse the bounds of a nation. All are inextricably connected, so that each is needed to explain the others. This is true especially of our modern world with its complex commerce and means of intellectual connection. In history, then, there is unity and continuity. Each age must be studied in the light of all the past; local history must be viewed in the light of world history.

Now, I think, we are in a position to consider the utility of historical studies. I will not dwell on the dignity of history considered as the self-consciousness of humanity; nor on the mental growth that comes from such a discipline; nor on the vastness of the field; all these occur to you, and their importance will impress you increasingly as you consider history from this point of view. To enable us to behold our own time and place as a part of the stupendous progress of the ages; to see primitive man; to recognize in our midst the undying ideas of Greece; to find Rome's majesty and power alive in present law and institution, still living in our superstitions and our folklore; to enable us to realize the richness of our inheritance, the possibility of our lives, the grandeur of the present—these are some of the priceless services of history.

But I must conclude my remarks with a few words upon the utility of history as affording a training for good citizenship. Doubtless good citizenship is the end for which the public schools exist. Were it otherwise there might be difficulty in justifying the support of them at public expense. The direct and important utility of the study of history in the achievement of this end hardly needs argument.

In the union of public service and historical study Germany has been pre-eminent. For certain governmental positions in that country a university training in historical studies is essential. Ex-President Andrew D. White affirms that a main cause of the efficiency of German administration is the training that officials get from the university study of history and politics. In Paris there is the famous School of Political Sciences which fits men for the public service of France. In the decade closing with 1887 competitive examinations showed the advantages of this training. Of sixty candidates appointed to the council of state, forty were graduates of this school. Of forty-two appointed to the inspection of finance, thirty-nine were from the school; sixteen of the seventeen appointees to the court of claims; and twenty of twenty-six appointees to the department of foreign affairs held diplomas from the School of Political Sciences. In these European countries not merely are the departmental officers required to possess historical training; the list of leading statesmen reveals many names eminent in historical science. I need hardly recall to you the great names of Niebuhr, the councilor, whose history of Rome gave the impetus to our new science; of Stein, the reconstructor of Germany and the projector of the *Monumenta Germanicae*, that priceless collection of original sources of medieval history. Read the roll of Germany's great public servants and you will find among them such eminent men as Gneist, the authority on English constitutional history; Bluntschli, the able historian of politics; Von Holst, the historian of our own political development; Knies, Roscher, and Wagner, the economists; and many more. I have given you Droysen's conception of history. But Droysen was not simply a historian; he belonged, with the famous historians Treitschke, Mommsen, Von Sybel, to what Lord Acton calls "that central band of writers and statesmen and soldiers who turned the tide that had run for six hundred years, and conquered the centrifugal forces that had reigned in Germany longer than the commons have sat at Westminster."

Nor does England fail to recognize the value of the union of history and politics, as is exemplified by such men as Macaulay, Dilke, Morley, and Bryce, all of whom have been eminent members of Parliament as well as distinguished historical writers. From France and Italy such illustrations could easily be multiplied.

When we turn to America and ask what marriages have occurred between history and statesmanship, we are filled with astonishment at the contrast. It is true that our country has tried to reward literary men: Motley, Irving, Bancroft, Lowell held official positions, but these positions were in the diplomatic service. The "literary fellow" was good enough for Europe. The state gave these men aid rather than called their services to its aid. To this statement I know of but one important exception—George Bancroft. In America statesmanship has been considered something of spontaneous generation, a miraculous birth from our republican institutions. To demand of the statesmen who debate such topics as the tariff, European and South American relations, immigration, labor and railroad problems, a scientific acquaintance with historical politics or economics would be to expose one's self to ridicule in the eyes of the public. I have said that the tribal stage of society demands tribal history and tribal politics. When a society is isolated it looks with contempt upon the history and institutions of the rest of the world. We shall not be altogether wrong if we say that such tribal ideas concerning our institutions and society have prevailed for many years in this country. Lately historians have turned to the comparative and historical study of our political institutions. The actual working of our constitution as contrasted with the literary theory of it has engaged the attention of able young men. Foreigners like Von Holst and Bryce have shown us a mirror of our political life in the light of the political life of other peoples. Little of this influence has yet attracted the attention of our public men. Count the roll in Senate and House, cabinet and diplomatic service—to say nothing of the state governments—and where are the names famous in history and politics? It is shallow to express satisfaction with this condition and to sneer at "literary fellows." To me it seems that we are approaching a pivotal point in our country's history.

In an earlier part of my remarks I quoted from Thorold Rogers to show how the Turkish conquest of far-off Egypt brought ruin to homes in Antwerp and Bruges. If this was true in that early day, when commercial threads were infinitely less complex than they are now, how profoundly is our present life interlocked with the events of all the world. Heretofore America has remained aloof from the Old World affairs. Under the influence of a wise policy she has avoided political relations with other powers. But it is one of the profoundest lessons that history has to teach, that political relations, in a highly developed civilization, are inextricably connected with economic relations. Already there are signs of a relaxation of our policy of commercial isolation. Reciprocity is a word that meets with increasing favor from all parties. But once fully afloat on the sea of worldwide economic interests, we shall soon develop political interests. Our fishery disputes furnish one example; our Samoan interests another; our Congo

How we develop our history depends in part!

relations a third. But perhaps most important are our present and future relations with South America, coupled with our Monroe Doctrine. It is a settled maxim of international law that the government of a foreign state whose subjects have lent money to another state may interfere to protect the rights of the bondholders, if they are endangered by the borrowing state. As Professor H. B. Adams has pointed out, South American states have close financial relations with many European money-lenders; they are also prone to revolutions. Suppose, now, that England, finding the interests of her bondholders in jeopardy, should step in to manage the affairs of some South American country as she has those of Egypt for the same reason. Would the United States abandon its popular interpretation of the Monroe Doctrine, or would she give up her policy of noninterference in the political affairs of the outer world? Or suppose our own bondholders in New York, say, to be in danger of loss from revolution in South America—and our increasing tendency to close connection with South American affairs makes this a supposable case—would our government stand idly by while her citizens' interests were sacrificed? Take another case, the protectorate of the proposed interoceanic canal. England will not be content to allow the control of this to rest solely in our hands. Will the United States form an alliance with England for the purpose of this protection? Such questions as these indicate that we are drifting out into European political relations, and that a new statesmanship is demanded, a statesmanship that shall clearly understand European history and present relations, which depend on history.

Again, consider the problems of socialism brought to our shores by European immigrants. We shall never deal rightly with such problems until we understand the historical conditions under which they grew. Thus we meet Europe not only outside our borders but in our very midst. The problem of immigration furnishes many examples of the need of historical study. Consider how our vast Western domain has been settled. Louis XIV devastates the Palatinate, and soon hundreds of its inhabitants are hewing down the forests of Pennsylvania. The bishop of Salzburg persecutes his Protestant subjects, and the woods of Georgia sound to the crack of Teutonic rifles. Presbyterians are oppressed in Ireland, and soon in Tennessee and Kentucky the fires of pioneers gleam. These were but advance guards of the mighty army that has poured into our midst ever since. Every economic change, every political change, every military conscription, every socialistic agitation in Europe, has sent us groups of colonists who have passed out onto our prairies to form new self-governing communities, or who have entered the life of our great cities. These men have come to us historical products, they have brought to us not merely so much bone and sinew, not merely so much money, not merely so much manual skill, they have brought with them deeply inrooted customs and ideas. They are important factors in the political and economic life of the nation. Our destiny is interwoven with theirs; how shall we understand American history without understanding European history? The story of the peopling of America has not yet been written. We do not understand ourselves.

One of the most fruitful fields of study in our country has been the process of growth of our own institutions, local and national. The town and the county, the germs of our political institutions, have been traced back to old Teutonic roots. Gladstone's remark that "the American constitution is the most wonderful work ever struck off at a given time by the brain and purpose of man" has been shown to be misleading, for the constitution was, with all the constructive powers of the fathers, still a growth; and our history is only to be understood as a growth from European history under the new conditions of the New World.

Says Dr. H. B. Adams: "American local history should be studied as a contribution to national history. This country will yet be viewed and reviewed as an organism of historic growth, developing from minute germs, from the very protoplasm of state-life. And some day this country will be studied in its international relations, as an organic part of a larger organism now vaguely called the World-State, but as surely developing through the operation of economic, legal, social, and scientific forces as the American Union, the German and British empires are evolving into higher forms.... The local consciousness must be expanded into a fuller sense of its historic worth and dignity. We must understand the cosmopolitan relations of modern local life, and its own wholesome conservative power in these days of growing centralization."

If any added argument were needed to show that good citizenship demands the careful study of history, it is in the examples and lessons that the history of other peoples has for us. It is profoundly true that each people makes its own history in accordance with its past. It is true that a purely artificial piece of legislation, unrelated to present and past conditions, is the most short-lived of things. Yet it is to be remembered that it was history that taught us this truth, and that there is, within the limits of the constructive action possible to a state, large scope for the use of this experience of foreign peoples.

I have aimed to offer, then, these considerations: History, I have said, is to be taken in no narrow sense. It is more than past literature, more than past politics, more than past economics. It is the self-consciousness of humanity—humanity's effort to understand itself through the study of its past. Therefore it is not confined to books; the *subject* is to be studied, not books simply. History has a unity and a continuity; the present needs the past to explain it; and local history must be read as a part of world history. The study has a utility as a mental discipline, and as expanding our ideas regarding the dignity of the present. But perhaps its most practical utility to us, as public school teachers, is its service in fostering good citizenship.

The ideals presented may at first be discouraging. Even to him who devotes his life to the study of history the ideal conception is impossible of attainment. He must select some field and till that thoroughly, be absolute master of it; for the rest he must seek the aid of others whose lives have been given in the true scientific spirit to the study of special fields. The public school teacher must do the best with the libraries at his disposal. We teachers must use all the resources we can obtain and not pin our faith to a single book; we must make history living instead of allowing it to seem mere literature, a mere narration of events that might have occurred in the moon. We must teach the history of a few countries thoroughly, rather than that of many countries superficially. The popularizing of scientific knowledge is one of the best achievements of this age of book-making. It is typical of that social impulse which has led university men to bring the fruits of their study home to the people. In England the social impulse has led to what is known as the university extension movement. University men have left their traditional cloister and gone to live among the working classes, in order to bring to them a new intellectual life. Chautauqua, in our own country, has begun to pass beyond the period of superficial work to a real union of the scientific and the popular. In their summer school they offer courses in American history. Our own state university carries on extensive work in various lines. I believe that this movement in the direction of popularizing historical and scientific knowledge will work a real revolution in our towns and villages as well as in our great cities.

The schoolteacher is called to do a work above and beyond the instruction in his school. He is called upon to be the apostle of the higher culture to the community in which he is placed. Given a good school or town library—such a one is now within the reach of every hamlet that is properly stimulated to the acquisition of one—and given an energetic, devoted teacher to direct and foster the study of history and politics and economics, we would have an intellectual regeneration of the state. Historical study has for its end to let the community see itself in the light of the past, to give it new thoughts and feelings, new aspirations and energies. Thoughts and feelings flow into deeds. Here is the motive power that lies behind institutions. This is therefore one of the ways to create good politics; here we can touch the very "age and body of the time, its form and pressure." Have you a thought of better things, a reform to accomplish? "Put it in the air," says the great teacher. Ideas have ruled, will rule. We must make university extension into state life felt in this country as did Germany. Of one thing beware. Avoid as the very unpardonable sin any one-sidedness, any partisan, any partial treatment of history. Do not misinterpret the past for the sake of the present. The man who enters the temple of history must respond devoutly to that invocation of the church, *Sursum corda*, lift up your hearts. No looking at history as an idle tale, a compend of anecdotes; no servile devotion to a textbook; no carelessness of truth about the dead that can no longer speak must be permitted in its sanctuary. "History," says Droysen, "is not the truth and the light; but a striving for it, a sermon on it, a consecration to it."

TWO

THE SIGNIFICANCE
OF THE FRONTIER IN
AMERICAN HISTORY

(1893)

In a recent bulletin of the Superintendent of the Census for 1890 appear these significant words: "Up to and including 1880 the country had a frontier of settlement, but at present the unsettled area has been so broken into by isolated bodies of settlement that there can hardly be said to be a frontier line. In the discussion of its extent, its westward movement, etc., it can not, therefore, any longer have a place in the census reports." This brief official statement marks the closing of a great historic movement. Up to our own day American history has been in a large degree the history of the colonization of the Great West. The existence of an area of free land, its continuous recession, and the advance of American settlement westward, explain American development.

Behind institutions, behind constitutional forms and modifications, lie the vital forces that call these organs into life and shape them to meet changing conditions. The peculiarity of

Reprinted from *Annual Report of the American Historical Association for the Year 1893* (Washington, D.C., 1894).

American institutions is the fact that they have been compelled to adapt themselves to the changes of an expanding people—to the changes involved in crossing a continent, in winning a wilderness, and in developing at each area of this progress out of the primitive economic and political conditions of the frontier into the complexity of city life. Said Calhoun in 1817, "We are great, and rapidly—I was about to say fearfully—growing!"[1] So saying, he touched the distinguishing feature of American life. All peoples show development; the germ theory of politics has been sufficiently emphasized. In the case of most nations, however, the development has occurred in a limited area; and if the nation has expanded, it has met other growing peoples whom it has conquered. But in the case of the United States we have a different phenomenon. Limiting our attention to the Atlantic coast, we have the familiar phenomenon of the evolution of institutions in a limited area, such as the rise of representative government; the differentiation of simple colonial governments into complex organs; the progress from primitive industrial society, without division of labor, up to manufacturing civilization. But we have in addition to this a recurrence of the process of evolution in each western area reached in the process of expansion. Thus American development has exhibited not merely advance along a single line, but a return to primitive conditions on a continually advancing frontier line, and a new development for that area. American social development has been continually beginning over again on the frontier. This perennial rebirth, this fluidity of American life, this expansion westward with its new opportunities, its continuous touch with the simplicity of primitive society, furnish the forces dominating American character. The true point of view in the history of this nation is not the Atlantic coast, it is the Great West. Even the slavery struggle, which is made so exclusive an object of attention by writers like Professor von Holst, occupies its important place in American history because of its relation to westward expansion.

In this advance, the frontier is the outer edge of the wave—the meeting point between savagery and civilization. Much has been written about the frontier from the point of view of border warfare and the chase, but as a field for the serious study of the economist and the historian it has been neglected.

The American frontier is sharply distinguished from the European frontier—a fortified boundary line running through dense populations. The most significant thing about the American frontier is that it lies at the hither edge of free land. In the census reports it is treated as the margin of that settlement which has a density of two or more to the square mile. The term is an elastic one, and for our purposes does not need sharp definition. We shall consider the whole frontier belt, including the Indian country and the outer margin of the "settled area" of the census reports. This paper will make no attempt to treat the subject exhaustively; its aim is simply to call attention to the frontier as a fertile field for investigation, and to suggest some of the problems which arise in connection with it.

In the settlement of America we have to observe how European life entered the continent, and how America modified and developed that life and reacted on Europe. Our early history is the study of European germs developing in an American environment. Too exclusive attention has been paid by institutional students to the Germanic origins, too little to the American factors. The frontier is the line of most rapid and effective Americanization. The wilderness masters the colonist. It finds him a European in dress, industries, tools, modes of travel, and thought. It takes him from the railroad car and puts him in the birch canoe. It strips off the garments of civilization and arrays him in the hunting shirt and the moccasin. It puts him in the log cabin of the Cherokee and Iroquois and runs an Indian palisade around him. Before long he has gone to planting Indian corn and plowing with a sharp stick; he shouts the war cry and takes the scalp in orthodox Indian fashion. In short, at the frontier the environment is at first too strong for the man. He must accept the conditions which it furnishes, or perish, and so he fits himself into the Indian clearings and follows the Indian trails. Little by little he transforms the wilderness, but the outcome is not the old Europe, not simply the development of

Germanic germs, any more than the first phenomenon was a case of reversion to the Germanic mark. The fact is, that here is a new product that is American. At first, the frontier was the Atlantic coast. It was the frontier of Europe in a very real sense. Moving westward, the frontier became more and more American. As successive terminal moraines result from successive glaciations, so each frontier leaves its traces behind it, and when it becomes a settled area the region still partakes of the frontier characteristics. Thus the advance of the frontier has meant a steady movement away from the influence of Europe, a steady growth of independence on American lines. And to study this advance, the men who grew up under these conditions, and the political, economic, and social results of it, is to study the really American part of our history.

In the course of the seventeenth century the frontier was advanced up the Atlantic river courses, just beyond the "fall line," and the tidewater region became the settled area. In the first half of the eighteenth century another advance occurred. Traders followed the Delaware and Shawnese Indians to the Ohio as early as the end of the first quarter of the century.[2] Gov. Spotswood, of Virginia, made an expedition in 1714 across the Blue Ridge. The end of the first quarter of the century saw the advance of the Scotch-Irish and the Palatine Germans up the Shenandoah Valley into the western part of Virginia, and along the Piedmont region of the Carolinas.[3] The Germans in New York pushed the frontier of settlement up the Mohawk to German Flats.[4] In Pennsylvania the town of Bedford indicates the line of settlement. Settlements had begun on New River, a branch of the Kanawha, and on the sources of the Yadkin and French Broad.[5] The King attempted to arrest the advance by his proclamation of 1763,[6] forbidding settlements beyond the sources of the rivers flowing into the Atlantic; but in vain. In the period of the Revolution the frontier crossed the Alleghanies into Kentucky and Tennessee, and the upper waters of the Ohio were settled.[7] When the first census was taken in 1790, the continuous settled area was bounded by a line which ran near the coast of Maine, and included New England except a portion of Vermont and New Hampshire, New York along the Hudson and up the Mohawk about Schenectady, eastern and southern Pennsylvania, Virginia well across the Shenandoah Valley, and the Carolinas and eastern Georgia.[8] Beyond this region of continuous settlement were the small settled areas of Kentucky and Tennessee, and the Ohio, with the mountains intervening between them and the Atlantic area, thus giving a new and important character to the frontier. The isolation of the region increased its peculiarly American tendencies, and the need of transportation facilities to connect it with the East called out important schemes of internal improvement, which will be noted farther on. The "West," as a self-conscious section, began to evolve.

From decade to decade distinct advances of the frontier occurred. By the census of 1820[9] the settled area included Ohio, southern Indiana and Illinois, southeastern Missouri, and about one-half of Louisiana. This settled area had surrounded Indian areas, and the management of these tribes became an object of political concern. The frontier region of the time lay along the Great Lakes, where Astor's American Fur Company operated in the Indian trade,[10] and beyond the Mississippi, where Indian traders extended their activity even to the Rocky Mountains; Florida also furnished frontier conditions. The Mississippi River region was the scene of typical frontier settlements.[11]

The rising steam navigation[12] on western waters, the opening of the Erie Canal, and the westward extension of cotton[13] culture added five frontier states to the Union in this period. Grund, writing in 1836, declares: "It appears then that the universal disposition of Americans to emigrate to the western wilderness, in order to enlarge their dominion over inanimate nature, is the actual result of an expansive power which is inherent in them, and which by continually agitating all classes of society is constantly throwing a large portion of the whole population on the extreme confines of the State, in order to gain space for its development. Hardly is a new State of Territory formed before the same principle manifests itself again and gives rise to a further emigration; and so is it destined to go on until a physical barrier must finally obstruct its progress."[14]

In the middle of this century the line indicated by the present eastern boundary of Indian Territory, Nebraska, and Kansas marked the frontier of the Indian country.[15] Minnesota and Wisconsin still exhibited frontier conditions,[16] but the distinctive frontier of the period is found in California, where the gold discoveries had sent a sudden tide of adventurous miners, and in Oregon, and the settlements in Utah.[17] As the frontier had leaped over the Alleghanies, so now it skipped the Great Plains and the Rocky Mountains; and in the same way that the advance of the frontiersmen beyond the Alleghanies had caused the rise of important questions of transportation and internal improvement, so now the settlers beyond the Rocky Mountains needed means of communication with the East, and in the furnishing of these arose the settlement of the Great Plains and the development of still another kind of frontier life. Railroads, fostered by land grants, sent an increasing tide of immigrants into the Far West. The United States Army fought a series of Indian wars in Minnesota, Dakota, and the Indian Territory.

By 1880 the settled area had been pushed into northern Michigan, Wisconsin, and Minnesota, along Dakota rivers, and in the Black Hills region, and was ascending the rivers of Kansas and Nebraska. The development of mines in Colorado had drawn isolated frontier settlements into that region, and Montana and Idaho were receiving settlers. The frontier was found in these mining camps and the ranches of the Great Plains. The superintendent of the census for 1890 reports, as previously stated, that the settlements of the West lie so scattered over the region that there can no longer be said to be a frontier line.

In these successive frontiers we find natural boundary lines which have served to mark and to affect the characteristics of the frontiers, namely: the "fall line"; the Alleghany Mountains; the Mississippi; the Missouri where its direction approximates north and south; the line of the arid lands, approximately the ninety-ninth meridian; and the

Rocky Mountains. The fall line marked the frontier of the seventeenth century; the Alleghanies that of the eighteenth; the Mississippi that of the first quarter of the nineteenth; the Missouri that of the middle of this century (omitting the California movement); and the belt of the Rocky Mountains and the arid tract, the present frontier. Each was won by a series of Indian wars.

At the Atlantic frontier one can study the germs of processes repeated at each successive frontier. We have the complex European life sharply precipitated by the wilderness into the simplicity of primitive conditions. The first frontier had to meet its Indian question, its question of the disposition of the public domain, of the means of intercourse with older settlements, of the extension of political organization, of religious and educational activity. And the settlement of these and similar questions for one frontier served as a guide for the next. The American student needs not to go to the "prim little townships of Sleswick" for illustrations of the law of continuity and development. For example, he may study the origin of our land policies in the colonial land policy; he may see how the system grew by adapting the statutes to the customs of the successive frontiers.[18] He may see how the mining experience in the lead regions of Wisconsin, Illinois, and Iowa was applied to the mining laws of the Sierras,[19] and how our Indian policy has been a series of experimentations on successive frontiers. Each tier of new States has found in the older ones material for its constitutions.[20] Each frontier has made similar contributions to American character, as will be discussed farther on.

But with all these similarities there are essential differences, due to the place element and the time element. It is evident that the farming frontier of the Mississippi Valley presents different conditions from the mining frontier of the Rocky Mountains. The frontier reached by the Pacific Railroad, surveyed into rectangles, guarded by the United States Army, and recruited by the daily immigrant ship, moves forward at a swifter pace and in a different way than the frontier reached by the birch canoe or the pack horse. The geologist traces patiently the shores of ancient seas, maps their areas, and compares the older and the newer. It would be a work worth the historian's labors to mark these various frontiers and in detail compare one with another. Not only would there result a more adequate conception of American development and charasteristics, but invaluable additions would be made to the history of society.

Loria,[21] the Italian economist, has urged the study of colonial life as an aid in understanding the stages of European development, affirming that colonial settlement is for economic science what the mountain is for geology, bringing to light primitive stratifications. "America," he says, "has the key to the historical enigma which Europe has sought for centuries in vain, and the land which has no history reveals luminously the course of universal history." There is much truth in this. The United States lies like a huge page in the history of society. Line by line as we read this continental page from West to East we find the record of social evolution. It begins with the Indian and the hunter; it goes on to tell of the disintegration of savagery by the entrance of the trader, the pathfinder of civilization; we read the annals of the pastoral stage in ranch life; the exploitation of the soil by the raising of unrotated crops of corn and wheat in sparsely settled farming communities; the intensive culture of the denser farm settlement; and finally the manufacturing organization with city and factory system.[22] This page is familiar to the student of census statistics, but how little of it has been used by our historians. Particularly in eastern States this page is a palimpsest. What is now a manufacturing State was in an earlier decade an area of intensive farming. Earlier yet it had been a wheat area, and still earlier the "range" had attracted the cattleherder. Thus Wisconsin, now developing manufacture, is a State with varied agricultural interests. But earlier it was given over to almost exclusive grain-raising, like North Dakota at the present time.

Each of these areas has had an influence in our economic and political history; the evolution of each into a higher stage has worked political transformations. But what constitutional historian has made any adequate attempt to interpret political facts by the light of these social areas and changes?[23]

The Atlantic frontier was compounded of fisherman, fur-trader, miner, cattle-raiser, and farmer. Excepting the fisherman, each type of industry was on the march toward the West, impelled by an irresistible attraction. Each passed in successive waves across the continent. Stand at Cumberland Gap and watch the procession of civilization, marching single file—the buffalo following the trail to the salt springs, the Indian, the fur-trader and hunter, the cattle-raiser, the pioneer farmer—and the frontier has passed by. Stand at South Pass in the Rockies a century later and see the same procession with wider intervals between. The unequal rate of advance compels us to distinguish the frontier into the trader's frontier, the rancher's frontier, or the miner's frontier, and the farmer's frontier. When the mines and the cow pens were still near the fall line the traders' pack trains were tinkling across the Alleghanies, and the French on the Great Lakes were fortifying their posts, alarmed by the British trader's birch canoe. When the trappers scaled the Rockies, the farmer was still near the mouth of the Missouri.

Why was it that the Indian trader passed so rapidly across the continent? What effects followed from the trader's frontier? The trade was coeval with American discovery. The Norsemen, Vespuccius, Verrazani, Hudson, John Smith, all trafficked for furs. The Plymouth pilgrims settled in Indian cornfields, and their first return cargo was of beaver and lumber. The records of the various New England colonies show how steadily exploration was carried into the wilderness by this trade. What is true for New England is, as would be expected, even plainer for the rest of the colonies. All along the coast from Maine to Georgia the Indian trade opened up the river courses. Steadily the trader passed westward, utilizing the older lines of French trade. The Ohio, the Great Lakes, the Mississippi, the Missouri, and the Platte, the lines of western advance, were ascended by traders. They found the passes in the Rocky Mountains and guided Lewis and Clark,[24]

Frémont, and Bidwell. The explanation of the rapidity of this advance is connected with the effects of the trader on the Indian. The trading post left the unarmed tribes at the mercy of those that had purchased fire-arms—a truth which the Iroquois Indians wrote in blood, and so the remote and unvisited tribes gave eager welcome to the trader. "The savages," wrote La Salle, "take better care of us French than of their own children; from us only can they get guns and goods." This accounts for the trader's power and the rapidity of his advance. Thus the disintegrating forces of civilization entered the wilderness. Every river valley and Indian trail became a fissure in Indian society, and so that society became honeycombed. Long before the pioneer farmer appeared on the scene, primitive Indian life had passed away. The farmers met Indians armed with guns. The trading frontier, while steadily undermining Indian power by making the tribes ultimately dependent on the whites, yet, through its sale of guns, gave to the Indian increased power of resistance to the farming frontier. French colonization was dominated by its trading frontier; English colonization by its farming frontier. There was an antagonism between the two frontiers as between the two nations. Said Duquesne to the Iroquois, "Are you ignorant of the difference between the king of England and the king of France? Go see the forts that our king has established and you will see that you can still hunt under their very walls. They have been placed for your advantage in places which you frequent. The English, on the contrary, are no sooner in possession of a place than the game is driven away. The forest falls before them as they advance, and the soil is laid bare so that you can scarce find the wherewithal to erect a shelter for the night."

And yet, in spite of this opposition of the interests of the trader and the farmer, the Indian trade pioneered the way for civilization. The buffalo trail became the Indian trail, and this became the trader's "trace"; the trails widened into roads, and the roads into turnpikes, and these in turn were transformed into railroads. The same origin can be shown for the railroads of the South, the Far West, and the Dominion of

Canada.[25] The trading posts reached by these trails were on the sites of Indian villages which had been placed in positions suggested by nature; and these trading posts, situated so as to command the water systems of the country, have grown into such cities as Albany, Pittsburgh, Detroit, Chicago, St. Louis, Council Bluffs, and Kansas City. Thus civilization in America has followed the arteries made by geology, pouring an ever richer tide through them, until at last the slender paths of aboriginal intercourse have been broadened and interwoven into the complex mazes of modern commercial lines; the wilderness has been interpenetrated by lines of civilization growing ever more numerous. It is like the steady growth of a complex nervous system for the originally simple, inert continent. If one would understand why we are to-day one nation, rather than a collection of isolated states, he must study this economic and social consolidation of the country. In this progress from savage conditions lie topics for the evolutionist.[26]

The effect of the Indian frontier as a consolidating agent in our history is important. From the close of the seventeenth century various intercolonial congresses have been called to treat with Indians and establish common measures of defense. Particularism was strongest in colonies with no Indian frontier. This frontier stretched along the western border like a cord of union. The Indian was a common danger, demanding united action. Most celebrated of these conferences was the Albany congress of 1754, called to treat with the Six Nations, and to consider plans of union. Even a cursory reading of the plan proposed by the congress reveals the importance of the frontier. The powers of the general council and the officers were, chiefly, the determination of peace and war with the Indians, the regulation of Indian trade, the purchase of Indian lands, and the creation and government of new settlements as a security against the Indians. It is evident that the unifying tendencies of the Revolutionary period were facilitated by the previous coöperation in the regulation of the frontier. In this connection may be mentioned the importance of the frontier, from that day to this, as a military training school, keeping alive the power of resistance to aggression, and developing the stalwart and rugged qualities of the frontiersman.

It would not be possible in the limits of this paper to trace the other frontiers across the continent. Travelers of the eighteenth century found the "cowpens" among the canebrakes and peavine pastures of the South, and the "cow drivers" took their droves to Charleston, Philadelphia, and New York.[27] Travelers at the close of the War of 1812 met droves of more than a thousand cattle and swine from the interior of Ohio going to Pennsylvania to fatten for the Philadelphia market.[28] The ranges of the Great Plains, with ranch and cowboy and nomadic life, are things of yesterday and of to-day. The experience of the Carolina cowpens guided the ranchers of Texas. One element favoring the rapid extension of the rancher's frontier is the fact that in a remote country lacking transportation facilities the product must be in small bulk, or must be able to transport itself, and the cattle raiser could easily drive his product to market. The effect of these great ranches on the subsequent agrarian history of the localities in which they existed should be studied.

The maps of the census reports show an uneven advance of the farmer's frontier, with tongues of settlement pushed forward and with indentations of wilderness. In part this is due to Indian resistance, in part to the location of river valleys and passes, in part to the unequal force of the centers of frontier attraction. Among the important centers of attraction may be mentioned the following: fertile and favorably situated soils, salt springs, mines, and army posts.

The frontier army post, serving to protect the settlers from the Indians, has also acted as a wedge to open the Indian country, and has been a nucleus for settlement.[29] In this connection mention should also be made of the government military and exploring expeditions in determining the lines of settlement. But all the more important expeditions were greatly indebted to the earliest pathmakers, the Indian guides, the traders and trappers, and the French voyageurs, who were inevitable parts of governmental expeditions from the days of Lewis and Clark.[30] Each expedition was an epitome of the previous factors in western advance.

In an interesting monograph, Victor Hehn[31] has traced the effect of salt upon early European development, and has pointed out how it affected the lines of settlement and the form of administration. A similar study might be made for the salt springs of the United States. The early settlers were tied to the coast by the need of salt, without which they could not preserve their meats or live in comfort. Writing in 1752, Bishop Spangenburg says of a colony for which he was seeking lands in North Carolina, "They will require salt & other necessaries which they can neither manufacture nor raise. Either they must go to Charleston, which is 300 miles distant . . . Or else they must go to Boling's Point in V^a on a branch of the James & is also 300 miles from here . . . Or else they must go down the Roanoke—I know not how many miles—where salt is brought up from the Cape Fear."[32] This may serve as a typical illustration. An annual pilgrimage to the coast for salt thus became essential. Taking flocks or furs and ginseng root, the early settlers sent their pack trains after seeding time each year to the coast.[33] This proved to be an important educational influence, since it was almost the only way in which the pioneer learned what was going on in the East. But when discovery was made of the salt springs of the Kanawha, and the Holston, and Kentucky, and central New York, the West began to be freed from dependence on the coast. It was in part the effect of finding these salt springs that enabled settlement to cross the mountains.

From the time the mountains rose between the pioneer and the seaboard, a new order of Americanism arose. The West and the East began to get out of touch of each other. The settlements from the sea to the mountains kept connection with the rear and had a certain solidarity. But the over-mountain men grew more and more independent. The East took a narrow view of American advance, and nearly lost these men. Kentucky and Tennessee history bears abundant witness to the truth of this statement. The East began to try to hedge and limit westward expansion. Though Webster could declare that there were no Alleghanies in his politics, yet in politics in general they were a very solid factor.

The exploitation of the beasts took hunter and trader to the west, the exploitation of the grasses took the rancher west, and the exploitation of the virgin soil of the river valleys and prairies attracted the farmer. Good soils have been the most continuous attraction to the farmer's frontier. The land hunger of the Virginians drew them down the rivers into Carolina, in early colonial days; the search for soils took the Massachusetts men to Pennsylvania and to New York. As the eastern lands were taken up migration flowed across them to the west. Daniel Boone, the great backwoodsman, who combined the occupations of hunter, trader, cattle-raiser, farmer, and surveyor—learning, probably from the traders, of the fertility of the lands of the upper Yadkin, where the traders were wont to rest as they took their way to the Indians, left his Pennsylvania home with his father, and passed down the Great Valley road to that stream. Learning from a trader of the game and rich pastures of Kentucky, he pioneered the way for the farmers to that region. Thence he passed to the frontier of Missouri, where his settlement was long a landmark on the frontier. Here again he helped to open the way for civilization, finding salt licks, and trails, and land. His son was among the earliest trappers in the passes of the Rocky Mountains, and his party are said to have been the first to camp on the present site of Denver. His grandson, Col. A. J. Boone, of Colorado, was a power among the Indians of the Rocky Mountains, and was appointed an agent by the government. Kit Carson's mother was a Boone.[34] Thus this family epitomizes the backwoodsman's advance across the continent.

The farmer's advance came in a distinct series of waves. In Peck's New Guide to the West, published in Boston in 1837, occurs this suggestive passage:

Generally, in all the western settlements, three classes, like the waves of the ocean, have rolled one after the other. First comes the pioneer, who depends for the subsistence of his family chiefly upon the natural growth of vegetation, called the "range," and the proceeds of hunting. His implements of agriculture are rude, chiefly of his own make, and his efforts directed mainly to a crop of corn and a "truck patch." The last is a rude garden for growing cabbage, beans, corn for roasting ears, cucumbers, and potatoes. A log cabin, and, occasionally, a stable and corn-crib, and a field of a dozen acres, the timber girdled or "deadened," and fenced, are enough for his occupancy. It is quite immaterial whether he ever becomes the owner of the soil. He is the occupant for the time being, pays no rent, and feels as independent as the "lord of the manor." With a horse, cow, and one or two breeders of swine, he strikes into the woods with his family, and becomes the founder of a new county, or perhaps state. He builds his cabin, gathers around him a few other families of similar tastes and habits, and occupies till the range is somewhat subdued, and hunting a little precarious, or, which is more frequently the case, till the neighbors crowd around, roads, bridges, and fields annoy him, and he lacks elbow room. The preëmption law enables him to dispose of his cabin and cornfield to the next class of emigrants; and, to employ his own figures, he "breaks for the high timber," "clears out for the New Purchase," or migrates to Arkansas or Texas, to work the same process over.

The next class of emigrants purchase the lands, add field to field, clear out the roads, throw rough bridges over the streams, put up hewn log houses with glass windows and brick or stone chimneys, occasionally plant orchards, build mills, schoolhouses, court-houses, etc., and exhibit the picture and forms of plain, frugal, civilized life.

Another wave rolls on. The men of capital and enterprise come. The settler is ready to sell out and take the advantage of the rise in property, push farther into the interior and become, himself, a man of capital and enterprise in turn. The small village rises to a spacious town or city; substantial edifices of brick, extensive fields, orchards, gardens, colleges, and churches are seen. Broadcloths, silks, leghorns, crapes, and all the refinements, luxuries, elegancies, frivolities, and fashions are in vogue. Thus wave after wave is rolling westward; the real Eldorado is still farther on.

A portion of the two first classes remain stationary amidst the general movement, improve their habits and condition, and rise in the scale of society.

The writer has traveled much amongst the first class, the real pioneers. He has lived many years in connection with the second grade; and now the third wave is sweeping over large districts of Indiana, Illinois, and Missouri. Migration has become almost a habit in the West. Hundreds of men can be found, not over 50 years of age, who have settled for the fourth, fifth, or sixth time on a new spot. To sell out and remove only a few hundred miles makes up a portion of the variety of backwoods life and manners.[35]

Omitting those of the pioneer farmers who move from the love of adventure, the advance of the more steady farmer is easy to understand. Obviously the immigrant was attracted by the cheap lands of the frontier, and even the native farmer felt their influence strongly. Year by year the farmers who lived on soil whose returns were diminished by unrotated crops were offered the virgin soil of the frontier at nominal prices. Their growing families demanded more lands, and these were dear. The competition of the unexhausted, cheap, and easily tilled prairie lands compelled the farmer either to go west and continue the exhaustion of the soil on a new frontier, or to adopt intensive culture. Thus the census of 1890 shows, in the Northwest, many counties in which there is an absolute or a relative decrease of population. These States have been sending farmers to advance the frontier on the plains, and have themselves begun to turn to intensive farming and to manufacture. A decade before this, Ohio had shown the same transition stage. Thus the demand for land and the love of wilderness freedom drew the frontier ever onward.

Having now roughly outlined the various kinds of frontiers, and their modes of advance, chiefly from the point of view of the frontier itself, we may next inquire what were the influences on the East and on the Old World. A rapid enumeration of some of the more noteworthy effects is all that I have time for.

First, we note that the frontier promoted the formation of a composite nationality for the American people. The coast was preponderantly English, but the later tides of continental immigration flowed across to the free lands. This was the case from the early colonial days. The Scotch-Irish and the Palatine Germans, or "Pennsylvania Dutch," furnished the dominant element in the stock of the colonial frontier. With these peoples were also the freed indented servants, or redemptioners, who at the expiration of their time of service passed to the frontier. Governor Spotswood of Virginia writes in 1717, "The inhabitants of our frontiers are composed generally of such as have been transported hither as servants, and, being out of their time, settle themselves where land is to be taken up and that will produce the necessarys of life with little labour."[36] Very generally these redemptioners were of non-English stock. In the crucible of the frontier the immigrants were Americanized, liberated, and fused into a mixed race, English in neither nationality nor characteristics. The process has gone on from the early days to our own. Burke and other writers in the middle of the eighteenth century believed that Pennsylvania[37] was "threatened with the danger of being wholly foreign in language, manners, and perhaps even inclinations." The German and Scotch-Irish elements in the frontier of the South were only less great. In the middle of the present century the German element in Wisconsin was already so considerable that leading publicists looked to the creation of a German state out of the commonwealth by concentrating their colonization.[38] Such examples teach us to beware of misinterpreting the fact that there is a common English speech in America into a belief that the stock is also English.

In another way the advance of the frontier decreased our dependence on England. The coast, particularly of the South, lacked diversified industries, and was dependent on England for the bulk of its supplies. In the South there was even a dependence on the Northern colonies for articles of food. Governor Glenn, of South Carolina, writes in the middle of the eighteenth century: "Our trade with New York and Philadelphia was of this sort, draining us of all the little money and bills we could gather from other places for their bread, flour, beer, hams, bacon, and other things of their produce, all which, except beer, our new townships begin to supply us with, which are settled with very industrious and thriving Germans. This no doubt diminishes the number of shipping and the appearance of our trade, but it is far from being a detriment to us."[39] Before long the frontier created a demand for merchants. As it retreated from the coast it became less and less possible for England to bring her supplies directly to the consumer's wharfs, and carry away staple crops, and staple crops began to give way to diversified agriculture for a time. The effect of this phase of the frontier action upon the northern section is perceived when we realize how the advance of the frontier aroused seaboard cities like Boston, New York, and Baltimore, to engage in rivalry for what Washington called "the extensive and valuable trade of a rising empire."

The legislation which most developed the powers of the national government, and played the largest part in its activity, was conditioned on the frontier. Writers have discussed the subjects of tariff, land, and internal improvement, as subsidiary to the slavery question. But when American history comes to be rightly viewed it will be seen that the slavery question is an incident. In the period from the end of the first half of the present century to the close of the Civil War slavery rose to primary, but far from exclusive, importance. But this does not justify Dr. von Holst (to take an example) in treating our constitutional history in its formative period down to 1828 in a single volume, giving six volumes chiefly to the history of slavery from 1828 to 1861, under the title "Constitutional History of the United States." The growth of nationalism and the evolution of American political institutions were dependent on the advance of the frontier. Even so recent a writer as Rhodes, in his "History of the United States since the Compromise of 1850," has treated the legislation called out by the western advance as incidental to the slavery struggle.

This is a wrong perspective. The pioneer needed the goods of the coast, and so the grand series of internal improvement and railroad legislation began, with potent nationalizing effects. Over internal improvements occurred great debates, in which grave constitutional questions were discussed. Sectional groupings appear in the votes, profoundly significant for the historian. Loose construction increased as the nation marched westward.[40] But the West was not content with bringing the farm to the factory. Under the lead of Clay—"Harry of the West"—protective tariffs were passed, with the cry of bringing the factory to the farm. The disposition of the public lands was a third important subject of national legislation influenced by the frontier.

The public domain has been a force of profound importance in the nationalization and development of the government. The effects of the struggle of the landed and the landless States, and of the Ordinance of 1787, need no discussion.[41] Administratively the frontier called out some of the highest and most vitalizing activities of the general government. The purchase of Louisiana was perhaps the constitutional turning point in the history of the Republic, inasmuch as it afforded both a new area for national legislation and the occasion of the downfall of the policy of strict construction. But the purchase of Louisiana was called out by frontier needs and demands. As frontier States accrued to the Union the national power grew. In a speech on the dedication of the Calhoun monument Mr. Lamar explained: "In 1789 the States were the creators of the Federal Government; in 1861 the Federal Government was the creator of a large majority of the States."

When we consider the public domain from the point of view of the sale and disposal of the public lands we are again brought face to face with the frontier. The policy of the United States in dealing with its lands is in sharp contrast with the European system of scientific administration. Efforts to make this domain a source of revenue, and to withhold it from emigrants in order that settlement might be compact, were in vain. The jealousy and the fears of the East were powerless in the face of the demands of the frontiersmen. John Quincy Adams was obliged to confess: "My own system of administration, which was to make the national domain the inexhaustible fund for progressive and unceasing internal improvement, has failed." The reason is obvious; a system of administration was not what the West demanded; it wanted land. Adams states the situation as follows: "The slaveholders of the South have bought the coöperation of the western country by the bribe of the western lands, abandoning to the new Western States their own proportion of the public property and aiding them in the design of grasping all the lands into their own hands. Thomas H. Benton was the author of this system, which he brought forward as a substitute for the American system of Mr. Clay, and to supplant him as the leading statesman of the West. Mr. Clay, by his tariff compromise with Mr. Calhoun, abandoned his own American system. At the same time he brought forward a plan for distributing among all the States of the Union the proceeds of the sales of the public lands. His bill for that purpose passed both Houses of Congress, but was vetoed by President Jackson, who, in his annual message of December, 1832, formally recommended that all public lands should be gratuitously given away to individual adventurers and to the States in which the lands are situated.[42]

"No subject," said Henry Clay, "which has presented itself to the present, or perhaps any preceding, Congress, is of greater magnitude than that of the public lands." When we consider the far-reaching effects of the government's land policy upon political, economic, and social aspects of American life, we are disposed to agree with him. But this legislation was framed under frontier influences, and under the lead of Western statesmen like Benton and Jackson. Said Senator Scott of Indiana in 1841: "I consider the preëmption law merely declaratory of the custom or common law of the settlers."

It is safe to say that the legislation with regard to land, tariff, and internal improvements—the American system of the nationalizing Whig party—was conditioned on frontier ideas and needs. But it was not merely in legislative action that the frontier worked against the sectionalism of the coast. The economic and social characteristics of the frontier worked against sectionalism. The men of the frontier had closer resemblances to the Middle region than to either of the other sections. Pennsylvania had been the seed-plot of frontier emigration, and, although she passed on her settlers along the Great Valley into the west of Virginia and the Carolinas, yet the industrial society of these Southern frontiersmen was always more like that of the Middle region than like that of the tide-water portion of the South, which later came to spread its industrial type throughout the South.

The Middle region, entered by New York harbor, was an open door to all Europe. The tide-water part of the South represented typical Englishmen, modified by a warm climate and servile labor, and living in baronial fashion on great plantations; New England stood for a special English movement—Puritanism. The Middle region was less English than the other sections. It had a wide mixture of nationalities, a varied society, the mixed town and county system of local government, a varied economic life, many religious sects. In short, it was a region mediating between New England and the South, and the East and the West. It represented that composite nationality which the contemporary United States exhibits, that juxtaposition of non-English groups, occupying a valley or a little settlement, and presenting reflections of the map of Europe in their variety. It was democratic and nonsectional, if not national; "easy, tolerant, and contented"; rooted strongly in material prosperity. It was typical of the modern United States. It was least sectional, not only because it lay between North and South, but also because with no barriers to shut out its frontiers from its settled region, and with a system of connecting waterways, the Middle region mediated between East and West as well as between North and South. Thus it became the typically American region. Even the New Englander, who was shut out from the frontier by the Middle region, tarrying in New York or Pennsylvania on his westward march, lost the acuteness of his sectionalism on the way.[43]

The spread of cotton culture into the interior of the South finally broke down the contrast between the "tide-water" region and the rest of the State, and based Southern interests on slavery. Before this process revealed its results the western portion of the South, which was akin to Pennsylvania in stock, society, and industry, showed tendencies to fall away from the faith of the fathers into internal improvement legislation and nationalism. In the Virginia convention of 1829–30, called to revise the constitution, Mr. Leigh, of Chesterfield, one of the tide-water counties, declared:

> One of the main causes of discontent which led to this convention, that which had the strongest influence in overcoming our veneration for the work of our fathers, which taught us to contemn the sentiments of Henry and Mason and Pendleton, which weaned us from our reverence for the constituted authorities of the State, was an overweening passion for internal improvement. I say this with perfect knowledge, for it has been avowed to me by gentlemen from the West over and over again. And let me tell the gentleman from Albemarle (Mr. Gordon) that it has been another principal object of those who set this ball of revolution in motion, to overturn the doctrine of State rights, of which Virginia has been the very pillar, and to remove the barrier she has interposed to the interference of the Federal Government in that same work of internal improvement, by so reorganizing the legislature that Virginia, too, may be hitched to the Federal car.

It was this nationalizing tendency of the West that transformed the democracy of Jefferson into the national republicanism of Monroe and the democracy of Andrew Jackson. The West of the War of 1812, the West of Clay, and Benton and Harrison, and Andrew Jackson, shut off by the Middle States and the mountains from the coast sections, had a solidarity of its own with national tendencies.[44] On the tide of the Father of Waters, North and South met and mingled into a nation. Interstate migration went steadily on—a process of cross-fertilization of ideas and institutions. The fierce struggle of the sections over slavery on the western frontier does not diminish the truth of this statement; it proves the truth of it. Slavery was a sectional trait that would not down, but in the West it could not remain sectional. It was the greatest of frontiersmen who declared: "I believe this Government can not endure permanently half slave and half free. It will become all of one thing or all of the other." Nothing works for nationalism like intercourse within the nation. Mobility of population is death to localism, and the western frontier worked irresistibly in unsettling population. The effect reached back from the frontier and affected profoundly the Atlantic coast and even the Old World.

But the most important effect of the frontier has been in the promotion of democracy here and in Europe. As has been indicated, the frontier is productive of individualism. Complex society is precipitated by the wilderness into a kind of primitive organization based on the family. The tendency is anti-social. It produces antipathy to control, and particularly to any direct control. The tax-gatherer is viewed as a representative of oppression. Prof. Osgood, in an able article,[45] has pointed out that the frontier conditions prevalent in the colonies are important factors in the explanation of the American Revolution, where individual liberty was sometimes confused with absence of all effective government. The same conditions aid in explaining the difficulty of instituting a strong government in the period of the confederacy. The frontier individualism has from the beginning promoted democracy.

The frontier States that came into the Union in the first quarter of a century of its existence came in with democratic suffrage provisions, and had reactive effects of the highest importance upon the older States whose peoples were being attracted there. An extension of the franchise became essential. It was *western* New York that forced an extension of suffrage in the constitutional convention of that State in 1821; and it was *western* Virginia that compelled the tide-water region to put a more liberal suffrage provision in the constitution framed in 1830, and to give to the frontier region a more nearly proportionate representation with the tide-water aristocracy. The rise of democracy as an effective force in the nation came in with western preponderance under Jackson and William Henry Harrison, and it meant the triumph of the frontier—with all of its good and with all of its evil elements.[46] An interesting illustration of the tone of frontier democracy in 1830 comes from the same debates in the Virginia convention already referred to. A representative from western Virginia declared:

But, sir, it is not the increase of population in the West which this gentleman ought to fear. It is the energy which the mountain breeze and western habits impart to those emigrants. They are regenerated, politically I mean, sir. They soon become *working politicians;* and the difference, sir, between a *talking* and a *working* politician is immense. The Old Dominion has long been celebrated for producing great orators; the ablest metaphysicians in policy; men that can split hairs in all abstruse questions of political economy. But at home, or when they return from Congress, they have negroes to fan them asleep. But a Pennsylvania, a New York, an Ohio, or a western Virginia statesman, though far inferior in logic, metaphysics, and rhetoric to an old Virginia statesman, has this advantage, that when he returns home he takes off his coat and takes hold of the plow. This gives him bone and muscle, sir, and preserves his republican principles pure and uncontaminated.

So long as free land exists, the opportunity for a competency exists, and economic power secures political power. But the democracy born of free land, strong in selfishness and individualism, intolerant of administrative experience and education, and pressing individual liberty beyond its proper bounds, has its dangers as well as its benefits. Individualism in America has allowed a laxity in regard to governmental affairs which has rendered possible the spoils system and all the manifest evils that follow from the lack of a highly developed civic spirit. In this connection may be noted also the influence of frontier conditions in permitting lax business honor, inflated paper currency and wild-cat banking. The colonial and revolutionary frontier was the region whence emanated many of the worst forms of an evil currency.[47] The West in the War of 1812 repeated the phenomenon on the frontier of that day, while the speculation and wild-cat banking of the period of the crisis of 1837 occurred on the new frontier belt of the next tier of States. Thus each one of the periods of lax financial integrity coincides with periods when a new set of frontier communities had arisen, and coincides in area with these successive frontiers, for the most part. The recent Populist agitation is a case in point. Many a State that now declines any connection with the tenets of the Populists, itself adhered to such ideas in an earlier stage of the development of the State. A primitive society can hardly be expected to show the intelligent appreciation of the complexity of business interests in a developed society. The continual recurrence of these areas of paper-money agitation is another evidence that the frontier can be isolated and studied as a factor in American history of the highest importance.[48]

The East has always feared the result of an unregulated advance of the frontier, and has tried to check and guide it. The English authorities would have checked settlement at the headwaters of the Atlantic tributaries and allowed the "savages to enjoy their deserts in quiet lest the peltry trade should decrease." This called out Burke's splendid protest:

If you stopped your grants, what would be the consequence? The people would occupy without grants. They have already so occupied in many places. You can not station garrisons in every part of these deserts. If you drive the people from one place, they will carry on their annual tillage and remove with their flocks and herds to another. Many of the people in the back settlements are already little attached to particular situations. Already they have topped the Appalachian Mountains. From thence they behold before them an immense plain, one vast, rich, level meadow; a square of five hundred miles. Over this they would wander without a possibility of restraint; they would change their manners with their habits of life; would soon forget a government by which they were disowned; would become hordes of English Tartars; and, pouring down upon your unfortified frontiers a fierce and irresistible cavalry, become masters of your governors and your counselers, your collectors and comptrollers, and of all the slaves that adhered to them. Such would, and in no long time must, be the effect of attempting to forbid as a crime and to suppress as an evil the command and blessing of Providence, "Increase and multiply." Such would be the happy result of an endeavor to keep as a lair of wild beasts that earth which God, by an express charter, has given to the children of men.

But the English Government was not alone in its desire to limit the advance of the frontier and guide its destinies. Tidewater Virginia[49] and South Carolina[50] gerrymandered those colonies to insure the dominance of the coast in their legislatures. Washington desired to settle a State at a time in the Northwest; Jefferson would reserve from settlement the territory of his Louisiana Purchase north of the thirty-second parallel, in order to offer it to the Indians in exchange for their settlements east of the Mississippi. "When we shall be full on this side," he writes, "we may lay off a range of States on the western bank from the head to the mouth, and so range after range, advancing compactly as we multiply." Madison went so far as to argue to the French minister that the United States had no interest in seeing population extend itself on the right bank of the Mississippi, but should rather fear it. When the Oregon question was under debate, in 1824, Smyth, of Virginia, would draw an unchangeable line for the limits of the United States at the outer limit of two tiers of States beyond the Mississippi, complaining that the seaboard States were being drained of the flower of their population by the bringing of too much land into market. Even Thomas Benton, the man of widest views of the destiny of the West, at this stage of his career declared that along the ridge of the Rocky mountains "the western limits of the Republic should be drawn, and the statue of the fabled god Terminus should be raised upon its highest peak, never to be thrown down."[51] But the attempts to limit the boundaries, to restrict land sales and settlement, and to deprive the West of its share of political power were all in vain. Steadily the frontier of settlement advanced and carried with it individualism, democracy, and nationalism, and powerfully affected the East and the Old World.

The most effective efforts of the East to regulate the frontier came through its educational and religious activity, exerted by interstate migration and by organized societies. Speaking in 1835, Dr. Lyman Beecher declared: "It is equally plain that the religious and political destiny of our nation is to be decided in the West," and he pointed out that the population of the West "is assembled from all the States of the Union and from all the nations of Europe, and is rushing in like the waters of the flood, demanding for its moral preservation the immediate and universal action of those institutions which discipline the mind and arm the conscience and the heart. And so various are the opinions and habits, and so recent and imperfect is the acquaintance, and so sparse are the settlements of the West, that no homogeneous public sentiment can be formed to legislate immediately into being the requisite institutions. And yet they are all needed immediately in their utmost perfection and power. A nation is being 'born in a day.' ... But what will become of the West if her prosperity rushes up to such a majesty of power, while those great institutions linger which are necessary to form the mind and the conscience and the heart of that vast world. It must not be permitted.... Let no man at the East quiet himself and dream of liberty, whatever may become of the West.... Her destiny is our destiny."[52]

With the appeal to the conscience of New England, he adds appeals to her fears lest other religious sects anticipate her own. The New England preacher and school-teacher left their mark on the West. The dread of Western emancipation from New England's political and economic control was paralleled by her fears lest the West cut loose from her religion. Commenting in 1850 on reports that settlement was rapidly extending northward in Wisconsin, the editor of the *Home Missionary* writes: "We scarcely know whether to rejoice or mourn over this extension of our settlements. While we sympathize in whatever tends to increase the physical resources and prosperity of our country, we can not forget that with all these dispersions into remote and still remoter corners of the land the supply of the means of grace is becoming relatively less and less." Acting in accordance with such ideas, home missions were established and Western colleges were erected. As seaboard cities like Philadelphia, New York, and Baltimore strove for the mastery of Western trade, so the various denominations strove for the possession of the West. Thus an intellectual stream from New England sources fertilized the West. Other sections sent their missionaries; but the real struggle was between sects. The contest for power and the expansive tendency furnished to the various sects by the existence of a moving frontier must have had important results on the character of religious organization in the United States. The multiplication of rival churches in the little frontier towns had deep and lasting social effects. The religious aspects of the frontier make a chapter in our history which needs study.

From the conditions of frontier life came intellectual traits of profound importance. The works of travelers along each frontier from colonial days onward describe certain common traits, and these traits have, while softening down, still persisted as survivals in the place of their origin, even when a higher social organization succeeded. The result is that to the frontier the American intellect owes its striking characteristics. That coarseness and strength combined with acuteness and inquisitiveness; that practical, inventive turn of mind, quick to find expedients; that masterful grasp of material things, lacking in the artistic but powerful to effect great ends; that restless, nervous energy;[53] that dominant individualism, working for good and for evil, and withal that buoyancy and exuberance which comes with freedom—these are traits of the frontier, or traits called out elsewhere because of the existence of the frontier. Since the days when the fleet of Columbus sailed into the waters of the New World, America has been another name for opportunity, and the people of the United States have taken their tone from the incessant expansion which has not only been open but has even been forced upon them. He would be a rash prophet who should assert that the expansive character of American life has now entirely ceased. Movement has been its dominant fact, and, unless this training has no effect upon a people, the American energy will continually demand a wider field for its exercise. But never again will such gifts of free land offer themselves. For a moment, at the frontier, the bonds of custom are broken and unrestraint is triumphant. There is not *tabula rasa*. The stubborn American environment is there with its imperious summons to accept its conditions; the inherited ways of doing things are also there; and yet, in spite of environment, and in spite of custom, each frontier did indeed furnish a new field of opportunity, a gate of escape from the bondage of the past; and freshness, and confidence, and scorn of older society, impatience of its restraints and its ideas, and indifference to its lessons, have accompanied the frontier. What the Mediterranean Sea was to the Greeks, breaking the bond of custom, offering new experiences, calling out new institutions and activities, that, and more, the ever retreating frontier has been to the United States directly, and to the nations of Europe more remotely. And now, four centuries from the discovery of America, at the end of a hundred years of life under the Constitution, the frontier has gone, and with its going has closed the first period of American history.

THREE

THE PROBLEM OF
THE WEST

(1896)

The problem of the West is nothing less than the problem of
American development. A glance at the map of the United
States reveals the truth. To write of a "Western sectionalism,"
bounded on the east by the Alleghanies, is, in itself, to proclaim the writer a provincial. What is the West? What has it
been in American life? To have the answers to these questions
is to understand the most significant features of the United
States of to-day.

The West, at bottom, is a form of society, rather than an
area. It is the term applied to the region whose social conditions result from the application of older institutions and ideas
to the transforming influences of free land. By this application,
a new environment is suddenly entered, freedom of opportunity is opened, the cake of custom is broken, and new activities, new lines of growth, new institutions and new ideals,
are brought into existence. The wilderness disappears, the
"West" proper passes on to a new frontier, and in the former

Reprinted by permission from *Atlantic Monthly* 77 (September 1896).

area, a new society has emerged from its contact with the backwoods. Gradually this society loses its primitive conditions, and assimilates itself to the type of the older social conditions of the East; but it bears within it enduring and distinguishing survivals of its frontier experience. Decade after decade, West after West, this rebirth of American society has gone on, has left its traces behind it, and has reacted on the East. The history of our political institutions, our democracy, is not a history of imitation, of simple borrowing; it is a history of the evolution and adaptation of organs in response to changed environment, a history of the origin of new political species. In this sense, therefore, the West has been a constructive force of the highest significance in our life. To use the words of that acute and widely informed observer, Mr. Bryce, "The West is the most American part of America.... What Europe is to Asia, what America is to England, that the Western States and Territories are to the Atlantic States."

The West, as a phase of social organization, began with the Atlantic coast, and passed across the continent. But the colonial tide-water area was in close touch with the Old World, and soon lost its Western aspects. In the middle of the eighteenth century, the newer social conditions appeared along the upper waters of the tributaries of the Atlantic. Here it was that the West took on its distinguishing features, and transmitted frontier traits and ideals to this area in later days. On the coast, were the fishermen and skippers, the merchants and planters, with eyes turned toward Europe. Beyond the falls of the rivers were the pioneer farmers, largely of non-English stock, Scotch-Irish and German. They constituted a distinct people, and may be regarded as an expansion of the social and economic life of the middle region into the back country of the South. These frontiersmen were the ancestors of Boone, Andrew Jackson, Calhoun, Clay, and Lincoln. Washington and Jefferson were profoundly affected by these frontier conditions. The forest clearings have been the seed plots of American character.

In the Revolutionary days, the settlers crossed the Alleghanies and put a barrier between them and the coast. They became, to use their phrases, "the men of the Western waters," the heirs of the "Western world." In this era, the backwoodsmen, all along the western slopes of the mountains, with a keen sense of the difference between them and the dwellers on the coast, demanded organization into independent States of the Union. Self-government was their ideal. Said one of their rude, but energetic petitions for statehood: "Some of our fellow-citizens may think we are not able to conduct our affairs and consult our interests; but if our society is rude, much wisdom is not necessary to supply our wants, and a fool can sometimes put on his clothes better than a wise man can do it for him." This forest philosophy is the philosophy of American democracy. But the men of the coast were not ready to admit its implications. They apportioned the State legislatures so that the property-holding minority of the tidewater lands were able to outvote the more populous back countries. A similar system was proposed by Federalists in the constitutional convention of 1787. Gouverneur Morris, arguing in favor of basing representation on property as well as numbers, declared that "he looked forward, also, to that range of new States which would soon be formed in the West. He thought the rule of representation ought to be so fixed, as to secure to the Atlantic States a prevalence in the national councils." "The new States," said he, "will know less of the public interest than these; will have an interest in many respects different; in particular will be little scrupulous of involving the community in wars, the burdens and operations of which would fall chiefly on the maritime States. Provision ought, therefore, to be made to prevent the maritime States from being hereafter outvoted by them." He added that the Western country "would not be able to furnish men equally enlightened to share in the administration of our common interests. The busy haunts of men, not the remote wilderness, was the proper school of political talents. If the Western people get power into their hands, they will ruin the Atlantic interest. The back members are always most averse to the best measures." Add to these utterances of Gouverneur Morris the impassioned protest of Josiah Quincy, of Massachusetts, in the debates in the House of Representatives, on the admission of Louisiana. Referring to the discussion over the slave votes and the West in the constitutional convention, he declared, "Suppose, then, that it had been distinctly foreseen that, in addition to the effect of this weight, the whole population of a world beyond the Mississippi was to be brought into this and the other branch of the legislature, to form our laws, control our rights, and decide our destiny. Sir, can it be pretended that the patriots of that day would for one moment have listened to it? . . . They had not taken degrees at the hospital of idiocy. . . . Why, sir, I have already heard of six States, and some say there will be, at no great distant time, more. I have also heard that the mouth of the Ohio will be far to the east of the center of the contemplated empire. . . . You have no authority to throw the rights and property of this people into 'hotch-pot' with the wild men on the Missouri, nor with the mixed, though more respectable, race of Anglo-Hispano-Gallo-Americans who bask on the sands in the mouth of the Mississippi. . . . Do you suppose the people of the Northern and Atlantic States will, or ought to, look on with patience and see Representatives and Senators from the Red River and Missouri, pouring themselves upon this and the other floor, managing the concerns of a seaboard fifteen hundred miles, at least, from their residence; and having a preponderancy in councils into which, constitutionally, they could never have been admitted?"

Like an echo from the fears expressed by the East at the close of the eighteenth century come the words of an eminent Eastern man of letters[1] at the end of the nineteenth century, in warning against the West: "Materialized in their temper; with few ideals of an ennobling sort; little instructed in the lessons of history; safe from exposure to the direct calamities and physical horrors of war; with undeveloped imaginations and sympathies—they form a community unfortunate and dangerous from the possession of power without a due sense of its corresponding responsibilities; a community in which the passion for war may easily be excited as the fancied means by which its greatness may be convincingly exhibited, and its ambitions gratified. . . . Some chance spark may fire the prairie."

Here, then, is the problem of the West, as it looked to New England leaders of thought in the beginning and at the end of this century. From the first, it was recognized that a new type was growing up beyond the seaboard, and that the time would come when the destiny of the nation would be in Western hands. The divergence of these societies became clear in the struggle over the ratification of the federal constitution. The up-country agricultural regions, the communities that were in debt and desired paper money, with some Western exceptions, opposed the instrument; but the areas of intercourse and property carried the day.

It is important to understand, therefore, what were some of the ideals of this early Western democracy. How did the frontiersman differ from the man of the coast?

The most obvious fact regarding the man of the Western Waters is that he had placed himself under influences destructive to many of the gains of civilization. Remote from the opportunity for systematic education, substituting a log hut in the forest-clearing for the social comforts of the town, he suffered hardships and privations, and reverted in many ways to primitive conditions of life. Engaged in a struggle to subdue the forest, working as an individual, and with little specie or capital, his interests were with the debtor class. At each stage of its advance, the West has favored an expansion of the currency. The pioneer had boundless confidence in the future of his own community, and when seasons of financial contraction and depression occurred, he, who had staked his all on confidence in Western development, and had fought the savage for his home, was inclined to reproach the conservative sections and classes. To explain this antagonism requires more than denunciation of dishonesty, ignorance, and boorishness as fundamental Western traits. Legislation in the United States has had to deal with two distinct social conditions. In some portions of the country there was, and is, an aggregation of property, and vested rights are in the foreground: in others, capital is lacking, more primitive conditions prevail, with different economic and social ideals, and the contentment of the average individual is placed in the foreground. That in the conflict between these two ideals an even hand has always been held by the government would be difficult to show.

The separation of the Western man from the seaboard, and his environment, made him in a large degree free from European precedents and forces. He looked at things independently and with small regard or appreciation for the best Old World experience. He had no ideal of a philosophical, eclectic nation, that should advance civilization by "intercourse with foreigners and familiarity with their point of view, and readiness to adopt whatever is best and most suitable in their ideas, manners, and customs." His was rather the ideal of conserving and developing what was original and valuable in this new country. The entrance of old society upon free lands meant to him opportunity for a new type of democracy and new popular ideals. The West was not conservative: buoyant self-confidence and self-assertion were distinguishing traits in its composition. It saw in its growth nothing less than a new order of society and state. In this conception were elements of evil and elements of good.

But the fundamental fact in regard to this new society was its relation to land. Professor Boutmy has said of the United States, "Their one primary and predominant object is to cultivate and settle these prairies, forests, and vast waste lands. The striking and peculiar characteristic of American society is that it is not so much a democracy as a huge commercial company for the discovery, cultivation, and capitalization of its enormous territory. The United States are primarily a commercial society, and only secondarily a nation." Of course, this involves a serious misapprehension. By the very fact of the task here set forth, far-reaching ideals of the state and of society have been evolved in the West, accompanied by loyalty to the nation representative of these ideals. But M. Boutmy's description hits the substantial fact, that the fundamental traits of the man of the interior were due to the free lands of the West. These turned his attention to the great task of subduing them to the purposes of civilization, and to the task of advancing his economic and social status in the new democracy which he was helping to create. Art, literature, refinement, scientific administration, all had to give way to this Titanic labor. Energy, incessant activity, became the lot of this new American. Says a traveler of the time of Andrew Jackson, "America is like a vast workshop, over the door of which is printed in blazing characters, 'No admittance here, except on business.' " The West of our own day reminds Mr. Bryce "of the crowd which Vathek found in the hall of Eblis, each darting hither and thither with swift steps and unquiet mien, driven to and fro by a fire in the heart. Time seems too short for what they have to do, and the result always to come short of their desire."

But free lands and the consciousness of working out their social destiny did more than turn the Westerner to material interests and devote him to a restless existence. They promoted equality among the Western settlers, and reacted as a check on the aristocratic influences of the East. Where everybody could have a farm, almost for taking it, economic equality easily resulted, and this involved political equality. Not without a struggle would the Western man abandon this ideal, and it goes far to explain the unrest in the remote West to-day.

Western democracy included individual liberty, as well as equality. The frontiersman was impatient of restraints. He knew how to preserve order, even in the absence of legal authority. If there were cattle thieves, lynch law was sudden and effective: the regulators of the Carolinas were the predecessors of the claims associations of Iowa and the vigilance committees of California. But the individual was not ready to submit to complex regulations. Population was sparse, there was no multitude of jostling interests, as in older settlements, demanding an elaborate system of personal restraints. Society became atomic. There was a reproduction of the primitive idea of the personality of the law, a crime was more an offense against the victim than a violation of the law of the land. Substantial justice, secured in the most direct way, was the ideal of the backwoodsman. He had little patience with finely drawn distinctions or scruples of method. If the thing was one proper to be done, then the most immediate, rough and ready, effective way was the best way.

It followed from the lack of organized political life, from the atomic conditions of the backwoods society, that the individual was exalted and given free play. The West was another name for opportunity. Here were mines to be seized, fertile valleys to be preëmpted, all the natural resources open to the shrewdest and the boldest. The United States is unique in the extent to which the individual has been given an open field, unchecked by restraints of an old social order, or of scientific administration of government. The self-made man was the Western man's ideal, was the kind of man that all men might become. Out of his wilderness experience, out of the freedom of his opportunities, he fashioned a formula for social regeneration—the freedom of the individual to seek his own. He did not consider that his conditions were exceptional and temporary.

Under such conditions, leadership easily develops—a leadership based on the possession of the qualities most serviceable to the young society. In the history of Western settlement, we see each forted village following its local hero. Clay, Jackson, Harrison, Lincoln, were illustrations of this tendency in periods when the Western hero rose to the dignity of national hero.

The Western man believed in the manifest destiny of his country. On his border, and checking his advance, were the Indian, the Spaniard, and the Englishman. He was indignant at Eastern indifference and lack of sympathy with his view of his relations to these peoples; at the short-sightedness of Eastern policy. The closure of the Mississippi by Spain, and the proposal to exchange our claim of freedom of navigating the river, in return for commercial advantages to New England, nearly led to the withdrawal of the West from the Union. It was the Western demands that brought about the purchase of Louisiana, and turned the scale in favor of declaring the War of 1812. Militant qualities were favored by the annual expansion of the settled area in the face of hostile Indians and the stubborn wilderness. The West caught the vision of the nation's continental destiny. Henry Adams, in his History of the United States, makes the American of 1800 exclaim to the foreign visitor, "Look at my wealth! See these solid mountains of salt and iron, of lead, copper, silver, and gold. See these magnificent cities scattered broadcast to the Pacific! See my cornfields rustling and waving in the summer breeze from ocean to ocean, so far that the sun itself is not high enough to mark where the distant mountains bound my golden seas. Look at this continent of mine, fairest of created worlds, as she lies turning up to the sun's never failing caress her broad and exuberant breasts, overflowing with milk for her hundred million children." And the foreigner saw only dreary deserts, tenanted by sparse, ague-stricken pioneers and savages. The cities were log huts and gambling dens. But the frontiersman's dream was prophetic. In spite of his rude, gross nature, this early Western man was an idealist withal. He dreamed dreams and beheld visions. He had faith in man, hope for democracy, belief in America's destiny, unbounded confidence in his ability to make his dreams come true. Said Harriet Martineau in 1834, "I regard the American people as a great embryo poet, now moody, now wild, but bringing out results of absolute good sense: restless and wayward in action, but with deep peace at his heart; exulting that he has caught the true aspect of things past, and the depth of futurity which lies before him, wherein to create something so magnificent as the world has scarcely begun to dream of. There is the strongest hope of a nation that is capable of being possessed with an idea."

It is important to bear this idealism of the West in mind. The very materialism that has been urged against the West was accompanied by ideals of equality, of the exaltation of the common man, of national expansion, that makes it a profound mistake to write of the West as though it were engrossed in mere material ends. It has been, and is, preëminently a region of ideals, mistaken or not.

It is obvious that these economic and social conditions were so fundamental in Western life that they might well dominate whatever accessions came to the West by immigration from the coast sections or from Europe. Nevertheless, the West cannot be understood without bearing in mind the fact that it has received the great streams from the North and from the South, and that the Mississippi compelled these currents to intermingle. Here it was that sectionalism first gave way under the pressure of unification. Ultimately the conflicting ideas and institutions of the old sections struggled for dominance in this area under the influence of the forces that made for uniformity, but this is merely another phase of the truth that the West must become unified, that it could not rest in sectional groupings. For precisely this reason the struggle occurred. In the period from the Revolution to the close of the War of 1812, the democracy of the Southern and Middle States contributed the main streams of settlement and social influence to the West. Even in Ohio political power was soon lost by the New England leaders. The democratic spirit of the Middle region left an indelible impress on the West in this its formative period. After the War of 1812, New England, its supremacy in the carrying trade of the world having vanished, became a hive from which swarms of settlers went out to western New York and the remoter regions.

These settlers spread New England ideals of education and character and political institutions, and acted as a leaven of great significance in the Northwest. But it would be a mistake to believe that an unmixed New England influence took possession of the Northwest. These pioneers did not come from the class that conserved the type of New England civilization pure and undefiled. They represented a less contented, less conservative influence. Moreover, by their sojourn in the Middle Region, on their westward march, they underwent modification, and when the farther West received them, they suffered a forest-change, indeed. The Westernized New England man was no longer the representative of the section that he left. He was less conservative, less provincial, more adaptable and approachable, less rigorous in his Puritan ideals, less a man of culture, more a man of action.

As might have been expected, therefore, the Western men, in the "era of good feeling," had much homogeneity throughout the Mississippi Valley, and began to stand as a new national type. Under the lead of Henry Clay they invoked the national government to break down the mountain barrier by internal improvements, and thus to give their crops an outlet to the coast. Under him they appealed to the national government for a protective tariff to create a home market. A group of frontier States entered the Union with democratic provisions respecting the suffrage, and with devotion to the nation that had given them their lands, built their roads and canals, regulated their territorial life, and made them equals in the sisterhood of States. At last these Western forces of aggressive nationalism and democracy took possession of the government in the person of the man who best embodied them, Andrew Jackson. This new democracy that captured the country and destroyed the ideals of statesmanship came from no theorist's dreams of the German forest. It came, stark and strong and full of life, from the American forest. But the triumph of this Western democracy revealed also the fact that it could rally to its aid the laboring classes of the coast, then just beginning to acquire self-consciousness and organization.

The next phase of Western development revealed forces of division between the northern and southern portions of the West. With the spread of the cotton culture went the slave system and the great plantation. The small farmer in his log cabin, raising varied crops, was displaced by the planter raising cotton. In all except the mountainous areas the industrial organization of the tidewater took possession of the Southwest, the unity of the back country was broken, and the solid South was formed. In the Northwest this was the era of railroads and canals, opening the region to the increasing stream of Middle State and New England settlement, and strengthening the opposition to slavery. A map showing the location of the men of New England ancestry in the Northwest would represent also the counties in which the Free Soil party cast its heaviest votes. The commercial connections of the Northwest likewise were reversed by the railroad. The result is stated by a writer in *De Bow's Review* in 1852 in these words:—

"What is New Orleans now? Where are her dreams of greatness and glory? . . . Whilst she slept, an enemy has sowed tares in her most prolific fields. Armed with energy, enterprise, and an indomitable spirit, that enemy, by a system of bold, vigorous, and sustained efforts, has succeeded in reversing the very laws of nature and of nature's God—rolled back the mighty tide of the Mississippi and its thousand tributary streams, until their mouth, practically and commercially, is more at New York or Boston than at New Orleans."

The West broke asunder, and the great struggle over the social system to be given to the lands beyond the Mississippi followed. In the Civil War the Northwest furnished the national hero—Lincoln was the very flower of frontier training and ideals—and it also took into its hands the whole power of the government. Before the war closed, the West could claim the President, Vice-President, Chief Justice, Speaker of the House, Secretary of the Treasury, Postmaster-General, Attorney-General, General of the army, and Admiral of the navy. The leading generals of the war had been furnished by the West. It was the region of action, and in the crisis it took the reins.

The triumph of the nation was followed by a new era of Western development. The national forces projected themselves across the prairies and plains. Railroads, fostered by government loans and land grants, opened the way for settlement and poured a flood of European immigrants and restless pioneers from all sections of the Union into the government lands. The army of the United States pushed back the Indian, rectangular Territories were carved into checkerboard States, creations of the federal government, without a history, without physiographical unity, without particularistic ideas. The later frontiersman leaned on the strong arm of national power.

At the same time the South underwent a revolution. The plantation, based on slavery, gave place to the farm, the gentry to the democratic elements. As in the West, new industries, of mining and of manufacture, sprang up as by magic. The New South, like the New West, was an area of construction, a debtor area, an area of unrest; and it, too, had learned the uses to which federal legislation might be put.

In the meantime the Old Northwest² passed through an economic and social transformation. The whole West furnished an area over which successive waves of economic development have passed. The State of Wisconsin, now much like parts of the State of New York, was at an earlier period like the State of Nebraska of to-day; the Granger movement and Greenback party had for a time the ascendancy; and in the northern counties of the State, where there is a sparser population, and the country is being settled, its sympathies are still with the debtor class. Thus the Old Northwest is a region where the older frontier conditions survive in parts, and where the inherited ways of looking at things are largely to be traced to its frontier days. At the same time it is a region in many ways assimilated to the East. It understands both sections. It is not entirely content with the existing structure of economic society in the sections where wealth has accumulated and corporate organizations are powerful; but neither has it seemed to feel that its interests lie in supporting the program of the prairies and the South. In the Fifty-third Congress it voted for the income tax, but it rejected free coinage. It is still affected by the ideal of the self-made man, rather than by the ideal of industrial nationalism. It is more American, but less cosmopolitan than the seaboard.

We are now in a position to see clearly some of the factors involved in the Western problem. For nearly three centuries the dominant fact in American life has been expansion. With the settlement of the Pacific coast and the occupation of the free lands, this movement has come to a check. That these energies of expansion will no longer operate would be a rash prediction; and the demands for a vigorous foreign policy, for an interoceanic canal, for a revival of our power upon the seas, and for the extension of American influence to outlying islands and adjoining countries, are indications that the movement will continue. The stronghold of these demands lies west of the Alleghanies.

In the remoter West, the restless, rushing wave of settlement has broken with a shock against the arid plains. The free lands are gone, the continent is crossed, and all this push and energy is turning into channels of agitation. Failures in one area can no longer be made good by taking up land on a new frontier; the conditions of a settled society are being reached with suddenness and with confusion. The West has been built up with borrowed capital, and the question of the stability of gold, as a standard of deferred payments, is eagerly agitated by the debtor West, profoundly dissatisfied with the industrial conditions that confront it, and actuated by frontier directness and rigor in its remedies. For the most part, the men who built up the West beyond the Mississippi, and who are now leading the agitation,[3] came as pioneers from the old Northwest, in the days when it was just passing from the stage of a frontier section. For example, Senator Allen of Nebraska, president of the recent national Populist Convention, and a type of the political leaders of his section, was born in Ohio in the middle of the century, went in his youth to Iowa, and not long after the Civil War made his home in Nebraska. As a boy, he saw the buffalo driven out by the settlers; he saw the Indian retreat as the pioneer advanced. His training is that of the old West, in its frontier days. And now the frontier opportunities are gone. Discontent is demanding an extension of governmental activity in its behalf. In these demands, it finds itself in touch with the depressed agricultural classes and the workingmen of the South and East. The Western problem is no longer a sectional problem: it is a social problem on a national scale. The greater West, extending from the Alleghanies to the Pacific, cannot be regarded as a unit; it requires analysis into regions and classes. But its area, its population, and its material resources would give force to its assertion that if there is a sectionalism in the country, the sectionalism is Eastern. The old West, united to the new South, would produce, not a new sectionalism, but a new Americanism. It would not mean sectional disunion, as some have speculated, but it might mean a drastic assertion of national government and imperial expansion under a popular hero.

This, then, is the real situation: a people composed of heterogeneous materials, with diverse and conflicting ideals and social interests, having passed from the task of filling up the vacant spaces of the continent, is now thrown back upon itself, and is seeking an equilibrium. The diverse elements are being fused into national unity. The forces of reorganization are turbulent and the nation seems like a witches' kettle.

But the West has its own centers of industrial life and culture not unlike those of the East. It has State universities, rivaling in conservative and scientific economic instruction those of any other part of the Union, and its citizens more often visit the East, than do Eastern men the West. As time goes on, its industrial development will bring it more into harmony with the East.

Moreover, the Old Northwest holds the balance of power, and is the battlefield on which these issues of American development are to be settled. It has more in common with all parts of the nation than has any other region. It understands the East, as the East does not understand the West. The White City which recently rose on the shores of Lake Michigan fitly typified its growing culture as well as its capacity for great achievement. Its complex and representative industrial organization and business ties, its determination to hold fast to what is original and good in its Western experience, and its readiness to learn and receive the results of the experience of other sections and nations, make it an open-minded and safe arbiter of the American destiny.

In the long run the "Center of the Republic" may be trusted to strike a wise balance between the contending ideals. But she does not deceive herself; she knows that the problem of the West means nothing less than the problem of working out original social ideals and social adjustments for the American nation.

FOUR

CONTRIBUTIONS OF THE WEST TO AMERICAN DEMOCRACY

(1903)

Political thought in the period of the French Revolution tended to treat democracy as an absolute system applicable to all times and to all peoples, a system that was to be created by the act of the people themselves on philosophical principles. Ever since that era there has been an inclination on the part of writers on democracy to emphasize the analytical and theoretical treatment to the neglect of the underlying factors of historical development.

If, however, we consider the underlying conditions and forces that create the democratic type of government, and at times contradict the external forms to which the name democracy is applied, we shall find that under this name there have appeared a multitude of political types radically unlike in fact.

The careful student of history must, therefore, seek the explanation of the forms and changes of political institutions in the social and economic forces that determine them. To know

Reprinted by permission from *Atlantic Monthly* 92 (January 1903).

that at any one time a nation may be called a democracy, an aristocracy, or a monarchy, is not so important as to know what are the social and economic tendencies of the state. These are the vital forces that work beneath the surface and dominate the external form. It is to changes in the economic and social life of a people that we must look for the forces that ultimately create and modify organs of political action. For the time, adaptation of political structure may be incomplete or concealed. Old organs will be utilized to express new forces, and so gradual and subtle will be the change that it may hardly be recognized. The pseudo-democracies under the Medici at Florence and under Augustus at Rome are familiar examples of this type. Or again, if the political structure be rigid, incapable of responding to the changes demanded by growth, the expansive forces of social and economic transformation may rend it in some catastrophe like that of the French Revolution. In all these changes both conscious ideals and unconscious social reorganization are at work.

These facts are familiar to the student, and yet it is doubtful if they have been fully considered in connection with American democracy. For a century at least, in conventional expression, Americans have referred to a "glorious Constitution" in explaining the stability and prosperity of their democracy. We have believed as a nation that other peoples had only to will our democratic institutions in order to repeat our own career.

In dealing with Western contributions to democracy, it is essential that the considerations which have just been mentioned shall be kept in mind. Whatever these contributions may have been, we find ourselves at the present time in an era of such profound economic and social transformation as to raise the question of the effect of these changes upon the democratic institutions of the United States. Within a decade four marked changes have occurred in our national development; taken together they constitute a revolution.

First, there is the exhaustion of the supply of free land and the closing of the movement of Western advance as an effective factor in

American development. The first rough conquest of the wilderness is accomplished, and that great supply of free lands which year after year has served to reinforce the democratic influences in the United States is exhausted. It is true that vast tracts of government land are still untaken, but they constitute the mountain and arid regions, only a small fraction of them capable of conquest, and then only by the application of capital and combined effort. The free lands that made the American pioneer have gone.

In the second place, contemporaneously with this there has been such a concentration of capital in the control of fundamental industries as to make a new epoch in the economic development of the United States. The iron, the coal, and the cattle of the country have all fallen under the domination of a few great corporations with allied interests, and by the rapid combination of the important railroad systems and steamship lines, in concert with these same forces, even the bread-stuffs and the manufactures of the nation are to some degree controlled in a similar way. This is largely the work of the last decade. The development of the greatest iron mines of Lake Superior occurred in the early nineties, and in the same decade came the combination by which the coal and the coke of the country, and the transportation systems that connect them with the iron mines, have been brought under a few concentrated managements. Side by side with this concentration of capital has gone the combination of labor in the same vast industries. The one is in a certain sense the concomitant of the other, but the movement acquires an additional significance because of the fact that during the past fifteen years the labor class has been so recruited by a tide of foreign immigration that this class is now largely made up of persons of foreign parentage, and the lines of cleavage which begin to appear in this country between capital and labor have been accentuated by distinctions of nationality.

A third phenomenon connected with the two just mentioned is the expansion of the United States politically and commercially into lands beyond the seas. A cycle of American development has been completed.

Up to the close of the War of 1812, this country was involved in the fortunes of the European state system. The first quarter of a century of our national existence was almost a continual struggle to prevent ourselves being drawn into the European wars. At the close of that era of conflict, the United States set its face toward the West. It began the settlement and improvement of the vast interior of the country. Here was the field of our colonization, here the field of our political activity. This process being completed, it is not strange that we find the United States again involved in world-politics. The revolution that occurred four years ago, when the United States struck down that ancient nation under whose auspices the New World was discovered, is hardly yet more than dimly understood. The insular wreckage of the Spanish War, Porto Rico and the Philippines, with the problems presented by the Hawaiian Islands, Cuba, the Isthmian Canal, and China, all are indications of the new direction of the ship of state, and while we thus turn our attention overseas, our concentrated industrial strength has given us a striking power against the commerce of Europe that is already producing consternation in the Old World. Having completed the conquest of the wilderness, and having consolidated our interests, we are beginning to consider the relations of democracy and empire.

And fourth, the political parties of the United States now tend to divide on issues that involve the question of Socialism. The rise of the Populist party in the last decade, and the acceptance of so many of its principles by the Democratic party under the leadership of Mr. Bryan, show in striking manner the birth of new political ideas, the reformation of the lines of political conflict.

It is doubtful if in any ten years of American history more significant factors in our growth have revealed themselves. The struggle of the pioneer farmers to subdue the arid lands of the Great Plains in the eighties was followed by the official announcement of the extinction of the frontier line in 1890. The dramatic outcome of the Chicago Convention of 1896 marked the rise into power of the representatives of Populistic change. Two years later came the battle of Manila, which broke down the old isolation of the nation, and started it on a path the goal of which no man can foretell; and finally, but two years ago came that concentration of which the billion and a half dollar steel trust and the union of the Northern continental railways are stupendous examples. Is it not obvious, then, that the student who seeks for the explanation of democracy in the social and economic forces that underlie political forms must make inquiry into the conditions that have produced our democratic institutions, if he would estimate the effect of these vast changes? As a contribution to this inquiry, let us now turn to an examination of the part that the West has played in shaping our democracy.

From the beginning of the settlement of America, the frontier regions have exercised a steady influence toward democracy. In Virginia, to take an example, it can be traced as early as the period of Bacon's Rebellion, a hundred years before our Declaration of Independence. The small landholders, seeing that their powers were steadily passing into the hands of the wealthy planters who controlled Church and State and lands, rose in revolt. A generation later, in the governorship of Alexander Spotswood, we find a contest between the frontier settlers and the property-holding classes of the coast. The democracy with which Spotswood had to struggle, and of which he so bitterly complained, was a democracy made up of small landholders, of the newer immigrants, and of indented servants, who at the expiration of their time of servitude passed into the interior to take up lands and engage in pioneer farming. The "War of the Regulation," just on the eve of the American Revolution, shows the steady persistence of this struggle between the classes of the interior and those of the coast. The Declaration of Grievances which the back counties of the Carolinas then drew up against the aristocracy that dominated the politics of those colonies exhibits the contest between the democracy of the frontier and the established classes who apportioned the legislature in such fashion as to secure effective control of government. Indeed, in a period before the outbreak of the American Revolution, one can trace a distinct belt of democratic territory extending from the back country of New England down through western New York, Pennsylvania, and the South.

In each colony this region was in conflict with the dominant classes of the coast. It constituted a quasi-revolutionary area before the days of the Revolution, and it formed the basis on which the Democratic party was afterwards established. It was, therefore, in the West, as it was in the period before the Declaration of Independence, that the struggle for democratic development first revealed itself, and in that area the essential ideas of American democracy had already appeared. Through the period of the Revolution and of the Confederation a similar contest can be noted. On the frontier of New England, along the western border of Pennsylvania, Virginia, and the Carolinas, and in the communities beyond the Alleghany Mountains, there arose a demand of the frontier settlers for independent statehood based on democratic provisions. There is a strain of fierceness in their energetic petitions demanding self-government under the theory that every people have the right to establish their own political institutions in an area which they have won from the wilderness. Those revolutionary principles based on natural rights, for which the seaboard colonies were contending, were taken up with frontier energy in an attempt to apply them to the lands of the West. No one can read their petitions denouncing the control exercised by the wealthy landholders of the coast, appealing to the record of their conquest of the wilderness, and demanding the possession of the lands for which they have fought the Indians, and which they had reduced by their ax to civilization, without recognizing in these frontier communities the cradle of a belligerent Western democracy. "A fool can sometimes put on his coat better than a wise man can do it for him,"—such is the philosophy of its petitioners. In this period also came the contests of the interior agricultural portion of New England against the coast-wise merchants and property-holders, of which Shays' Rebellion is the best known, although by no means an isolated instance.

By the time of the constitutional convention, this struggle for democracy had effected a fairly well-defined division into parties. Although these parties did not at first recognize their interstate connections, there were similar issues on which they split in almost all the States. The demands for an issue of paper money, the stay of execution against debtors, and the relief against excessive taxation were found in every colony in the interior agricultural regions. The rise of this significant movement wakened the apprehensions of the men of means, and in the debates over the basis of suffrage for the House of Representatives in the constitutional convention of 1787 leaders of the conservative party did not hesitate to demand that safeguards to the property should be furnished the coast against the interior. The outcome of the debate left the question of suffrage for the House of Representatives dependent upon the policy of the separate States. This was in effect imposing a property qualification throughout the nation as a whole, and it was only as the interior of the country developed that these restrictions gradually gave way in the direction of manhood suffrage.

All of these scattered democratic tendencies Jefferson combined, in the period of Washington's presidency, into the Democratic-Republican party. Jefferson was the first prophet of American democracy, and when we analyse the essential features of his gospel, it is clear that the Western influence was the dominant element. Jefferson himself was born in the frontier region of Virginia, on the edge of the Blue Ridge, in the middle of the eighteenth century. His father was a pioneer. Jefferson's "Notes on Virginia" reveal clearly his conception that democracy should have an agricultural basis, and that manufacturing development and city life were dangerous to the purity of the body politic. Simplicity and economy in government, the right of revolution, the freedom of the individual, the belief that those who win the vacant lands are entitled to shape their own government in their own way—these are all parts of the platform of political principles to which he gave his adhesion, and they are all elements eminently characteristic of the Western democracy into which he was born.

In the period of the Revolution he had brought in a series of measures which tended to throw the power of Virginia into the hands of the settlers in the interior rather than of the coastwise aristocracy. The repeal of the laws of entail and primogeniture would have destroyed the great estates on which the planting aristocracy based its power. The abolition of the Established Church would still further have diminished the influence of the coastwise party in favor of the dissenting sects of the interior. His scheme of general public education reflected the same tendency, and his demand for the abolition of slavery was characteristic of a representative of the West rather than of the old-time aristocracy of the coast. His sympathy with the Western expansion culminated in the Louisiana Purchase. In short, the tendencies of Jefferson's legislation were to replace the dominance of the planting aristocracy by the dominance of the interior class, which had sought in vain to achieve its liberties in the period of Bacon's Rebellion.

Nevertheless, Thomas Jefferson was the John the Baptist of democracy, not its Moses. Only with the slow setting of the tide of settlement farther and farther toward the interior did the democratic influence grow strong enough to take actual possession of the government. The period from 1800 to 1820 saw a steady increase in these tendencies. The established classes in New England and the South began to take alarm. Perhaps no better illustration of the apprehensions of the old-time Federal conservative can be given than these utterances of President Dwight, of Yale College, in the book of travels which he published in that period:—

The class of pioneers cannot live in regular society. They are too idle, too talkative, too passionate, too prodigal, and too shiftless to acquire either property or character. They are impatient of the restraints of law, religion, and morality, and grumble about the taxes by which the Rulers, Ministers, and Schoolmasters are supported. . . . After exposing the injustice of the community in neglecting to invest persons of such superior merit in public offices, in many an eloquent harangue uttered by many a kitchen fire, in every blacksmith shop, in every corner of the streets, and finding all their efforts vain, they become at length discouraged, and under the pressure of poverty, the fear of the gaol, and consciousness of public contempt, leave their native places and betake themselves to the wilderness.

Such was a conservative's impression of that pioneer movement of New England colonists who had spread up the valley of the Connecticut into New Hampshire, Vermont, and western New York in the period of which he wrote, and who afterwards went on to possess the Northwest. New England Federalism looked with a shudder at the democratic ideas of those who refused to recognize the established order. But in that period there came into the Union a sisterhood of frontier States—Ohio, Indiana, Illinois, Missouri—with provisions for the franchise that brought in complete democracy.

Even the newly created States of the Southwest showed the tendency. The wind of democracy blew so strongly from the West, that even in the older States of New York, Massachusetts, Connecticut, and Virginia, conventions were called, which liberalized their constitutions by strengthening the democratic basis of the State. In the same time the labor population of the cities began to assert its power and its determination to share in government. Of this frontier democracy which now took possession of the nation, Andrew Jackson was the very personification. He was born in the backwoods of the Carolinas in the midst of the turbulent democracy that preceded the Revolution, and he grew up in the frontier State of Tennessee. In the midst of this region of personal feuds and frontier ideals of law, he quickly rose to leadership. The appearance of this frontiersman on the floor of

Congress was an omen full of significance. He reached Philadelphia at the close of Washington's administration, having ridden on horseback nearly eight hundred miles to his destination. Gallatin, himself a Western man, describes Jackson as he entered the halls of Congress: "A tall, lank, uncouth-looking personage, with long locks of hair hanging over his face and a cue down his back tied in an eel-skin; his dress singular; his manners those of a rough backwoodsman." And Jefferson testified: "When I was President of the Senate he was a Senator, and he could never speak on account of the rashness of his feelings. I have seen him attempt it repeatedly and as often choke with rage." At last the frontier in the person of its typical man had found a place in the Government. This six-foot backwoodsman, with blue eyes that could blaze on occasion, this choleric, impetuous, self-willed Scotch-Irish leader of men, this expert duelist, and ready fighter, this embodiment of the tenacious, vehement, personal West, was in politics to stay. The frontier democracy of that time had the instincts of the clansman in the days of Scotch border warfare. Vehement and tenacious as the democracy was, strenuously as each man contended with his neighbor for the spoils of the new country that opened before them, they all had respect for the man who best expressed their aspirations and their ideas. Every community had its hero. In the War of 1812 and the subsequent Indian fighting Jackson made good his claim, not only to the loyalty of the people of Tennessee, but of the whole West, and even of the nation. He had the essential traits of the Kentucky and Tennessee frontier. It was a frontier free from the influence of European ideas and institutions. The men of the "Western World" turned their backs upon the Atlantic Ocean, and with a grim energy and self-reliance began to build up a society free from the dominance of ancient forms.

The Westerner defended himself and resented governmental restrictions. The duel and the blood-feud found congenial soil in Kentucky and Tennessee. The idea of the personality of law was often dominant over the organized machinery of justice. That method was best which was most direct and effective. The backwoodsman was intolerant of men who split hairs, or scrupled over the method of reaching the right. In a word, the unchecked development of the individual was the significant product of this frontier democracy. It sought rather to express itself by choosing a man of the people, than by the formation of elaborate governmental institutions.

It was because Andrew Jackson personified these essential Western traits that in his presidency he became the idol and the mouthpiece of the popular will. In his assault upon the Bank as an engine of aristocracy, and in his denunciation of nullification, he went directly to his object with the ruthless energy of a frontiersman. For formal law and the subleties of State sovereignty he had the contempt of a backwoodsman. Nor is it without significance that this typical man of the new democracy will always be associated with the triumph of the spoils system in national politics. To the new democracy of the West, office was an opportunity to exercise natural rights as an equal citizen of the community. Rotation in office served not simply to allow the successful man to punish his enemies and reward his friends, but it also furnished the training in the actual conduct of political affairs which every American claimed as his birthright. Only in a primitive democracy of the type of the United States in 1830 could such a system have existed without the ruin of the State. National government in that period was no complex and nicely adjusted machine, and the evils of the system were long in making themselves fully apparent.

The triumph of Andrew Jackson marked the end of the old era of trained statesmen for the Presidency. With him began the era of the popular hero. Even Martin Van Buren, whom we think of in connection with the East, was born in a log house under conditions that were not unlike parts of the older West. Harrison was the hero of the Northwest, as Jackson had been of the Southwest. Polk was a typical Tennesseean, eager to expand the nation, and Zachary Taylor was what Webster called a "frontier colonel." During the period that followed Jackson, power passed from the region of Kentucky and Tennessee to the border of the Mississippi. The natural democratic tendencies that had earlier shown themselves in the Gulf States were destroyed, however, by the spread of cotton culture, and the development of great plantations in that region. What had been typical of the democracy of the Revolutionary frontier and of the frontier of Andrew Jackson was now to be seen in the States between the Ohio and the Mississippi. As Andrew Jackson is the typical democrat of the former region, so Abraham Lincoln is the very embodiment of the pioneer period of the Old Northwest. Indeed, he is the embodiment of the democracy of the West. How can one speak of him except in the words of Lowell's great "Commemoration Ode":—

"For him her Old-World moulds aside she threw,
And, choosing sweet clay from the breast
    Of the unexhausted West,
With stuff untainted shaped a hero new,
Wise, steadfast in the strength of God, and true.

. . . .

His was no lonely mountain-peak of mind,
Thrusting to thin air o'er our cloudy bars,
A sea-mark now, now lost in vapors blind;
Broad prairie rather, genial, level-lined,
Fruitful and friendly for all human kind,
Yet also nigh to heaven and loved of loftiest stars.
    Nothing of Europe here,
Or, then, of Europe fronting mornward still,
Ere any names of Serf and Peer,
Could Nature's equal scheme deface;
New birth of our new soil, the first American."

The pioneer life from which Lincoln came differed in important respects from the frontier democracy typified by Andrew Jackson. Jackson's democracy was contentious, individualistic, and it sought the ideal of local self-government and expansion. Lincoln represents rather the pioneer folk who entered the forest of the great Northwest to chop out a home, to build up their fortunes in the midst of a continually ascending industrial movement. In the democracy of the Southwest, industrial development and city life were only minor factors, but to the democracy of the Northwest they were its very life. To widen the area of the clearing, to contend with one another for the mastery of the industrial resources of the rich provinces, to struggle for a place in the ascending movement of society, to transmit to one's offspring the chance for education, for industrial betterment, for the rise in life which the hardships of the pioneer existence denied to the pioneer himself, these were some of the ideals of the region to which Lincoln came. The men were commonwealth builders, industry builders. Whereas the type of hero in the Southwest was militant, in the Northwest he was industrial. It was in the midst of these "plain people," as he loved to call them, that Lincoln grew to manhood. As Emerson says: "He is the true history of the American people in his time." The years of his early life were the years when the democracy of the Northwest came into struggle with the institution of slavery which threatened to forbid the expansion of the democratic pioneer life in the West. In President Eliot's essay on "Five American Contributions to Civilization," he instances as one of the supreme tests of American democracy its attitude upon the question of slavery. But if democracy chose wisely and worked effectively toward the solution of this problem, it must be remembered that Western democracy took the lead. The rail-splitter himself became the nation's President in that fierce time of struggle, and armies of the woodsmen and pioneer farmers recruited in the Old Northwest made free the Father of Waters, marched through Georgia, and helped to force the struggle to a conclusion at Appomattox. The free pioneer democracy struck down the slave-holding aristocracy on its march to the West.

The last chapter in the development of Western democracy is the one that deals with its conquest over the vast spaces of the new West. At each new stage of Western development, the people have had to grapple with larger areas, with bigger combinations. The little colony of Massachusetts veterans that settled at Marietta received a land grant as large as the State of Rhode Island. The band of Connecticut pioneers that followed Moses Cleaveland to the Connecticut Reserve occupied a region as large as the parent State. The area which settlers of New England stock occupied on the prairies of northern Illinois surpassed the combined area of Massachusetts, Connecticut, and Rhode Island. Men who had become accustomed to the narrow valleys and the little towns of the East found themselves out on the boundless spaces of the West dealing with units of such magnitude as dwarfed their former experience. The Great Lakes, the Prairies, the Great Plains, the Rocky Mountains, the Mississippi and the Missouri, furnished new standards of measurement for the achievement of this industrial democracy. Individualism began to give way to cooperation and to governmental activity. Even in the earlier days of the democratic conquest of the wilderness, demands had been made upon the government for support in internal improvements, but this new West showed a growing tendency to call to its assistance the powerful arm of national authority. In the period since the Civil War, the vast public domain has been donated to the individual farmer, to States for education, to railroads for the construction of transportation lines.

Moreover, with the advent of democracy in the last fifteen years upon the Great Plains, new physical conditions have presented themselves which have accelerated the social tendency of Western democracy. The pioneer farmer of the days of Lincoln could place his family on a flatboat, strike into the wilderness, cut out his clearing, and with little or no capital go on to the achievement of industrial independence. Even the homesteader on the Western prairies found it possible to work out a similar independent destiny, although the factor of transportation made a serious and increasing impediment to the free working-out of his individual career. But when the arid lands and the mineral resources of the Far West were reached, no conquest was possible by the old individual pioneer methods. Here expensive irrigation works must be constructed, coöperative activity was demanded in utilization of the water supply, capital beyond the reach of the small farmer was required. In a word, the physiographic province itself decreed that the destiny of this new frontier should be social rather than individual.

Magnitude of social achievement is the watchword of the democracy since the Civil War. From petty towns built in the marshes, cities arose whose greatness and industrial power are the wonder of our time. The conditions were ideal for the production of captains of industry. The old democratic admiration for the self-made man, its old deference to the rights of competitive individual development, together with the stupendous natural resources that opened to the conquest of the keenest and the strongest, gave such conditions of mobility as enabled the development of the large corporate industries which in our own decade have marked the West.

Thus, in brief, have been outlined the chief phases of the development of Western democracy in the different areas which it has conquered. There has been a steady development of the industrial ideal, and a steady increase of the social tendency, in this later movement of Western democracy. While the individualism of the frontier, so prominent in the earliest days of the Western advance, has been preserved as an ideal, more and more these individuals struggling each with the other, dealing with vaster and vaster areas, with larger and larger problems, have found it necessary to combine under the leadership of the strongest. This is the explanation of the rise of those preëminent captains of industry whose genius has concentrated capital to control the fundamental resources of the nation. If now in the way of recapitulation, we try to pick out from the influences that have gone to the making of Western democracy the factors which constitute the net result of this movement, we shall have to mention at least the following:—

Most important of all has been the fact that an area of free land has continually lain on the western border of the settled area of the United

States. Whenever social conditions tended to crystallize in the East, whenever capital tended to press upon labor or political restraints to impede the freedom of the mass, there was this gate of escape to the free conditions of the frontier. These free lands promoted individualism, economic equality, freedom to rise, democracy. Men would not accept inferior wages and a permanent position of social subordination when this promised land of freedom and equality was theirs for the taking. Who would rest content under oppressive legislative conditions when with a slight effort he might reach a land wherein to become a co-worker in the building of free cities and free States on the lines of his own ideal? In a word, then, free lands meant free opportunities. Their existence has differentiated the American democracy from the democracies which have preceded it, because ever, as democracy in the East took the form of highly specialized and complicated industrial society, in the West it kept in touch with primitive conditions, and by action and reaction these two forces have shaped our history.

In the next place, these free lands and this treasury of industrial resources have existed over such vast spaces that they have demanded of democracy increasing spaciousness of design and power of execution. Western democracy is contrasted with the democracy of all other times in the largeness of the tasks to which it has set its hand, and in the vast achievements which it has wrought out in the control of nature and of politics. It would be difficult to over-emphasize the importance of this training upon democracy. Never before in the history of the world has a democracy existed on so vast an area and handled things in the gross with such success, with such largeness of design, and such grasp upon the means of execution. In short, democracy has learned in the West of the United States how to deal with the problem of magnitude. The old historic democracies were but little states with primitive economic conditions.

But the very task of dealing with vast resources, over vast areas, under the conditions of free competition furnished by the West, has produced the rise of those captains of industry whose success in consolidating economic power now raises the question as to whether democracy under such conditions can survive. For the old military type of Western leaders like George Rogers Clark, Andrew Jackson, and William Henry Harrison have been substituted such industrial leaders as James J. Hill, John D. Rockefeller, and Andrew Carnegie.

The question is imperative, then, What ideals persist from this democratic experience of the West; and have they acquired sufficient momentum to sustain themselves under conditions so radically unlike those in the days of their origin? In other words, the question put at the beginning of this discussion becomes pertinent. Under the forms of the American democracy is there in reality evolving such a concentration of economic and social power in the hands of a comparatively few men as may make political democracy an appearance rather than a reality? The free lands are gone. The material forces that gave vitality to Western democracy are passing away. It is to the realm of the spirit, to the domain of ideals and legislation, that we must look for Western influence upon democracy in our own days.

Western democracy has been from the time of its birth idealistic. The very fact of the wilderness appealed to men as a fair, blank page on which to write a new chapter in the story of man's struggle for a higher type of society. The Western wilds, from the Alleghanies to the Pacific, constituted the richest free gift that was ever spread out before civilized man. To the peasant and artisan of the Old World, bound by the chains of social class, as old as custom and as inevitable as fate, the West offered an exit into a free life and greater well-being among the bounties of nature, into the midst of resources that demanded manly exertion, and that gave in return the chance for indefinite ascent in the scale of social advance. "To each she offered gifts after his will." Never again can such an opportunity come to the sons of men. It was unique, and the thing is so near us, so much a part of our lives, that we do not even yet comprehend its full significance. The existence of this land of opportunity has made America the goal of idealists from the days of

the Pilgrim Fathers. With all the materialism of the pioneer movements, this idealistic conception of the vacant lands as an opportunity
for a new order of things is unmistakably present. Kipling's "Song of
the English" has given it expression:—

"We were dreamers, dreaming greatly, in the man-stifled town;
We yearned beyond the sky-line where the strange roads go down.
Came the Whisper, came the Vision, came the Power with the
Need,
Till the Soul that is not man's soul was lent us to lead.
As the deer breaks—as the steer breaks—from the herd where they
graze,
In the faith of little children we went on our ways.
Then the wood failed—then the food failed—then the last water
dried—
In the faith of little children we lay down and died.

"On the sand-drift—on the veldt-side—in the fern-scrub we lay,
That our sons might follow after by the bones on the way.
Follow after—follow after! We have watered the root
And the bud has come to blossom that ripens for fruit!
Follow after—we are waiting by the trails that we lost
For the sound of many footsteps, for the tread of a host.

"Follow after—follow after—for the harvest is sown:
By the bones about the wayside ye shall come to your own!"

This was the vision that called to Roger Williams—that "prophetic
soul ravished of truth disembodied," "unable to enter into treaty with
its environment," and forced to seek the wilderness. "Oh, how sweet,"
wrote William Penn, from his forest refuge, "is the quiet of these parts,
freed from the troubles and perplexities of woeful Europe." And here
he projected what he called his "Holy Experiment in Government."

If the later West offers few such striking illustrations of the relation of the wilderness to idealistic schemes, and if some of the designs were fantastic and abortive, none the less the influence is a fact. Hardly a Western State but has been the Mecca of some sect or band of social reformers, anxious to put into practice their ideals, in vacant land, far removed from the checks of a settled form of social organization. Consider the Dunkards, the Icarians, the Fourierists, the Mormons, and similar idealists who sought our Western wilds. But the idealistic influence is not limited to the dreamers' conception of a new State. It gave to the pioneer farmer and city builder a restless energy, a quick capacity for judgment and action, a belief in liberty, freedom of opportunity, and a resistance to the domination of class which infused a vitality and power into the individual atoms of this democratic mass. Even as he dwelt among the stumps of his newly-cut clearing, the pioneer had the creative vision of a new order of society. In imagination he pushed back the forest boundary to the confines of a mighty Commonwealth; he willed that log cabins should become the lofty buildings of great cities. He decreed that his children should enter into a heritage of education, comfort, and social welfare, and for this ideal he bore the scars of the wilderness. Possessed with this idea he ennobled his task and laid deep foundations for a democratic State. Nor was this idealism by any means limited to the American pioneer.

To the old native democratic stock has been added a vast army of recruits from the Old World. There are in the Middle West alone four million persons of German parentage out of a total of seven millions in the country. Over a million persons of Scandinavian parentage live in the same region. The democracy of the newer West is deeply affected by the ideals brought by these immigrants from the Old World. To them America was not simply a new home; it was a land of opportunity, of freedom, of democracy. It meant to them, as to the American pioneer that preceded them, the opportunity to destroy the bonds of social caste that bound them in their older home, to hew out for themselves in a new country a destiny proportioned to the powers that

God had given them, a chance to place their families under better conditions and to win a larger life than the life that they had left behind. He who believes that even the hordes of recent immigrants from southern Italy are drawn to these shores by nothing more than a dull and blind materialism has not penetrated into the heart of the problem. The idealism and expectation of these children of the Old World, the hopes which they have formed for a newer and freer life across the seas, are almost pathetic when one considers how far they are from the possibility of fruition. He who would take stock of American democracy must not forget the accumulation of human purposes and ideals which immigration has added to the American populace.

In this connection it must also be remembered that these democratic ideals have existed at each stage of the advance of the frontier, and have left behind them deep and enduring effects on the thinking of the whole country. Long after the frontier period of a particular region of the United States has passed away, the conception of society, the ideals and aspirations which it produced, persist in the minds of the people. So recent has been the transition of the greater portion of the United States from frontier conditions to conditions of settled life, that we are, over the large portion of the United States, hardly a generation removed from the primitive conditions of the West. If, indeed, we ourselves were not pioneers, our fathers were, and the inherited ways of looking at things, the fundamental assumptions of the American people, have all been shaped by this experience of democracy on its westward march. This experience has been wrought into the very warp and woof of American thought.

Even those masters of industry and capital who have risen to power by the conquest of Western resources came from the midst of this society and still profess its principles. John D. Rockefeller was born on a New York farm, and began his career as a young business man in St. Louis. Marcus Hanna was a Cleveland grocer's clerk at the age of twenty. Claus Spreckles, the sugar king, came from Germany as a steerage passenger to the United States in 1848. Marshall Field was a farmer boy in Conway, Massachusetts, until he left to grow up with the young Chicago. Andrew Carnegie came as a ten-year-old boy from Scotland to Pittsburgh, then a distinctively Western town. He built up his fortunes through successive grades until he became the dominating factor in the great iron industries, and paved the way for that colossal achievement, the Steel Trust. Whatever may be the tendencies of this corporation, there can be little doubt of the democratic ideals of Mr. Carnegie himself. With lavish hand he has strewn millions through the United States for the promotion of libraries. The effect of this library movement in perpetuating the democracy that comes from an intelligent and self-respecting people can hardly be measured. In his "Triumphant Democracy," published in 1886, Mr. Carnegie, the ironmaster, said, in reference to the mineral wealth of the United States: "Thank God, these treasures are in the hands of an intelligent people, the Democracy, to be used for the general good of the masses, and not made the spoils of monarchs, courts, and aristocracy, to be turned to the base and selfish ends of a privileged hereditary class." It would be hard to find a more rigorous assertion of democratic doctrine than the celebrated utterance, attributed to the same man, that he should feel it a disgrace to die rich.

In enumerating the services of American democracy, President Eliot included the corporation as one of its achievements, declaring that "freedom of incorporation, though no longer exclusively a democratic agency, has given a strong support to democratic institutions." In one sense this is doubtless true, since the corporation has been one of the means by which small properties can be aggregated into an effective working body. Socialistic writers have long been fond of pointing out also that these various concentrations pave the way for and make possible social control. From this point of view it is possible that the masters of industry may prove to be not so much an incipient aristocracy as the pathfinders for democracy in reducing the industrial world to systematic consolidation suited to democratic control. The great geniuses that have built up the modern industrial concentration were trained in the midst of democratic society. They were the product of these democratic conditions. Freedom to rise was the very condition of their existence. Whether they will be followed by successors who will adopt the exploitation of the masses, and who will be capable of retaining under efficient control these vast resources, is one of the questions which we shall have to face.

This, at least, is clear: American democracy is fundamentally the outcome of the experiences of the American people in dealing with the West. Western democracy through the whole of its earlier period tended to the production of a society of which the most distinctive fact was the freedom of the individual to rise under conditions of social mobility, and whose ambition was the liberty and well-being of the masses. This conception has vitalized all American democracy, and has brought it into sharp contrasts with the democracies of history, and with those modern efforts of Europe to create an artificial democratic order by legislation. The problem of the United States is not to create democracy, but to conserve democratic institutions and ideals. In the later period of its development, Western democracy has been gaining experience in the problem of social control. It has steadily enlarged the sphere of its action and the instruments for its perpetuation. By its system of public schools, from the grades to the graduate work of the great universities, the West has created a larger single body of intelligent plain people than can be found elsewhere in the world. Its political tendencies, whether we consider Democracy, Populism, or Republicanism, are distinctly in the direction of greater social control and the conservation of the old democratic ideals.

To these ideals the West adheres with even a passionate determination. If, in working out its mastery of the resources of the interior, it has produced a type of industrial leader so powerful as to be the wonder of the world, nevertheless, it is still to be determined whether these men constitute a menace to democratic institutions, or the most efficient factor for adjusting democratic control to the new conditions.

Whatever shall be the outcome of the rush of this huge industrial modern United States to its place among the nations of the earth, the formation of its Western democracy will always remain one of the wonderful chapters in the history of the human race. Into this vast shaggy continent of ours poured the first feeble tide of European settlement. European men, institutions, and ideas were lodged in the American wilderness, and this great American West took them to her bosom, taught them a new way of looking upon the destiny of the common man, trained them in adaptation to the conditions of the New World, to the creation of new institutions to meet new needs; and ever as society on her eastern border grew to resemble the Old World in its social forms and its industry, ever, as it began to lose faith in the ideals of democracy, she opened new provinces, and dowered new democracies in her most distant domains with her material treasures and with the ennobling influence that the fierce love of freedom, the strength that came from hewing out a home, making a school and a church, and creating a higher future for his family, furnished to the pioneer.

She gave to the world such types as the farmer Thomas Jefferson, with his Declaration of Independence, his statute for religious toleration, and his purchase of Louisiana. She gave us Andrew Jackson, that fierce Tennessee spirit who broke down the traditions of conservative rule, swept away the privacies and privileges of officialdom, and, like a Gothic leader, opened the temple of the nation to the populace. She gave us Abraham Lincoln, whose gaunt frontier form and gnarled, massive hand told of the conflict with the forest, whose grasp of the ax-handle of the pioneer was no firmer than his grasp of the helm of the ship of state as it breasted the seas of civil war. She has furnished to this new democracy her stores of mineral wealth, that dwarf of those of the Old World, and her provinces that in themselves are vaster and more productive than most of the nations of Europe. Out of her bounty has come a nation whose industrial competition alarms the Old World, and the masters of whose resources wield wealth and power vaster than the wealth and power of kings. Best of all, the West gave, not only to the American, but to the unhappy and oppressed of all lands, a vision of hope, and assurance that the world held a place where were to be found high faith in man and the will and power to furnish him the opportunity to grow to the full measure of his own capacity. Great and powerful as are the new sons of her loins, the Republic is greater than they. The paths of the pioneer have widened into broad highways. The forest clearing has expanded into affluent commonwealths. Let us see to it that the ideals of the pioneer in his log cabin shall enlarge into the spiritual life of a democracy where civic power shall dominate and utilize individual achievement for the common good.

FIVE

PIONEER IDEALS AND THE STATE UNIVERSITY

(1910)

The ideals of a people, their aspirations and convictions, their hopes and ambitions, their dreams and determinations, are assets in their civilization as real and important as per capita wealth or industrial skill.

This nation was formed under pioneer ideals. During three centuries after Captain John Smith struck the first blow at the American forest on the eastern edge of the continent, the pioneers were abandoning settled society for the wilderness, seeking, for generation after generation, new frontiers. Their experiences left abiding influences upon the ideas and purposes of the nation. Indeed the older settled regions themselves were shaped profoundly by the very fact that the whole nation was pioneering and that in the development of the West the East had its own part.

The first ideal of the pioneer was that of conquest. It was his task to fight with nature for the chance to exist. Not as in older countries did this contest take place in a mythical past,

Commencement address at the University of Indiana, 1910.

told in folk lore and epic. It has been continuous to our own day. Facing each generation of pioneers was the unmastered continent. Vast forests blocked the way; mountainous ramparts interposed; desolate, grass-clad prairies, barren oceans of rolling plains, arid deserts, and a fierce race of savages, all had to be met and defeated. The rifle and the ax are the symbols of the backwoods pioneer. They meant a training in aggressive courage, in domination, in directness of action, in destructiveness.

To the pioneer the forest was no friendly resource for posterity, no object of careful economy. He must wage a hand-to-hand war upon it, cutting and burning a little space to let in the light upon a dozen acres of hard-won soil, and year after year expanding the clearing into new woodlands against the stubborn resistance of primeval trunks and matted roots. He made war against the rank fertility of the soil. While new worlds of virgin land lay ever just beyond, it was idle to expect the pioneer to stay his hand and turn to scientific farming. Indeed, as Secretary Wilson has said, the pioneer would, in that case, have raised wheat that no one wanted to eat, corn to store on the farm, and cotton not worth the picking.

Thus, fired with the ideal of subduing the wilderness, the destroying pioneer fought his way across the continent, masterful and wasteful, preparing the way by seeking the immediate thing, rejoicing in rude strength and wilful achievement.

But even this backwoodsman was more than a mere destroyer. He had visions. He was finder as well as fighter—the trailmaker for civilization, the inventor of new ways. Although Rudyard Kipling's "Foreloper"[1] deals with the English pioneer in lands beneath the Southern Cross, yet the poem portrays American traits as well:

"The gull shall whistle in his wake, the blind wave break in fire,
He shall fulfill God's utmost will, unknowing his desire;
And he shall see old planets pass and alien stars arise,
And give the gale his reckless sail in shadow of new skies.

"Strong lust of gear shall drive him out and hunger arm his hand
To wring food from desert nude, his foothold from the sand.
His neighbors' smoke shall vex his eyes, their voices break his rest;
He shall go forth till south is north, sullen and dispossessed;
He shall desire loneliness and his desire shall bring
Hard on his heels, a thousand wheels, a people and a king.

"He shall come back on his own track, and by his scarce cool camp,
There shall he meet the roaring street, the derrick and the stamp;
For he must blaze a nation's way with hatchet and with brand,
Till on his last won wilderness an empire's bulwarks stand."

This quest after the unknown, this yearning "beyond the sky line, where the strange roads go down," is of the very essence of the backwoods pioneer, even though he was unconscious of its spiritual significance.

The pioneer was taught in the school of experience that the crops of one area would not do for a new frontier; that the scythe of the clearing must be replaced by the reaper of the prairies. He was forced to make old tools serve new uses; to shape former habits, institutions and ideas to changed conditions; and to find new means when the old proved inapplicable. He was building a new society as well as breaking new soil; he had the ideal of nonconformity and of change. He rebelled against the conventional.

Besides the ideals of conquest and of discovery, the pioneer had the ideal of personal development, free from social and governmental constraint. He came from a civilization based on individual competition, and he brought the conception with him to the wilderness where a wealth of resources and innumerable opportunities gave it a new scope. The prizes were for the keenest and the strongest; for them were the best bottom lands, the finest timber tracts, the best salt-springs, the richest ore beds; and not only these natural gifts, but also the opportunities afforded in the midst of a forming society. Here were mill sites, town sites, transportation lines, banking centers, openings in the law, in politics—all the varied chances for advancement afforded in a rapidly developing society where everything was open to him who knew how to seize the opportunity.

The squatter enforced his claim to lands even against the government's title by the use of extra-legal combinations and force. He appealed to lynch law with little hesitation. He was impatient of any governmental restriction upon his individual right to deal with the wilderness.

In our own day we sometimes hear of congressmen sent to jail for violating land laws; but the different spirit in the pioneer days may be illustrated by a speech of Delegate Sibley of Minnesota in Congress in 1852. In view of the fact that he became the State's first governor, a regent of its university, president of its historical society, and a doctor of laws of Princeton, we may assume that he was a pillar of society. He said:

> The government has watched its public domain with jealous eye, and there are now enactments upon your statute books, aimed at the trespassers upon it, which should be expunged as a disgrace to the country and to the nineteenth century. Especially is he pursued with unrelenting severity, who has dared to break the silence of the primeval forest by the blows of the American ax. The hardy lumberman who has penetrated to the remotest wilds of the Northwest, to drag from their recesses the materials for building up towns and cities in the great valley of the Mississippi, has been particularly marked out as a victim. After enduring all the privations and subjecting himself to all the perils incident to his vocation—when he has toiled for months to add by his honest labor to the comfort of his fellow men, and to the aggregate wealth of the nation, he finds himself suddenly in the clutches of the law for trespassing on the public domain. The proceeds of his long winter's work are reft from him, and exposed to public sale for the benefit of his paternal

government ... and the object of this oppression and wrong is further harassed by vexatious law proceedings against him.

Sibley's protest in congress against these "outrages" by which the northern lumbermen were "harassed" in their work of what would now be called stealing government timber, aroused no protest from his colleagues. No president called this congressman an undesirable citizen or gave him over to the courts.

Thus many of the pioneers, following the ideal of the right of the individual to rise, subordinated the rights of the nation and posterity to the desire that the country should be "developed" and that the individual should advance with as little interference as possible. Squatter doctrines and individualism have left deep traces upon American conceptions.

But quite as deeply fixed in the pioneer's mind as the ideal of individualism was the ideal of democracy. He had a passionate hatred for aristocracy, monopoly and special privilege; he believed in simplicity, economy and in the rule of the people. It is true that he honored the successful man, and that he strove in all ways to advance himself. But the West was so free and so vast, the barriers to individual achievement were so remote, that the pioneer was hardly conscious that any danger to equality could come from his competition for natural resources. He thought of democracy as in some way the result of our political institutions, and he failed to see that it was primarily the result of the free lands and immense opportunities which surrounded him. Occasional statesmen voiced the idea that American democracy was based on the abundance of unoccupied land, even in the first debates on the public domain.

This early recognition of the influence of abundance of land in shaping the economic conditions of American democracy is peculiarly significant to-day in view of the practical exhaustion of the supply of cheap arable public lands open to the poor man, and the coincident development of labor unions to keep up wages.

Certain it is that the strength of democratic movements has chiefly lain in the regions of the pioneer. "Our governments tend too much to democracy," wrote Izard, of South Carolina, to Jefferson, in 1785. "A handicraftsman thinks an apprenticeship necessary to make him acquainted with his business. But our backcountrymen are of the opinion that a politician may be born just as well as a poet."

The Revolutionary ideas, of course, gave a great impetus to democracy, and in substantially every colony there was a double revolution, one for independence and the other for the overthrow of aristocratic control. But in the long run the effective force behind American democracy was the presence of the practically free land into which men might escape from oppression or inequalities which burdened them in the older settlements. This possibility compelled the coastwise States to liberalize the franchise; and it prevented the formation of a dominant class, whether based on property or on custom. Among the pioneers one man was as good as his neighbor. He had the same chance; conditions were simple and free. Economic equality fostered political equality. An optimistic and buoyant belief in the worth of the plain people, a devout faith in man prevailed in the West. Democracy became almost the religion of the pioneer. He held with passionate devotion the idea that he was building under freedom a new society, based on self government, and for the welfare of the average man.

And yet even as he proclaimed the gospel of democracy the pioneer showed a vague apprehension lest the time be short—lest equality should not endure—lest he might fall behind in the ascending movement of Western society. This led him on in feverish haste to acquire advantages as though he only half believed his dream. "Before him lies a boundless continent," wrote De Tocqueville, in the days when pioneer democracy was triumphant under Jackson, "and he urges forward as if time pressed and he was afraid of finding no room for his exertions."

Even while Jackson lived, labor leaders and speculative thinkers were demanding legislation to place a limit on the amount of land which one person might acquire and to provide free farms. De Tocqueville saw the signs of change. "Between the workman and the master," he said, "there are frequent relations but no real association. . . . I am of the opinion, upon the whole, that the manufacturing aristocracy which is growing up under our eyes is one of the harshest which ever existed in the world; . . . if ever a permanent inequality, of conditions and aristocracy again penetrate into the world, it may be predicted that this is the gate by which they will enter." But the sanative influences of the free spaces of the West were destined to ameliorate labor's condition, to afford new hopes and new faith to pioneer democracy, and to postpone the problem.

As the settlers advanced into provinces whose area dwarfed that of the older sections, pioneer democracy itself began to undergo changes, both in its composition and in its processes of expansion. At the close of the Civil War, when settlement was spreading with greatest vigor across the Mississippi, the railways began their work as colonists. Their land grants from the government, amounting altogether by 1871 to an area five times that of the State of Pennsylvania, demanded purchasers, and so the railroads pioneered the way for the pioneer.

The homestead law increased the tide of settlers. The improved farm machinery made it possible for him to go boldly out on to the prairie and to deal effectively with virgin soil in farms whose cultivated area made the old clearings of the backwoodsman seem mere garden plots. Two things resulted from these conditions, which profoundly modified pioneer ideals. In the first place the new form of colonization demanded an increasing use of capital; and the rapidity of the formation of towns, the speed with which society developed, made men the more eager to secure bank credit to deal with the new West. This made the pioneer more dependent on the eastern economic forces. In the second place the farmer became dependent as never before on transportation companies. In this speculative movement the railroads, finding that they had pressed too far in advance and had issued stock too freely for their earnings to justify the face of the investment, came into collision with the pioneer on the question of rates and of discriminations. The Greenback movement and the Granger movements were appeals to government to prevent what the pioneer thought to be invasions of pioneer democracy.

As the western settler began to face the problem of magnitude in the areas he was occupying; as he began to adjust his life to the modern forces of capital and to complex productive processes; as he began to see that, go where he would, the question of credit and currency, of transportation and distribution in general conditioned his success, he sought relief by legislation. He began to lose his primitive attitude of individualism, government began to look less like a necessary evil and more like an instrument for the perpetuation of his democratic ideals. In brief, the defenses of the pioneer democrat began to shift from free land to legislation, from the ideal of individualism to the ideal of social control through regulation by law. He had no sympathy with a radical reconstruction of society by the revolution of socialism; even his alliances with the movement of organized labor, which paralleled that of organized capital in the East, were only half-hearted. But he was becoming alarmed over the future of the free democratic ideal. The wisdom of his legislation it is not necessary to discuss here. The essential point is that his conception of the right of government to control social process had undergone a change. He was coming to regard legislation as an instrument of social construction. The individualism of the Kentucky pioneer of 1796 was giving way to the Populism of the Kansas pioneer of 1896.

The later days of pioneer democracy are too familiar to require much exposition. But they are profoundly significant. As the pioneer doctrine of free competition for the resources of the nation revealed its tendencies; as individual, corporation and trust, like the pioneer, turned increasingly to legal devices to promote their contrasting ideals, the natural resources were falling into private possession. Tides of alien immigrants were surging into the country to replace the old

American stock in the labor market, to lower the standard of living and to increase the pressure of population upon the land. These recent foreigners have lodged almost exclusively in the dozen great centers of industrial life, and there they have accented the antagonisms between capital and labor by the fact that the labor supply has become increasingly foreign born, and recruited from nationalities who arouse no sympathy on the part of capital and little on the part of the general public. Class distinctions are accented by national prejudices, and democracy is thereby invaded. But even in the dull brains of great masses of these unfortunates from southern and eastern Europe the idea of America as the land of freedom and of opportunity to rise, the land of pioneer democratic ideals, has found lodgment, and if it is given time and is not turned into revolutionary lines it will fructify.

As the American pioneer passed on in advance of this new tide of European immigration, he found lands increasingly limited. In place of the old lavish opportunity for the settler to set his stakes where he would, there were frantic rushes of thousands of eager pioneers across the line of newly opened Indian reservations. Even in 1889, when Oklahoma was opened to settlement, twenty thousand settlers crowded at the boundaries, like straining athletes, waiting the bugle note that should start the race across the line. To-day great crowds gather at the land lotteries of the government as the remaining fragments of the public domain are flung to hungry settlers.

Hundreds of thousands of pioneers from the Middle West have crossed the national boundary into Canadian wheat fields eager to find farms for their children, although under an alien flag. And finally the government has taken to itself great areas of arid land for reclamation by costly irrigation projects whereby to furnish twenty-acre tracts in the desert to settlers under careful regulation of water rights. The government supplies the capital for huge irrigation dams and reservoirs and builds them itself. It owns and operates quarries, coal mines and timber to facilitate this work. It seeks the remotest regions of the earth for crops suitable for these areas. It analyzes the soils and tells the farmer what and when and how to plant. It has even considered the rental to manufacturers of the surplus water, electrical and steam power generated in its irrigation works and the utilization of this power to extract nitrates from the air to replenish worn-out soils. The pioneer of the arid regions must be both a capitalist and the protégé of the government.

Consider the contrast between the conditions of the pioneers at the beginning and at the end of this period of development. Three hundred years ago adventurous Englishmen on the coast of Virginia began the attack on the wilderness. Three years ago the President of the United States summoned the governors of forty-six states to deliberate upon the danger of the exhaustion of the natural resources of the nation.[2]

The pressure of population upon the food supply is already felt and we are at the beginning only of this transformation. It is profoundly significant that at the very time when American democracy is becoming conscious that its pioneer basis of free land and sparse population is giving way, it is also brought face to face with the startling outcome of its old ideals of individualism and exploitation under competition uncontrolled by government. Pioneer society itself was not sufficiently sophisticated to work out to its logical result the conception of the self-made man. But the captains of industry by applying squatter doctrines to the evolution of American industrial society, have made the process so clear that he who runs may read. Contests imply alliances as well as rivalries. The increasing magnitude of the areas to be dealt with and the occurrences of times of industrial stress furnished occasion for such unions. The panic of 1873 was followed by an unprecedented combination of individual businesses and partnerships into corporations. The panic of 1893 marked the beginning of an extraordinary development of corporate combinations into pools and trusts, agreements and absorptions, until, by the time of the panic of 1907, it seemed not impossible that the outcome of free competition under individualism was to be monopoly of the most important natural resources and processes by a limited group of men whose vast fortunes were so invested in allied and dependent industries that they constituted the dominating force in the industrial life of the nation. The development of large scale factory production, the benefit of combination in the competitive struggle, and the tremendous advantage of concentration in securing possession of the unoccupied opportunities, were so great that vast accumulations of capital became the normal agency of the industrial world. In almost exact ratio to the diminution of the supply of unpossessed resources, combinations of capital have increased in magnitude and in efficiency of conquest. The solitary backwoodsman wielding his ax at the edge of a measureless forest is replaced by companies capitalized at millions, operating railroads, sawmills, and all the enginery of modern machinery to harvest the remaining trees.

A new national development is before us without the former safety valve of abundant resources open to him who would take. Classes are becoming alarmingly distinct: There is the demand on the one side voiced by Mr. Harriman so well and by others since, that nothing must be done to interfere with the early pioneer ideals of the exploitation and the development of the country's wealth; that restrictive and reforming legislation must on no account threaten prosperity even for a moment. In fact, we sometimes hear in these days, from men of influence, serious doubts of democracy, and intimations that the country would be better off if it freely resigned itself to guidance by the geniuses who are mastering the economic forces of the nation, and who, it is alleged, would work out the prosperity of the United States more effectively, if unvexed by politicians and people.

On the other hand, an inharmonious group of reformers are sounding the warning that American democratic ideals and society are menaced and already invaded by the very conditions that make this apparent prosperity; that the economic resources are no longer limitless and free; that the aggregate national wealth is increasing at the cost of present social justice and moral health, and the future well-being of the American people. The Granger and the Populist were prophets of this reform movement. Mr. Bryan's Democracy, Mr. Debs'

Socialism, and Mr. Roosevelt's Republicanism all had in common the emphasis upon the need of governmental regulation of industrial tendencies in the interest of the common man; the checking of the power of those business Titans who emerged successful out of the competitive individualism of pioneer America. As land values rise, as meat and bread grow dearer, as the process of industrial consolidation goes on, and as Eastern industrial conditions spread across the West, the problems of traditional American democracy will become increasingly grave.

The time has come when University men may well consider pioneer ideals, for American society has reached the end of the first great period in its formation. It must survey itself, reflect upon its origins, consider what freightage of purposes it carried in its long march across the continent, what ambitions it had for the man, what rôle it would play in the world. How shall we conserve what was best in pioneer ideals? How adjust the old conceptions to the changed conditions of modern life?

Other nations have been rich and prosperous and powerful. But the United States has believed that it had an original contribution to make to the history of society by the production of a self-determining, self-restrained, intelligent democracy. It is in the Middle West that society has formed on lines least like those of Europe. It is here, if anywhere, that American democracy will make its stand against the tendency to adjust to a European type.

This consideration gives importance to my final topic, the relation of the University to pioneer ideals and to the changing conditions of American democracy. President Pritchett of the Carnegie Foundation has recently declared that in no other form of popular activity does a nation or State so clearly reveal its ideals or the quality of its civilization as in its system of education; and he finds, especially in the State University, "a conception of education from the standpoint of the whole people." "If our American democracy were to-day called to give proof of its constructive ability," he says, "the State University and the public school system which it crowns would be the strongest evidence of its fitness which it could offer."

It may at least be conceded that an essential characteristic of the State University is its democracy in the largest sense. The provision in the Constitution of Indiana of 1816, so familiar to you all, for a "general system of education ascending in regular gradations from township schools to a State University, wherein tuition shall be gratis and equally open to all," expresses the Middle Western conception born in the days of pioneer society and doubtless deeply influenced by Jeffersonian democracy.

The most obvious fact about these universities, perhaps, lies in their integral relation with the public schools, whereby the pupil has pressed upon him the question whether he shall go to college, and whereby the road is made open and direct to the highest training. By this means the State offers to every class the means of education, and even engages in propaganda to induce students to continue. It sinks deep shafts through the social strata to find the gold of real ability in the underlying rock of the masses. It fosters that due degree of individualism which is implied in the right of every human being to have opportunity to rise in whatever directions his peculiar abilities entitle him to go, subordinate to the welfare of the state. It keeps the avenues of promotion to the highest offices, the highest honors, open to the humblest and most obscure lad who has the natural gifts, at the same time that it aids in the improvement of the masses.

Nothing in our educational history is more striking than the steady pressure of democracy upon its universities to adapt them to the requirements of all the people. From the State Universities of the Middle West, shaped under pioneer ideals, have come the fuller recognition of scientific studies, and especially those of applied science devoted to the conquest of nature; the breaking down of the traditional required curriculum; the union of vocational and college work in the same institution; the development of agricultural and engineering colleges and business courses; the training of lawyers, administrators, public men, and journalists—all under the ideal of service to democracy rather than of individual advancement alone. Other universities do the same thing; but the head springs and the main current of this great stream of tendency come from the land of the pioneers, the democratic states of the Middle West. And the people themselves, through their boards of trustees and the legislature, are in the last resort the court of appeal as to the directions and conditions of growth, as well as have the fountain of income from which these universities derive their existence.

The State University has thus both a peculiar power in the directness of its influence upon the whole people and a peculiar limitation in its dependence upon the people. The ideals of the people constitute the atmosphere in which it moves, though it can itself affect this atmosphere. Herein is the source of its strength and the direction of its difficulties. For to fulfil its mission of uplifting the state to continuously higher levels the University must, in the words of Mr. Bryce, "serve the time without yielding to it"; it must recognize new needs without becoming subordinate to the immediately practical, to the short-sightedly expedient. It must not sacrifice the higher efficiency for the more obvious but lower efficiency. It must have the wisdom to make expenditures for results which pay manifold in the enrichment of civilization, but which are not immediate and palpable.

In the transitional condition of American democracy which I have tried to indicate, the mission of the university is most important. The times call for educated leaders. General experience and rule-of-thumb information are inadequate for the solution of the problems of a democracy which no longer owns the safety fund of an unlimited quantity of untouched resources. Scientific farming must increase the yield of the field, scientific forestry must economize the woodlands, scientific experiment and construction by chemist, physicist, biologist and engineer must be applied to all of nature's forces in our complex modern society. The test tube and the microscope are needed rather than ax and rifle in this new ideal of conquest. The very discoveries of science in such fields as public health and manufacturing processes have made it necessary to depend upon the expert, and if the ranks of experts are to be recruited broadly from the democratic masses as well as from those of larger means, the State Universities must furnish at least as liberal opportunities for research and training as the universities based on private endowments furnish. It needs no argument to show that it is not to the advantage of democracy to give over the training of the expert exclusively to privately endowed institutions.

But quite as much in the field of legislation and of public life in general as in the industrial world is the expert needed. The industrial conditions which shape society are too complex, problems of labor, finance, social reform too difficult to be dealt with intelligently and wisely without the leadership of highly educated men familiar with the legislation and literature on social questions in other States and nations.

By training in science, in law, politics, economics and history the universities may supply from the ranks of democracy administrators, legislators, judges and experts for commissions who shall disinterestedly and intelligently mediate between contending interests. When the words "capitalistic classes" and "the proletariate" can be used and understood in America it is surely time to develop such men, with the ideal of service to the State, who may help to break the force of these collisions, to find common grounds between the contestants and to possess the respect and confidence of all parties which are genuinely loyal to the best American ideals.

The signs of such a development are already plain in the expert commissions of some States; in the increasing proportion of university men in legislatures; in the university men's influence in federal departments and commissions. It is hardly too much to say that the best hope of intelligent and principled progress in economic and social legislation and administration lies in the increasing influence of American universities. By sending out these open-minded experts, by furnishing well-fitted legislators, public leaders and teachers, by graduating successive armies of enlightened citizens accustomed to deal dispassionately with the problems of modern life, able to think for themselves, governed not by ignorance, by prejudice or by impulse, but by knowledge and reason and high-mindedness, the State Universities will safeguard democracy. Without such leaders and followers democratic reactions may create revolutions, but they will not be able to produce industrial and social progress. America's problem is not violently to introduce democratic ideals, but to preserve and entrench them by courageous adaptation to new conditions. Educated leadership sets bulwarks against both the passionate impulses of the mob and the sinister designs of those who would subordinate public welfare to private greed. Lord Bacon's splendid utterance still rings true: "The learning of the few is despotism; the learning of the many is liberty. And intelligent and principled liberty is fame, wisdom and power."

There is a danger to the universities in this very opportunity. At first pioneer democracy had scant respect for the expert. He believed that "a fool can put on his coat better than a wise man can do it for him." There is much truth in the belief; and the educated leader, even he who has been trained under present university conditions, in direct contact with the world about him, will still have to contend with this inherited suspicion of the expert. But if he be well trained and worthy of his training, if he be endowed with creative imagination and personality, he will make good his leadership.

A more serious danger will come when the universities are fully recognized as powerful factors in shaping the life of the State—not mere cloisters, remote from its life, but an influential element in its life. Then it may easily happen that the smoke of the battle-field of political and social controversy will obscure their pure air, that efforts will be made to stamp out the exceptional doctrine and the exceptional man. Those who investigate and teach within the university walls must respond to the injunction of the church, *"Sursum corda"*—lift up the heart to high thinking and impartial search for the unsullied truth in the interests of all the people; this is the holy grail of the universities.

That they may perform their work they must be left free, as the pioneer was free, to explore new regions and to report what they find; for like the pioneers they have the ideal of investigation, they seek new horizons. They are not tied to past knowledge; they recognize the fact that the universe still abounds in mystery, that science and society have not crystallized, but are still growing and need their pioneer trailmakers. New and beneficent discoveries in nature, new and beneficial discoveries in the processes and directions of the growth of society, substitutes for the vanishing material basis of pioneer democracy may be expected if the university pioneers are left free to seek the trail.

In conclusion, the university has a duty in adjusting pioneer ideals to the new requirements of American democracy, even more important than those which I have named. The early pioneer was an individualist and a seeker after the undiscovered; but he did not understand the richness and complexity of life as a whole; he did not fully realize his opportunities of individualism and discovery. He stood in his somber forest as the traveler sometimes stands in a village on the Alps when the mist has shrouded everything, and only the squalid hut, the stony field, the muddy pathway are in view. But suddenly a wind sweeps the fog away. Vast fields of radiant snow and sparkling ice lie before him; profound abysses open at his feet; and as he lifts his eyes the unimaginable peak of the Matterhorn cleaves the thin air, far, far above. A new and unsuspected world is revealed all about him. Thus it is the function of the university to reveal to the individual the mystery and the glory of life as a whole—to open all the realms of rational human enjoyment and achievement; to preserve the consciousness of the past; to spread before the eye the beauty of the universe; and to throw wide its portals of duty and of power to the human soul. It must honor the poet and painter, the writer and the teacher, the scientist and the inventor, the musician and the prophet of righteousness—the men of genius in all fields who make life nobler. It must call forth anew, and for finer uses, the pioneer's love of creative individualism and provide for it a spiritual atmosphere friendly to the development of personality in all uplifting ways. It must check the tendency to act in mediocre social masses with undue emphasis upon the ideals of prosperity and politics. In short, it must summon ability of all kinds to joyous and earnest effort for the welfare and the spiritual enrichment of society. It must awaken new tastes and ambitions among the people.

The light of these university watch towers should flash from State to State until American democracy itself is illuminated with higher and broader ideals of what constitutes service to the State and to mankind; of what are prizes; of what is worthy of praise and reward. So long as success in amassing great wealth for the aggrandizement of the individual is the exclusive or the dominant standard of success, so long as material prosperity, regardless of the conditions of its cost, or the civilization which results, is the shibboleth, American democracy, that faith in the common man which the pioneer cherishes, is in danger. For the strongest will make their way unerringly to whatever goal society sets up as the mark of conceded preëminence. What more effective agency is there for the cultivation of the seed wheat of ideals than the university? Where can we find a more promising body of sowers of the grain?

The pioneer's clearing must be broadened into a domain where all that is worthy of human endeavor may find fertile soil on which to grow; and America must exact of the constructive business geniuses who owe their rise to the freedom of pioneer democracy supreme allegiance and devotion to the commonweal. In fostering such an outcome and in tempering the asperities of the conflicts that must precede its fulfilment, the nation has no more promising agency than the State Universities, no more hopeful product than their graduates.

SIX

SOCIAL FORCES IN
AMERICAN HISTORY

(1910)

The transformations through which the United States is passing in our own day are so profound, so far-reaching, that it is hardly an exaggeration to say that we are witnessing the birth of a new nation in America. The revolution in the social and economic structure of this country during the past two decades is comparable to what occurred when independence was declared and the constitution was formed, or to the changes wrought by the era which began half a century ago, the era of Civil War and Reconstruction.

These changes have been long in preparation and are, in part, the result of world-wide forces of reorganization incident to the age of steam production and large-scale industry, and, in part, the result of the closing of the period of the colonization of the West. They have been prophesied, and the course of the movement partly described by students of American development; but after all, it is with a shock that the people of the

Presidential address to the American Historical Association, Indianapolis, December 28, 1910. Reprinted by permission from *American Historical Review* 17 (January 1911).

United States are coming to realize that the fundamental forces which have shaped their society up to the present are disappearing. Twenty years ago, as I have before had occasion to point out, the Superintendent of the Census declared that the frontier line, which its maps had depicted for decade after decade of the westward march of the nation, could no longer be described. To-day we must add that the age of free competition of individuals for the unpossessed resources of the nation is nearing its end. It is taking less than a generation to write the chapter which began with the disappearance of the line of the frontier—the last chapter in the history of the colonization of the United States, the conclusion to the annals of its pioneer democracy.

It is a wonderful chapter, this final rush of American energy upon the remaining wilderness. Even the bare statistics become eloquent of a new era. They no longer derive their significance from the exhibit of vast proportions of the public domain transferred to agriculture, of wildernesses equal to European nations changed decade after decade into the farm area of the United States. It is true there was added to the farms of the nation between 1870 and 1880 a territory equal to that of France, and between 1880 and 1900 a territory equal to the European area of France, Germany, England, and Wales combined. The records of 1910 are not yet available, but whatever they reveal they will not be so full of meaning as the figures which tell of upleaping wealth and organization and concentration of industrial power in the East in the last decade. As the final provinces of the Western empire have been subdued to the purposes of civilization and have yielded their spoils, as the spheres of operation of the great industrial corporations have extended, with the extension of American settlement, production and wealth have increased beyond all precedent.

The total deposits in all national banks have more than trebled in the present decade; the money in circulation has doubled since 1890. The flood of gold makes it difficult to gage the full meaning of the incredible increase in values, for in the decade ending with 1909 over 41,600,000 ounces of gold were mined in the United States alone. Over four million ounces have been produced every year since 1905, whereas between 1880 and 1894 no year showed a production of two million ounces. As a result of this swelling stream of gold and instruments of credit, aided by a variety of other causes, prices have risen until their height has become one of the most marked features and influential factors in American life, producing social readjustments and contributing effectively to party revolutions.

But if we avoid those statistics which require analysis because of the changing standard of value, we still find that the decade occupies an exceptional place in American history. More coal was mined in the United States in the ten years after 1897 than in all the life of the nation before that time.[1] Fifty years ago we mined less than fifteen million long tons of coal. In 1907 we mined nearly 429,000,000. At the present rate it is estimated that the supply of coal would be exhausted at a date no farther in the future than the formation of the constitution is in the past. Iron and coal are the measures of industrial power. The nation has produced three times as much iron ore in the past two decades as in all its previous history; the production of the past ten years was more than double that of the prior decade. Pig-iron production is admitted to be an excellent barometer of manufacture and of transportation. Never until 1898 had this reached an annual total of ten million long tons. But in the five years beginning with 1904 it averaged over twice that. By 1907 the United States had surpassed Great Britain, Germany, and France combined in the production of pig-iron and steel together, and in the same decade a single great corporation has established its domination over the iron mines and steel manufacture of the United States. It is more than a mere accident that the United States Steel Corporation with its stocks and bonds aggregating $1,400,000,000 was organized at the beginning of the present decade. The former wilderness about Lake Superior has, principally in the past two decades, established its position as overwhelmingly the preponderant source of iron ore, present and prospective, in the United States—a treasury from which Pittsburgh has drawn wealth and extended its unparalleled industrial empire in these years. The tremendous energies thus liberated at this center of industrial power in the United States revolutionized methods of manufacture in general, and in many indirect ways profoundly influenced the life of the nation.

Railroad statistics also exhibit unprecedented development, the formation of a new industrial society. The number of passengers carried one mile more than doubled between 1890 and 1908; freight carried one mile has nearly trebled in the same period and has doubled in the past decade. Agricultural products tell a different story. The corn crop has only risen from about two billion bushels in 1891 to two and seven-tenths billions in 1909; wheat from six hundred and eleven million bushels in 1891 to only seven hundred and thirty-seven million in 1909; and cotton from about nine million bales in 1891 to ten and three-tenths million bales in 1909. Population has increased in the United States proper from about sixty-two and one-half millions in 1890 to seventy-five and one-half millions in 1900 and to over ninety millions in 1910.

It is clear from these statistics that the ratio of the nation's increased production of immediate wealth by the enormously increased exploitation of its remaining natural resources vastly exceeds the ratio of increase of population and still more strikingly exceeds the ratio of increase of agricultural products. Already population is pressing upon the food supply while capital consolidates in billion-dollar organizations. The "Triumphant Democracy" whose achievements the iron-master celebrated has reached a stature even more imposing than he could have foreseen; but still less did he perceive the changes in democracy itself and the conditions of its life which have accompanied this material growth.

Having colonized the Far West, having mastered its internal resources, the nation turned at the conclusion of the nineteenth and the beginning of the twentieth century to deal with the Far East to engage in the world-politics of the Pacific Ocean. Having continued its historic expansion into the lands of the old Spanish empire by the successful outcome of the recent war, the United States became the mistress of the Philippines at the same time that it came into possession of the Hawaiian Islands, and the controlling influence in the Gulf of Mexico. It provided early in the present decade for connecting its Atlantic and Pacific coasts by the Isthmian Canal, and became an imperial republic with dependencies and protectorates—admittedly a new world-power, with a potential voice in the problems of Europe, Asia, and Africa.

This extension of power, this undertaking of grave responsibilities in new fields, this entry into the sisterhood of world-states, was no isolated event. It was, indeed, in some respects the logical outcome of the nation's march to the Pacific, the sequence to the era in which it was engaged in occupying the free lands and exploiting the resources of the West. When it had achieved this position among the nations of the earth, the United States found itself confronted, also, with the need of constitutional readjustment, arising from the relations of federal government and territorial acquisitions. It was obliged to reconsider questions of the rights of man and traditional American ideals of liberty and democracy, in view of the task of government of other races politically inexperienced and undeveloped.

If we turn to consider the effect upon American society and domestic policy in these two decades of transition we are met with palpable evidences of the invasion of the old pioneer democratic order. Obvious among them is the effect of unprecedented immigration to supply the mobile army of cheap labor for the centers of industrial life. In the past ten years, beginning with 1900, over eight million immigrants have arrived. The newcomers of the eight years since 1900 would, according to a writer in 1908, "repopulate all the five older New England States as they stand to-day; or, if properly disseminated over the newer parts of the country they would serve to populate no less than nineteen states of the Union as they stand." In 1907 "there were one and one-quarter million arrivals. This number would entirely populate both New Hampshire and Maine, two of our oldest States." "The arrivals of this one year would found a State with more inhabitants than any one of twenty-one of our other existing commonwealths which could be named." Not only has the addition to the population from Europe been thus extraordinary, it has come in increasing measure from southern and eastern Europe. For the year 1907, Professor Ripley,[2] whom I am quoting, has redistributed the incomers on the basis of physical type and finds that one-quarter of them were of the Mediterranean race, one-quarter of the Slavic race, one-eighth Jewish, and only one-sixth of the Alpine, and one-sixth of the Teutonic. In 1882 Germans had come to the amount of 250,000; in 1907 they were replaced by 330,000 South Italians. Thus it is evident that the ethnic elements of the United States have undergone startling changes; and instead of spreading over the nation these immigrants have concentrated especially in the cities and great industrial centers in the past decade. The composition of the labor class and its relation to wages and to the native American employer have been deeply influenced thereby; the sympathy of the employers with labor has been unfavorably affected by the pressure of great numbers of immigrants of alien nationality and of lower standards of life.

The familiar facts of the massing of population in the cities and the contemporaneous increase of urban power, and of the massing of capital and production in fewer and vastly greater industrial units, especially attest the revolution. "It is a proposition too plain to require elucidation," wrote Richard Rush, Secretary of the Treasury, in his report of 1827, "that the creation of capital is retarded rather than accelerated by the diffusion of a thin population over a great surface of soil." Thirty years before Rush wrote these words Albert Gallatin declared in Congress that "if the cause of the happiness of this country were examined into, it would be found to arise as much from the great plenty of land in proportion to the inhabitants which their citizens enjoyed as from the wisdom of their political institutions." Possibly both of these Pennsylvania financiers were right under the conditions of the time; but it is at least significant that capital and labor entered upon a new era as the end of the free lands approached. A contemporary of Gallatin in Congress had replied to the argument that cheap lands would depopulate the Atlantic coast by saying that if a law were framed to prevent ready access to western lands it would be tantamount to saying that there is some class which must remain "and by law be obliged to serve the others for such wages as they pleased to give." The passage of the arable public domain into private possession has raised this question in a new form and has brought forth new answers. This is peculiarly the era when competitive individualism in the midst of vast unappropriated opportunities changed into the monopoly of the fundamental industrial processes by huge aggregations of capital as the free lands disappeared. All the tendencies of the large-scale production of the twentieth century, all the trend to the massing of capital in large combinations, all of the energies of the age of steam, found in America exceptional freedom of action and were offered regions of activity equal to the states of all Western Europe. Here they reached their highest development.

The decade following 1897 is marked by the work of Mr. Harriman and his rivals in building up the various railroads into a few great groups, a process that had gone so far that before his death Mr. Harriman was ambitious to concentrate them all under his single control. High finance under the leadership of Mr. Morgan steadily achieved the consolidation of the greater industries into trusts or combinations and effected a community of interests between them and a few dominant banking organizations, with allied insurance companies and trust companies. In New York City have been centered, as never before, the banking reserves of the nation, and here, by the financial management of capital and speculative promotion, there has grown up a unified control over the nation's industrial life. Colossal private fortunes have arisen. No longer is the per capita wealth of the nation a real index to the prosperity of the average man. Labor on the other hand has shown an increasing self-consciousness, is combining and increasing its demands. In a word, the old pioneer individualism is disappearing, while the forces of social combination are manifesting themselves as never before. The self-made man has become, in popular speech, the coal baron, the steel king, the oil king, the cattle king, the railroad magnate, the master of high finance, the monarch of trusts. The world has never before seen such huge fortunes exercising combined control over the economic life of a people, and such luxury as has come out of the individualistic pioneer democracy of America in the course of competitive evolution.

At the same time the masters of industry, who control interests which represent billions of dollars, do not admit that they have broken with pioneer ideals. They regard themselves as pioneers under changed conditions, carrying on the old work of developing the natural resources of the nation, compelled by the constructive fever in their veins, even in ill-health and old age and after the accumulation of wealth beyond their power to enjoy, to seek new avenues of action and of power, to chop new clearings, to find new trails, to expand the horizon of the nation's activity, and to extend the scope of their dominion. "This country," said the late Mr. Harriman in an interview a few years ago, "has been developed by a wonderful people, flush with enthusiasm, imagination and speculative bent.... They have been magnificent pioneers. They saw into the future and adapted their work to the possibilities.... Stifle that enthusiasm, deaden that imagination and prohibit that speculation by restrictive and cramping conservative law, and you tend to produce a moribund and conservative people and country." This is an appeal to the historic ideals of Americans who viewed the republic as the guardian of individual freedom to compete for the control of the natural resources of the nation.

On the other hand, we have the voice of the insurgent West, recently given utterance in the New Nationalism of ex-President Roosevelt, demanding increase of federal authority to curb the special interests, the powerful industrial organizations, and the monopolies, for the sake of the conservation of our natural resources and the preservation of American democracy.

The past decade has witnessed an extraordinary federal activity in limiting individual and corporate freedom for the benefit of society. To that decade belong the conservation congresses and the effective organization of the Forest Service, and the Reclamation Service. Taken together these developments alone would mark a new era, for over three hundred million acres are, as a result of this policy, reserved from entry and sale, an area more than equal to that of all the states which established the constitution, if we exclude their western claims; and these reserved lands are held for a more beneficial use of their forests, minerals, arid tracts, and water rights, by the nation as a whole. Another example is the extension of the activity of the Department of Agriculture, which seeks the remotest regions of the earth for crops suitable to the areas reclaimed by the government, maps and analyzes the soils, fosters the improvement of seeds and animals, tells the farmer when and how and what to plant, and makes war upon diseases of plants and animals and insect pests. The recent legislation for pure food and meat inspection, and the whole mass of regulative law under the Interstate Commerce clause of the constitution, further illustrates the same tendency.

Two ideals were fundamental in traditional American thought, ideals that developed in the pioneer era. One was that of individual freedom to compete unrestrictedly for the resources of a continent— the squatter ideal. To the pioneer government was an evil. The other was the ideal of a democracy—"government of the people, by the people and for the people." The operation of these ideals took place contemporaneously with the passing into private possession of the free public domain and the natural resources of the United States. But American democracy was based on an abundance of free lands; these were the very conditions that shaped its growth and its fundamental traits. Thus time has revealed that these two ideals of pioneer democracy had elements of mutual hostility and contained the seeds of its dissolution. The present finds itself engaged in the task of readjusting its old ideals to new conditions and is turning increasingly to government to preserve its traditional democracy. It is not surprising that socialism shows noteworthy gains as elections continue; that parties are forming on new lines; that the demand for primary elections, for popular choice of senators, initiative, referendum, and recall, is spreading, and that the regions once the center of pioneer democracy exhibit these tendencies in the most marked degree. They are efforts to find substitutes for that former safeguard of democracy, the disappearing free lands. They are the sequence to the extinction of the frontier.

It is necessary next to notice that in the midst of all this national energy, and contemporaneous with the tendency to turn to the national government for protection to democracy, there is clear evidence of the persistence and the development of sectionalism.[3] Whether we observe the grouping of votes in Congress and in general elections, or the organization and utterances of business leaders, or the association of scholars, churches, or other representatives of the things of the spirit, we find that American life is not only increasing in its national intensity but that it is integrating by sections. In part this is due to the factor of great spaces which make sectional rather than national organization the line of least resistance; but, in part, it is also the expression of the separate economic, political, and social interests and the separate spiritual life of the various geographic provinces or sections. The votes on the tariff, and in general the location of the strongholds of the Progressive Republican movement, illustrate this fact. The difficulty of a national adjustment of railway rates to the diverse interests of different sections is another example. Without attempting to enter upon a more extensive discussion of sectionalism, I desire simply to point out that there are evidences that now, as formerly, the separate geographical interests have their leaders and spokesmen, that much Congressional legislation is determined by the contests, triumphs, or compromises between the rival sections, and that the real federal relations of the United States are shaped by the interplay of sectional with national forces rather than by the relation of State and Nation. As time goes on and the nation adjusts itself more durably to the conditions of the differing geographic sections which make it up, they are coming to a new self-consciousness and a revived self-assertion. Our national character is a composite of these sections.[4]

Obviously in attempting to indicate even a portion of the significant features of our recent history we have been obliged to take note of a complex of forces. The times are so close at hand that the relations between events and tendencies force themselves upon our attention. We have had to deal with the connections of geography, industrial growth, politics, and government. With these we must take into consideration the changing social composition, the inherited beliefs and habitual attitude of the masses of the people, the psychology of the nation and of the separate sections, as well as of the leaders. We must see how these leaders are shaped partly by their time and section, and how they are in part original, creative, by virtue of their own genius and initiative. We cannot neglect the moral tendencies and the ideals. All are related parts of the same subject and can no more be properly understood in isolation than the movement as a whole can be understood by neglecting some of these important factors, or by the use of a single method of investigation. Whatever be the truth regarding European history, American history is chiefly concerned with social forces, shaping and reshaping under the conditions of a nation changing as it adjusts to its environment. And this environment progressively reveals new aspects of itself, exerts new influences, and calls out new social organs and functions.

I have undertaken this rapid survey of recent history for two purposes. First, because it has seemed fitting to emphasize the significance of American development since the passing of the frontier, and, second, because in the observation of present conditions we may find assistance in our study of the past.

It is a familiar doctrine that each age studies its history anew and with interests determined by the spirit of the time. Each age finds it necessary to reconsider at least some portion of the past, from points of view furnished by new conditions which reveal the influence and significance of forces not adequately known by the historians of the previous generation. Unquestionably each investigator and writer is influenced by the times in which he lives and while this fact exposes the historian to a bias, at the same time it affords him new instruments and new insight for dealing with his subject.

If recent history, then, gives new meaning to past events, if it has to deal with the rise into a commanding position of forces, the origin and growth of which may have been inadequately described or even overlooked by historians of the previous generation, it is important to study the present and the recent past, not only for themselves but also as the source of new hypotheses, new lines of inquiry, new criteria of the perspective of the remoter past. And, moreover, a just public opinion and a statesmanlike treatment of present problems demand that they be seen in their historical relations in order that history may hold the lamp for conservative reform.

Seen from the vantage-ground of present developments what new light falls upon past events! When we consider what the Mississippi Valley has come to be in American life, and when we consider what it is yet to be, the young Washington, crossing the snows of the wilderness to summon the French to evacuate the portals of the great valley, becomes the herald of an empire. When we recall the huge industrial power that has centered at Pittsburgh, Braddock's advance to the forks of the Ohio takes on new meaning. Even in defeat, he opened a road to what is now the center of the world's industrial energy. The modifications which England proposed in 1794 to John Jay in the northwestern boundary of the United States from the Lake of the Woods to the Mississippi, seemed to him, doubtless, significant chiefly as a matter of principle and as a question of the retention or loss of beaver grounds. The historians hardly notice the proposals. But they involved, in fact, the ownership of the richest and most extensive deposits of iron ore in America, the all-important source of a fundamental industry of the United States, the occasion for the rise of some of the most influential forces of our time.

What continuity and meaning are furnished by the outcome in present times of the movements of minor political parties and reform agitations! To the historian they have often seemed to be mere curious side eddies, vexatious distractions to the course of his literary craft as it navigated the stream of historical tendency. And yet, by the revelation of the present, what seemed to be side eddies have not seldom proven to be the concealed entrances to the main current, and the course which seemed the central one has led to blind channels and stagnant waters, important in their day, but cut off like oxbow lakes from the mighty river of historical progress by the mere permanent and compelling forces of the neglected currents.

We may trace the contest between the capitalist and the democratic pioneer from the earliest colonial days. It is influential in colonial parties. It is seen in the vehement protests of Kentucky frontiersmen in petition after petition to the Congress of the Confederation against the "nabobs" and men of wealth who took out titles to the pioneers' farms while they themselves were too busy defending those farms from the Indians to perfect their claims. It is seen in the attitude of the Ohio Valley in its backwoods days before the rise of the Whig party, as when in 1811 Henry Clay denounced the Bank of the United States as a corporation which throve on special privileges—"a special association of favored individuals taken from the mass of society, and invested with exemptions and surrounded by immunities and privileges." Benton voiced the same contest twenty years later when he denounced the bank as

a company of private individuals, many of them foreigners, and the mass of them residing in a remote and narrow corner of the Union, unconnected by any sympathy with the fertile regions of the Great Valley in which the natural power of this Union, the power of numbers, will be found to reside long before the renewed term of the second charter would expire.

"And where," he asked, "would all this power and money center? In the great cities of the Northeast, which have been for forty years and that by force of federal legislation, the lion's den of Southern and Western money—that den into which all the tracks point inward; from which the returning track of a solitary dollar has never yet been seen." Declaring, in words that have a very modern sound, that the bank tended to multiply nabobs and paupers, and that "a great moneyed power is favorable to great capitalists, for it is the principle of capital to favor capital," he appealed to the fact of the country's extent and its sectional divergences against the nationalizing of capital.

What a condition for a confederacy of states! What grounds for alarm and terrible apprehension when in a confederacy of such vast extent, so many rival commercial cities, so much sectional jealousy, such violent political parties, such fierce contests for power, there should be but one moneyed tribunal before which all the rival and contending elements must appear.

Even more vehement were the words of Jackson in 1837. "It is now plain," he wrote, "that the war is to be carried on by the monied aristocracy of the few against the democracy of numbers; the [prosperous] to make the honest laborers hewers of wood and drawers of water through the credit and paper system."

Van Buren's administration is usually passed hastily over with hardly more than mention of his Independent Treasury plan, and with particular consideration of the slavery discussion. But some of the most important movements in American social and political history began in these years of Jackson and Van Buren. Read the demands of the obscure labor papers and the reports of labor's open-air meetings anew, and you will find in the utterances of so-called labor visionaries and the Locofoco champions of "equal rights for all and special privileges for none," like Evans and Jacques, Byrdsall and Leggett, the finger points to the currents that now make the main channel of our history; you will find in them some of the important planks of the platforms of the triumphant parties of our own day. As Professor Commons has shown by his papers and the documents which he has published on labor history, an idealistic but widespread and influential humanitarian movement, strikingly similar to that of the present, arose in the years between 1830 and 1850, dealing with social forces in American life, animated by a desire to apply the public lands to social amelioration, eager to find new forms of democratic development. But the flood of the slavery struggle swept all of these movements into its mighty inundation for the time. After the war, other influences de-layed the revival of the movement. The railroads opened the wide prairies after 1850 and made it easy to reach them; and decade after decade new sections were reduced to the purposes of civilization and to the advantages of the common man as well as the promotion of great individual fortunes. The nation centered its interests in the develop-ment of the West. It is only in our own day that this humanitarian democratic wave has reached the level of those earlier years. But in the meantime there are clear evidences of the persistence of the forces, even though under strange guise. Read the platforms of the Greenback-Labor, the Granger, and the Populist parties, and you will find in those platforms, discredited and reprobated by the major par-ties of the time, the basic proposals of the Democratic party after its revolution under the leadership of Mr. Bryan, and of the Republican party after its revolution by Mr. Roosevelt. The Insurgent movement is so clearly related to the areas and elements that gave strength to this progressive assertion of old democratic ideals with new weapons, that it must be regarded as the organized refusal of these persistent tendencies to be checked by the advocates of more moderate mea-sures.

I have dealt with these fragments of party history, not, of course, with the purpose of expressing any present judgment upon them, but to emphasize and give concreteness to the fact that there is disclosed by present events a new significance to these contests of radical democracy and conservative interests; that they are rather a continuing expression of deep-seated forces than fragmentary and sporadic curios for the historical museum.

If we should survey the history of our lands from a similar point of view, considering the relations of legislation and administration of the public domain to the structure of American democracy, it would yield a return far beyond that offered by the formal treatment of the subject in most of our histories. We should find in the squatter doctrines and practices, the seizure of the best soils, the taking of public timber on the theory of a right to it by the labor expended on it, fruitful material for understanding the atmosphere and ideals under which the great corporations developed the West. Men like Senator Benton and Delegate Sibley in successive generations defended the trespasses of the pioneer and the lumberman upon the public forest lands, and denounced the paternal government that "harassed" these men, who were engaged in what we should call stealing government timber. It is evident that at some time between the middle of the nineteenth century and the present time, when we impose jail sentences upon Congressmen caught in such violations of the land laws, a change came over the American conscience and the civic ideals were modified. That our great industrial enterprises developed in the midst of these changing ideals is important to recall when we write the history of their activity.

We should find also that we cannot understand the land question without seeing its relations to the struggle of sections and classes bidding against each other and finding in the public domain a most important topic of political bargaining. We should find, too, that the settlement of unlike geographic areas in the course of the nation's progress resulted in changes in the effect of the land laws; that a system intended for the humid prairies was ill-adjusted to the grazing lands and coal fields and to the forests in the days of large-scale exploitation by corporations commanding great capital. Thus changing geographic factors as well as the changing character of the forces which occupied the public domain must be considered, if we would understand the bearing of legislation and policy in this field.[5] It is fortunate that suggestive studies of democracy and the land policy have already begun to appear.

The whole subject of American agriculture viewed in relation to the economic, political, and social life of the nation has important contributions to make. If, for example, we study the maps showing the transition of the wheat belt from the East to the West, as the virgin soils were conquered and made new bases for destructive competition with the older wheat States, we shall see how deeply they affected not only land values, railroad building, the movement of population, and the supply of cheap food, but also how the regions once devoted to single cropping of wheat were forced to turn to varied and intensive agriculture and to diversified industry, and we shall see also how these transformations affected party politics and even the ideals of the Americans of the regions thus changed. We shall find in the over-production of wheat in the provinces thus rapidly colonized, and in the over-production of silver in the mountain provinces which were contemporaneously exploited, important explanations of the peculiar form which American politics took in the period when Mr. Bryan mastered the Democratic party, just as we shall find in the opening of the new gold fields in the years immediately following, and in the passing of the era of almost free virgin wheat soils, explanations of the more recent period when high prices are giving new energy and aggressiveness to the demands of the new American industrial democracy.

Enough has been said, it may be assumed, to make clear the point which I am trying to elucidate, namely that a comprehension of the United States of to-day, an understanding of the rise and progress of the forces which have made it what it is, demands that we should rework our history from the new points of view afforded by the present. If this is done, it will be seen, for example, that the progress of the struggle between North and South over slavery and the freed negro, which held the principal place in American interest in the two decades after 1850, was, after all, only one of the interests in the time. The pages of the Congressional debates, the contemporary newspapers, the public documents of those twenty years, remain a rich mine for those who will seek therein the sources of movements dominant in the present day.

The final consideration to which I ask your attention in this discussion of social forces in American life, is with reference to the mode of investigating them and the bearing of these investigations upon the relations and the goal of history. It has become a precedent, fairly well established by the distinguished scholars who have held the office which I am about to lay down, to state a position with reference to the relations of history and its sister-studies, and even to raise the question of the attitude of the historian toward the laws of thermodynamics and to seek to find the key of historical development or of historical degradation. It is not given to all to bend the bow of Ulysses. I shall attempt a lesser task.

We may take some lessons from the scientist. He has enriched knowledge especially in recent years by attacking the no-man's lands left unexplored by the too sharp delimitation of spheres of activity. These new conquests have been especially achieved by the combination of old sciences. Physical chemistry, electro-chemistry, geophysics, astro-physics, and a variety of other scientific unions have led to audacious hypotheses, veritable flashes of vision, which open new regions of activity for a generation of investigators. Moreover they have promoted such investigations by furnishing new instruments of research. Now in some respects there is an analogy between geology and history. The new geologist aims to describe the inorganic earth dynamically in terms of natural law, using chemistry, physics, mathematics, and even botany and zoölogy so far as they relate to paleontology. But he does not insist that the relative importance of physical or chemical factors shall be determined before he applies the methods and data of these sciences to his problem. Indeed, he has learned that a geological area is too complex a thing to be reduced to a single explanation. He has abandoned the single hypothesis for the multiple hypothesis. He creates a whole family of possible explanations of a given problem and thus avoids the warping influence of partiality for a simple theory.

Have we not here an illustration of what is possible and necessary for the historian? Is it not well, before attempting to decide whether history requires an economic interpretation, or a psychological, or any other ultimate interpretation, to recognize that the factors in human society are varied and complex; that the political historian handling his subject in isolation is certain to miss fundamental facts and relations in his treatment of a given age or nation; that the economic historian is exposed to the same danger; and so of all of the other special historians?

Those who insist that history is simply the effort to tell the thing exactly as it was, to state the facts, are confronted with the difficulty that the fact which they would represent is not planted on the solid ground of fixed conditions; it is in the midst and is itself a part of the changing currents, the complex and interacting influences of the time, deriving its significance as a fact from its relations to the deeper-seated movements of the age, movements so gradual that often only the passing years can reveal the truth about the fact and its right to a place on the historian's page.

The economic historian is in danger of making his analysis and his statement of a law on the basis of present conditions and then passing to history for justificatory appendixes to his conclusions. An American economist of high rank has recently expressed his conception of "the full relation of economic theory, statistics, and history" in these words:

> A principle is formulated by *a priori* reasoning concerning facts of common experience; it is then tested by statistics and promoted to the rank of a known and acknowledged truth;

illustrations of its action are then found in narrative history and, on the other hand, the economic law becomes the interpreter of records that would otherwise be confusing and comparatively valueless; the law itself derives its final confirmation from the illustrations of its working which the records afford; but what is at least of equal importance is the parallel fact that the law affords the decisive test of the correctness of those assertions concerning the causes and the effects of past events which it is second nature to make and which historians almost invariably do make in connection with their narrations.[6]

There is much in this statement by which the historian may profit, but he may doubt also whether the past should serve merely as the "illustration" by which to confirm the law deduced from common experience by *a priori* reasoning tested by statistics. In fact the pathway of history is strewn with the wrecks of the "known and acknowledged truths" of economic law, due not only to defective analysis and imperfect statistics, but also to the lack of critical historical methods, of insufficient historical-mindedness on the part of the economist, to failure to give due attention to the relativity and transiency of the conditions from which his laws were deduced.

But the point on which I would lay stress is this. The economist, the political scientist, the psychologist, the sociologist, the geographer, the student of literature, of art, of religion—all the allied laborers in the study of society—have contributions to make to the equipment of the historian. These contributions are partly of material, partly of tools, partly of new points of view, new hypotheses, new suggestions of relations, causes, and emphasis. Each of these special students is in some danger of bias by his particular point of view, by his exposure to see simply the thing in which he is primarily interested, and also by his effort to deduce the universal laws of his separate science. The historian, on the other hand, is exposed to the danger of dealing with the complex and interacting social forces of a period or of a country, from some single point of view to which his special training or interest inclines him. If the truth is to be made known, the historian must so far familiarize himself with the work, and equip himself with the training of his sister-subjects that he can at least avail himself of their results and in some reasonable degree master the essential tools of their trade. And the followers of the sister-studies must likewise familiarize themselves and their students with the work and the methods of the historians, and coöperate in the difficult task.

It is necessary that the American historian shall aim at this equipment, not so much that he may possess the key to history or satisfy himself in regard to its ultimate laws. At present a different duty is before him. He must see in American society with its vast spaces, its sections equal to European nations, its geographic influences, its brief period of development, its variety of nationalities and races, its extraordinary industrial growth under the conditions of freedom, its institutions, culture, ideals, social psychology, and even its religions forming and changing almost under his eyes, one of the richest fields ever offered for the preliminary recognition and study of the forces that operate and interplay in the making of society.

SEVEN

THE WEST AND AMERICAN IDEALS

(1914)

True to American traditions that each succeeding generation ought to find in the Republic a better home, once in every year the colleges and universities summon the nation to lift its eyes from the routine of work, in order to take stock of the country's purposes and achievements, to examine its past and consider its future.

This attitude of self-examination is hardly characteristic of the people as a whole. Particularly it is not characteristic of the historic American. He has been an opportunist rather than a dealer in general ideas. Destiny set him in a current which bore him swiftly along through such a wealth of opportunity that reflection and well-considered planning seemed wasted time. He knew not where he was going, but he was on his way, cheerful, optimistic, busy and buoyant.

Commencement Address, University of Washington, June 17, 1914. Reprinted by permission from *The Washington Historical Quarterly*, October 1914.

To-day we are reaching a changed condition, less apparent perhaps, in the newer regions than in the old, but sufficiently obvious to
extend the commencement frame of mind from the college to the
country as a whole. The swift and inevitable current of the upper
reaches of the nation's history has borne it to the broader expanse and
slower stretches which mark the nearness of the level sea. The vessel,
no longer carried along by the rushing waters, finds it necessary to
determine its own directions on this new ocean of its future, to give
conscious consideration to its motive power and to its steering gear.

It matters not so much that those who address these college men
and women upon life, give conflicting answers to the questions of
whence and whither: the pause for remembrance, for reflection and for
aspiration is wholesome in itself.

Although the American people are becoming more self-conscious,
more responsive to the appeal to act by deliberate choices, we should
be over-sanguine if we believed that even in this new day these
commencement surveys were taken to heart by the general public, or
that they were directly and immediately influential upon national
thought and action.

But even while we check our enthusiasm by this realization of the
common thought, we must take heart. The University's peculiar privilege and distinction lie in the fact that it is not the passive instrument
of the State to voice its current ideas. Its problem is not that of
expressing tendencies. Its mission is to create tendencies and to direct
them. Its problem is that of leadership and of ideals. It is called, of
course, to justify the support which the public gives it, by working in
close and sympathetic touch with those it serves. More than that,
it would lose [an] important element of strength if it failed to recognize the fact that improvement and creative movement often come
from the masses themselves, instinctively moving toward a better
order. The University's graduates must be fitted to take their places
naturally and effectually in the common life of the time.

But the University is called especially to justify its existence by giving to its sons and daughters something which they could not well have gotten through the ordinary experiences of the life outside its walls. It is called to serve the time by independent research and by original thought. If it were a mere recording instrument of conventional opinion and average information, it is hard to see why the University should exist at all. To clasp hands with the common life in order that it may lift that life, to be a radiant center enkindling the society in which it has its being, these are primary duties of the University. Fortunate the State which gives free play to this spirit of inquiry. Let it "grubstake" its intellectual prospectors and send them forth where "the trails run out and stop." A famous scientist holds that the universal ether bears vital germs which impinging upon a dead world would bring life to it. So, at least it is, in the world of thought, where energized ideals put in the air and carried here and there by the waves and currents of the intellectual atmosphere, fertilize vast inert areas.

The University, therefore, has a double duty. On the one hand it must aid in the improvement of the general economic and social environment. It must help in the work of scientific discovery and of making such conditions of existence, economic, political and social, as will produce more fertile and responsive soil for a higher and better life. It must stimulate a wider demand on the part of the public for right leadership. It must extend its operations more widely among the people and sink deeper shafts through social strata to find new supplies of intellectual gold in popular levels yet untouched. And on the other hand, it must find and fit men and women for leadership. It must both awaken new demands and it must satisfy those demands by trained leaders with new motives, with new incentives to ambition, with higher and broader conception of what constitute the prize in life, of what constitutes success. The University has to deal with both the soil and sifted seed in the agriculture of the human spirit.

Its efficiency is not the efficiency which the business engineer is fitted to appraise. If it is a training ship, it is a training ship bound on a voyage of discovery, seeking new horizons. The economy of the University's consumption can only be rightly measured by the later times which shall possess those new realms of the spirit which its voyage shall reveal. If the ships of Columbus had engaged in a profitable coastwise traffic between Palos and Cadiz they might have saved sail cloth, but their keels would never have grated on the shores of a New World.

The appeal of the undiscovered is strong in America. For three centuries the fundamental process in its history was the westward movement, the discovery and occupation of the vast free spaces of the continent. We are the first generation of Americans who can look back upon that era as a historic movement now coming to its end. Other generations have been so much a part of it that they could hardly comprehend its significance. To them it seemed inevitable. The free land and the natural resources seemed practically inexhaustible. Nor were they aware of the fact that their most fundamental traits, their institutions, even their ideals were shaped by this interaction between the wilderness and themselves.

American democracy was born of no theorist's dream; it was not carried in the *Susan Constant* to Virginia, nor in the *Mayflower* to Plymouth. It came out of the American forest, and it gained new strength each time it touched a new frontier. Not the constitution, but free land and an abundance of natural resources open to a fit people, made the democratic type of society in America for three centuries while it occupied its empire.

To-day we are looking with a shock upon a changed world. The national problem is no longer how to cut and burn away the vast screen of the dense and daunting forest; it is how to save and wisely use the remaining timber. It is no longer how to get the great spaces of fertile prairie land in humid zones out of the hands of the government into the hands of the pioneer; these lands have already passed into private possession. No longer is it a question of how to avoid or cross the Great Plains and the arid desert. It is a question of how to con-

quer those rejected lands by new method of farming and by culti-
vating new crops from seed collected by the government and by
scientists from the cold, dry steppes of Siberia, the burning sands of
Egypt, and the remote interior of China. It is a problem of how to
bring the precious rills of water on to the alkali and sage brush.
Population is increasing faster than the food supply.

New farm lands no longer increase decade after decade in areas
equal to those of European states. While the ratio of increase of
improved land declines, the value of farm lands rise and the price of
food leaps upward, reversing the old ratio between the two. The cry
of scientific farming and the conservation of natural resources replaces
the cry of rapid conquest of the wilderness. We have so far won our
national home, wrested from it its first rich treasures, and drawn to it
the unfortunate of other lands, that we are already obliged to compare
ourselves with settled states of the Old World. In place of our attitude
of contemptuous indifference to the legislation of such countries as
Germany and England, even Western States like Wisconsin send commissions to study their systems of taxation, workingmen's insurance,
old age pensions and a great variety of other remedies for social ills.

If we look about the periphery of the nation, everywhere we see
the indications that our world is changing. On the streets of Northeastern cities like New York and Boston, the faces which we meet are
to a surprising extent those of Southeastern Europe. Puritan New
England, which turned its capital into factories and mills and drew to
its shores an army of cheap labor, governed these people for a time by a
ruling class like an upper stratum between which and the lower strata
there was no assimilation. There was no such evolution into an assimilated commonwealth as is seen in Middle Western agricultural States,
where immigrant and old native stock came in together and built up a
homogeneous society on the principle of give and take. But now the
Northeastern coast finds its destiny, politically and economically, passing away from the descendants of the Puritans. It is the little Jewish
boy, the Greek or the Sicilian, who takes the traveler through historic

streets, now the home of these newer people, to the Old North Church or to Paul Revere's house, or to Tea Wharf, and tells you in his strange patois the story of revolution against oppression.

Along the Southern Atlantic and the Gulf coast, in spite of the preservative influence of the negro, whose presence has always called out resistance to change on the part of the whites, the forces of social and industrial transformation are at work. The old tidewater aristocracy has surrendered to the up-country democrats. Along the line of the Alleghanies like an advancing column, the forces of Northern capital, textile and steel mills, year after year extend their invasion into the lower South. New Orleans, once the mistress of the commerce of the Mississippi Valley, is awakening to new dreams of world commerce. On the southern border, similar invasions of American capital have been entering Mexico. At the same time, the opening of the Panama Canal has completed the dream of the ages of the Straits of Anian between Atlantic and Pacific. Four hundred years ago, Balboa raised the flag of Spain at the edge of the Sea of the West and we are now preparing to celebrate both that anniversary, and the piercing of the continent. New relations have been created between Spanish America and the United States and the world is watching the mediation of Argentina, Brazil and Chile between the contending forces of Mexico and the Union. Once more alien national interests lie threatening at our borders, but we no longer appeal to the Monroe Doctrine and send our armies of frontiersmen to settle our concerns off-hand. We take council with European nations and with the sisterhood of South America, and propose a remedy of social reorganization in place of imperious will and force. Whether the effort will succeed or not, it is a significant indication that an old order is passing away, when such a solution is undertaken by a President of Scotch Presbyterian stock, born in the State of Virginia.

If we turn to the Northern border, where we are about to celebrate a century of peace with England, we see in progress, like a belated procession of our own history the spread of pioneers, the opening of new wildernesses, the building of new cities, the growth of a new and mighty nation. That old American advance of the wheat farmer from the Connecticut to the Mohawk, and the Genesee, from the Great Valley of Pennsylvania to the Ohio Valley and the prairies of the Middle West, is now by its own momentum and under the stimulus of Canadian homesteads and the high price of wheat, carried across the national border to the once lone plains where the Hudson Bay dog trains crossed the desolate snows of the wild North Land. In the Pacific Northwest the era of construction has not ended, but it is so rapidly in progress that we can already see the closing of the age of the pioneer. Already Alaska beckons on the north, and pointing to her wealth of natural resources asks the nation on what new terms the new age will deal with her. Across the Pacific looms Asia, no longer a remote vision and a symbol of the unchanging, but borne as by mirage close to our shores and raising grave questions of the common destiny of the people of the ocean. The dreams of Benton and of Seward of a regenerated Orient, when the long march of westward civilization should complete its circle, seem almost to be in process of realization. The age of the Pacific Ocean begins, mysterious and unfathomable in its meaning for our own future.

Turning to view the interior, we see the same picture of change. When the Superintendent of the Census in 1890 declared the frontier line no longer traceable, the beginning of the rush into Oklahoma had just occurred. Here where the broken fragments of Indian nations from the East had been gathered and where the wilder tribes of the Southwest were being settled, came the rush of the land-hungry pioneer. Almost at a blow the old Indian territory passed away, populous cities came into being and it was not long before gushing oil wells made a new era of sudden wealth. The farm lands of the Middle West taken as free homesteads or bought for a mere pittance, have risen so in value that the original owners have in an increasing degree either sold them in order to reinvest in the newer cheap lands of the West, or have moved into the town and have left the tillage to tenant farmers. The growth of absentee ownership of the soil is producing a serious problem in the former centers of the Granger and the Populist. Along the old Northwest the Great Lakes are becoming a new Mediterranean Sea joining the realms of wheat and iron ore, at one end with the coal and furnaces of the forks of the Ohio, where the most intense and wide-reaching center of industrial energy exists. City life like that of the East, manufactures and accumulated capital, seem to be reproducing in the center of the Republic the tendencies already so plain on the Atlantic Coast.

Across the Great Plains where buffalo and Indian held sway successive industrial waves are passing. The old free range gave place to the ranch, the ranch to the homestead and now in places in the arid lands the homestead is replaced by the ten or twenty acre irrigated fruit farm. The age of cheap land, cheap corn and wheat, and cheap cattle has gone forever. The federal government has undertaken vast paternal enterprises of reclamation of the desert.

In the Rocky Mountains where at the time of Civil War, the first important rushes to gold and silver mines carried the frontier backward on a march toward the east, the most amazing transformations have occurred. Here, where prospectors made new trails, and lived the wild free life of mountain men, here where the human spirit seemed likely to attain the largest measure of individual freedom, and where fortune beckoned to the common man, have come revolutions wrought by the demand for organized industry and capital. In the regions where the popular tribunal and the free competitive life flourished, we have seen law and order break down in the unmitigated collision of great aggregations of capital, with each other and with organized socialistic labor. The Cripple Creek strikes, the contests at Butte, the Goldfield mobs, the recent Colorado fighting, all tell a similar story—the solid impact of contending forces in regions where civic power and loyalty to the State have never fully developed. Like the Grand Cañon, where in dazzling light the huge geologic history is written so large that none may fail to read it, so in the

Rocky Mountains the dangers of modern American industrial tendencies have been exposed.

As we crossed the Cascades on our way to Seattle, one of the passengers was moved to explain his feeling on the excellence of Puget Sound in contrast with the remaining visible Universe. He did it well in spite of irreverent interruptions from those fellow travelers who were unconverted children of the East, and at last he broke forth in passionate challenge, "Why should I not love Seattle! It took me from the slums of the Atlantic Coast, a poor Swedish boy with hardly fifteen dollars in my pocket. It gave me a home by the beautiful sea; it spread before my eyes a vision of snow-capped peaks and smiling fields; it brought abundance and a new life to me and my children and I love it, I love it! If I were a multi-millionaire I would charter freight cars and carry away from the crowded tenements and noisome alleys of the eastern cities and the Old World the toiling masses, and let them loose in our vast forests and ore-laden mountains to learn what life really is!" And my heart was stirred by his words and by the whirling spaces of woods and peaks through which we passed.

But as I looked and listened to this passionate outcry, I remembered the words of Talleyrand, the exiled Bishop of Autun, in Washington's administration. Looking down from an eminence not far from Philadelphia upon a wilderness which is now in the heart of that huge industrial society where population presses on the means of life, even the cold-blooded and cynical Talleyrand, gazing on those unpeopled hills and forests, kindled with the vision of coming clearings, the smiling farms and grazing herds that were to be, the populous towns that should be built, the newer and finer social organization that should there arise. And then I remembered the hall in Harvard's museum of social ethics through which I pass to my lecture room when I speak on the history of the Westward movement. That hall is covered with an exhibit of the work in Pittsburgh steel mills, and of the congested tenements. Its charts and diagrams tell of the long hours of work, the death rate, the relation of typhoid to the slums, the gathering of the poor of all Southeastern Europe to make a civilization at that center of American industrial energy and vast capital that is a social tragedy. As I enter my lecture room through that hall, I speak of the young Washington leading his Virginia frontiersmen to the magnificent forest at the forks of the Ohio. Where Braddock and his men, "carving a cross on the wilderness rim," were struck by the painted savages in the primeval woods, huge furnaces belch forth perpetual fires and Huns and Bulgars, Poles and Sicilians struggle for a chance to earn their daily bread, and live a brutal and degraded life. Irresistibly there rushed across my mind the memorable words of Huxley:

> Even the best of modern civilization appears to me to exhibit a condition of mankind which neither embodies any worthy ideal nor even possesses the merit of stability. I do not hesitate to express the opinion that, if there is no hope of a large improvement of the condition of the greater part of the human family; if it is true that the increase of knowledge, the winning of a greater dominion over Nature, which is its consequence, and the wealth which follows upon that dominion, are to make no difference in the extent and the intensity of Want, with its concomitant physical and moral degradation, among the masses of the people, I should hail the advent of some kindly comet, which would sweep the whole affair away, as a desirable consummation.

But if there is disillusion and shock and apprehension as we come to realize these changes, to strong men and women there is challenge and inspiration in them too. In place of old frontiers of wilderness, there are new frontiers of unwon fields of science, fruitful for the needs of the race; there are frontiers of better social domains yet unexplored. Let us hold to our attitude of faith and courage, and creative zeal. Let us dream as our fathers dreamt and let us make our dreams come true.

"Daughters of Time, the hypocritic days,
Muffled and dumb like barefoot dervishes,
And marching single in an endless file,
Bear diadems and fagots in their hands.
To each they offer gifts after his will
Bread, kingdoms, stars, and sky that hold them all.
I, in my pleached garden watched the pomp,
Forgot my morning wishes, hastily
Took a few herbs and apples and the day
Turned and departed silent. I, too late,
Under her solemn fillet, saw the scorn!"

What were America's "morning wishes"? From the beginning of that long westward march of the American people America has never been the home of mere contented materialism. It has continuously sought new ways and dreamed of a perfected social type.

In the fifteenth century when men dealt with the New World which Columbus found, the ideal of discovery was dominant. Here was placed within the reach of men whose ideas had been bounded by the Atlantic, new realms to be explored. America became the land of European dreams, its Fortunate Islands were made real, where, in the imagination of old Europe, peace and happiness, as well as riches and eternal youth, were to be found. To Sir Edwin Sandys and his friends of the London Company, Virginia offered an opportunity to erect the Republic for which they had longed in vain in England. To the Puritans, New England was the new land of freedom, wherein they might establish the institutions of God, according to their own faith. As the vision died away in Virginia toward the close of the seventeenth century, it was taken up anew by the fiery Bacon with his revolution to establish a real democracy in place of the rule of the planter aristocracy that formed along the coast. Hardly had he been overthrown when in the eighteenth century, the democratic ideal was rejuvenated by the strong frontiersmen, who pressed beyond the New England

Coast into the Berkshires and up the valleys of the Green Mountains of Vermont, and by the Scotch-Irish and German pioneers who followed the Great Valley from Pennsylvania into the Upland South. In both the Yankee frontiersmen and the Scotch-Irish Presbyterians of the South, the Calvinistic conception of the importance of the individual, bound by free covenant to his fellow men and to God, was a compelling influence, and all their wilderness experience combined to emphasize the ideals of opening new ways, of giving freer play to the individual, and of constructing democratic society.

When the backwoodsmen crossed the Alleghanies they put between themselves and the Atlantic Coast a barrier which seemed to separate them from a region already too much like the Europe they had left, and as they followed the courses of the rivers that flowed to the Mississippi, they called themselves "Men of the Western Waters," and their new home in the Mississippi Valley was the "Western World." Here, by the thirties, Jacksonian democracy flourished, strong in the faith of the intrinsic excellence of the common man, in his right to make his own place in the world, and in his capacity to share in government. But while Jacksonian democracy demanded these rights, it was also loyal to leadership as the very name implies. It was ready to follow to the uttermost the man in whom it placed its trust, whether the hero were frontier fighter or president, and it even rebuked and limited its own legislative representatives and recalled its senators when they ran counter to their chosen executive. Jacksonian democracy was essentially rural. It was based on the good fellowship and genuine social feeling of the frontier, in which classes and inequalities of fortune played little part. But it did not demand equality of condition, for there was abundance of natural resources and the belief that the self-made man had a right to his success in the free competition which western life afforded was as prominent in their thought as was the love of democracy. On the other hand, they viewed governmental restraints with suspicion as a limitation on their right to work out their own individuality.

For the banking institutions and capitalists of the East they had an instinctive antipathy. Already they feared that the "money power" as Jackson called it, was planning to make hewers of wood and drawers of water of the common people.

In this view they found allies among the labor leaders of the East, who in the same period began their fight for better conditions of the wage earner. These Locofocos were the first Americans to demand fundamental social changes for the benefit of the workers in the cities. Like the Western pioneers, they protested against monopolies and special privilege. But they also had a constructive policy, whereby society was to be kept democratic by free gifts of the public land, so that surplus labor might not bid against itself, but might find an outlet in the West. Thus to both the labor theorist and the practical pioneer, the existence of what seemed inexhaustible cheap land and un-possessed resources was the condition of democracy. In these years of the thirties and forties, Western democracy took on its distinctive form. Travelers like De Tocqueville and Harriet Martineau came to study and to report it enthusiastically to Europe.

Side by side with this westward marching army of individualistic liberty-loving democratic backwoodsmen, went a more northern stream of pioneers, who cherished similar ideas, but added to them the desire to create new industrial centers, to build up factories, to build railroads, and to develop the country by founding cities and extending prosperity. They were ready to call upon legislatures to aid in this, by subscriptions to stock, grants of franchises, promotion of banking and internal improvements. These were the Whig followers of that other Western leader, Henry Clay, and their early strength lay in the Ohio Valley, and particularly among the well-to-do. In the South their strength was found among the aristocracy of the Cotton Kingdom.

Both of these Western groups, Whigs and Democrats alike, had one common ideal: the desire to leave their children a better heritage than they themselves had received, and both were fired with devotion to the ideal of creating in this New World a home more worthy of mankind. Both were ready to break with the past, to boldly strike out new lines of social endeavor, and both believed in American expansion.

Before these tendencies had worked themselves out, three new forces entered. In the sudden extension of our boundaries to the Pacific Coast, which took place in the forties, the nation won so vast a domain that its resources seemed illimitable and its society seemed able to throw off all its maladies by the very presence of these vast new spaces. At the same period the great activity of railroad building to the Mississippi Valley occurred, making these lands available and diverting attention to the task of economic construction. The third influence was the slavery question which, becoming acute, shaped the American ideals and public discussion for nearly a generation. Viewed from one angle, this struggle involved the great question of national unity. From another it involved the question of the relations of labor and capital, democracy and aristocracy. It was not without significance that Abraham Lincoln became the very type of American pioneer democracy, the first adequate and elemental demonstration to the world that that democracy could produce a man who belonged to the ages.

After the war, new national energies were set loose, and new construction and development engaged the attention of the Westerners as they occupied prairies and Great Plains and mountains. Democracy and capitalistic development did not seem antagonistic.

With the passing of the frontier, Western social and political ideals took new form. Capital began to consolidate in even greater masses, and increasingly attempted to reduce to system and control the processes of industrial development. Labor with equal step organized its forces to destroy the old competitive system. It is not strange that the Western pioneers took alarm for their ideals of democracy as the outcome of the free struggle for the national resources became apparent. They espoused the cause of governmental activity.

It was a new gospel, for the Western radical became convinced that he must sacrifice his ideal of individualism and free competition in order to maintain his ideal of democracy. Under this conviction the Populist revised the pioneer conception of government. He saw in government no longer something outside of him, but the people themselves shaping their own affairs. He demanded therefore an extension of the powers of governments in the interest of his historic ideal of democratic society. He demanded not only free silver, but the ownership of the agencies of communication and transportation, the income tax, the postal savings bank, the provision of means of credit for agriculture, the construction of more effective devices to express the will of the people, primary nominations, direct elections, initiative, referendum and recall. In a word, capital, labor, and the Western pioneer, all deserted the ideal of competitive individualism in order to organize their interests in more effective combinations. The disappearance of the frontier, the closing of the era which was marked by the influence of the West as a form of society, brings with it new problems of social adjustment, new demands for considering our past ideals and our present needs.

Let us recall the conditions of the foreign relations along our borders, the dangers that wait us if we fail to unite in the solution of our domestic problems. Let us recall those internal evidences of the destruction of our old social order. If we take to heart this warning, we shall do well also to recount our historic ideals, to take stock of those purposes and fundamental assumptions that have gone to make the American spirit and the meaning of America in world history.

First of all, there was the ideal of discovery, the courageous determination to break new paths, indifference to the dogma that because an institution or a condition exists, it must remain. All American experience has gone to the making of the spirit of innovation; it is in the blood and will not be repressed.

Then, there was the ideal of democracy, the ideal of a free self-directing people, responsive to leadership in the forming of programs and their execution, but insistent that the procedure should be that of free choice, not of compulsion.

But there was also the ideal of individualism. This democratic society was not a disciplined army, where all must keep step and where the collective interests destroyed individual will and work. Rather it was a mobile mass of freely circulating atoms, each seeking its own place and finding play for its own powers and for its own original initiative. We cannot lay too much stress upon this point, for it was at the very heart of the whole American movement. The world was to be made a better world by the example of a democracy in which there was freedom of the individual, in which there was the vitality and mobility productive of originality and variety.

Bearing in mind the far-reaching influence of the disappearance of unlimited resources open to all men for the taking, and considering the recoil of the common man when he saw the outcome of the competitive struggle for these resources as the supply came to its end over most of the nation, we can understand the reaction against individualism and in favor of drastic assertion of the powers of government. Legislation is taking the place of the free lands as the means of preserving the ideal of democracy. But at the same time it is endangering the other pioneer ideal of creative and competitive individualism. Both were essential and constituted what was best in America's contribution to history and to progress. Both must be preserved if the nation would be true to its past, and would fulfil its highest destiny. It would be a grave misfortune if these people so rich in experience, in self-confidence and aspiration, in creative genius, should turn to some Old World discipline of socialism or plutocracy, or despotic rule, whether by class or by dictator. Nor shall we be driven to these alternatives. Our ancient hopes, our courageous faith, our underlying good humor and love of fair play will triumph in the end. There will be give and take in all directions. There will be disinterested leadership, under loyalty to the best American ideals. Nowhere is this leadership more likely to arise than among the men trained in the Universities, aware of the promise of the past and the possibilities of the future. The times call for new ambitions and new motives.

In a most suggestive essay on the Problems of Modern Democracy, Mr. Godkin has said:

M. de Tocqueville and all his followers take it for granted that the great incentive to excellence, in all countries in which excellence is found, is the patronage and encouragement of an aristocracy; that democracy is generally content with mediocrity. But where is the proof of this? The incentive to exertion which is widest, most constant, and most powerful in its operations in all civilized countries, is the desire of distinction; and this may be composed either of love of fame or love of wealth or of both. In literary and artistic and scientific pursuits, sometimes the strongest influence is exerted by a love of the subject. But it may safely be said that no man has ever labored in any of the higher colleges to whom the applause and appreciation of his fellows was not one of the sweetest rewards of his exertions.

What is there we would ask, in the nature of democratic institutions, that should render this great spring of action powerless, that should deprive glory of all radiance, and put ambition to sleep? Is it not notorious, on the contrary, that one of the most marked peculiarities of democratic society, or of a society drifting toward democracy, is the fire of competition which rages in it, the fevered anxiety which possesses all its members to rise above the dead level to which the law is ever seeking to confine them, and by some brilliant stroke become something higher and more remarkable than their fellows? The secret of that great restlessness which is one of the most disagreeable accompaniments of life in democratic countries, is in fact due to the eagerness of everybody to grasp the prizes of which in aristocratic countries, only the few have much chance. And in no other society is success more worshiped, is distinction of any kind more widely flattered and caressed.

In democratic societies, in fact, excellence is the first title to distinction; in aristocratic ones there are two or three others which are far stronger and which must be stronger or aristocracy could not exist. The moment you acknowledge that the highest social position ought to be the reward of the man who has the most talent, you make aristocratic institutions impossible.

All that was buoyant and creative in American life would be lost if we gave up the respect for distinct personality, and variety in genius, and came to the dead level of common standards. To be "socialized into an average" and placed "under the tutelage of the mass of us," as a recent writer has put it, would be an irreparable loss. Nor is it necessary in a democracy, as these words of Godkin well disclose. What is needed is the multiplication of motives for ambition and the opening of new lines of achievement for the strongest. As we turn from the task of the first rough conquest of the continent there lies before us a whole wealth of unexploited resources in the realm of the spirit. Arts and letters, science and better social creation, loyalty and political service to the commonweal— these and a thousand other directions of activity are open to the men, who formerly under the incentive of attaining distinction by amassing extraordinary wealth, saw success only in material display. Newer and finer careers will open to the ambitious when once public opinion shall award the laurels to those who rise above their fellows in these new fields of labor. It has not been the gold, but the getting of the gold, that has caught the imaginations of our captains of industry. Their real enjoyment lay not in the luxuries which wealth brought, but in the work of construction and in the place which society awarded them. A new era will come if schools and universities can only widen the intellectual horizon of the people, help to lay the foundations of a better industrial life, show them new goals for endeavor, inspire them with more varied and higher ideals.

The Western spirit must be invoked for new and nobler achievements. Of that matured Western spirit, Tennyson's Ulysses is a
symbol.

> "... *I am become a name*
> *For always roaming with an hungry heart,*
> *Much have I seen and known ...*
> *I am a part of all that I have met;*
> *Yet all experience is an arch, where thro'*
> *Gleams that untravelled world, whose margin fades*
> *Forever and forever when I move.*
> *How dull it is to pause, to make an end.*
> *To rust unburnished, not to shine in use!*
>
> .   .   .   .
>
> *And this gray spirit yearning in desire*
> *To follow knowledge like a shining star*
> *Beyond the utmost bound of human thought.*
> *... Come my friends,*
> *'Tis not too late to seek a newer world.*
> *Push off, and sitting well in order smite*
> *The sounding furrows; for my purpose holds*
> *To sail beyond the sunset, and the baths*
> *Of all the Western stars until I die*
>
> .   .   .   .
>
> *To strive, to seek, to find and not to yield."*

EIGHT

MIDDLE WESTERN
PIONEER DEMOCRACY

~

(1918)

In time of war, when all that this nation has stood for, all the things in which it passionately believes, are at stake, we have met to dedicate this beautiful home for history.

There is a fitness in the occasion. It is for historic ideals that we are fighting. If this nation is one for which we should pour out our savings, postpone our differences, go hungry, and even give up life itself, it is not because it is a rich, extensive, well-fed and populous nation; it is because from its early days America has pressed onward toward a goal of its own; that it has followed an ideal, the ideal of a democracy developing under conditions unlike those of any other age or country.

We are fighting not for an Old World ideal, not for an abstraction, not for a philosophical revolution. Broad and generous as are our sympathies, widely scattered in origin as are our people, keenly as we feel the call of kinship, the thrill of

An address delivered at the dedication of the building of the State Historical Society of Minnesota, May 11, 1918. Printed by permission of the Society.

sympathy with the stricken nations across the Atlantic, we are fighting for the historic ideals of the United States, for the continued existence of the type of society in which we believe, because we have proved it good, for the things which drew European exiles to our shores, and which inspired the hopes of the pioneers.

We are at war that the history of the United States, rich with the record of high human purposes, and of faith in the destiny of the common man under freedom, filled with the promises of a better world, may not become the lost and tragic story of a futile dream.

Yes, it is an American ideal and an American example for which we fight; but in that ideal and example lies medicine for the healing of the nations. It is the best we have to give to Europe, and it is a matter of vital import that we shall safeguard and preserve our power to serve the world, and not be overwhelmed in the flood of imperialistic force that wills the death of democracy and would send the freeman under the yoke. Essential as are our contributions of wealth, the work of our scientists, the toil of our farmers and our workmen in factory and shipyard, priceless as is the stream of young American manhood which we pour forth to stop the flood which flows like moulten lava across the green fields and peaceful hamlets of Europe toward the sea and turns to ashes and death all that it covers, these contributions have their deeper meaning in the American spirit. They are born of the love of Democracy.

Long ago in prophetic words Walt Whitman voiced the meaning of our present sacrifices:

"*Sail, sail thy best, ship of Democracy,*
Of value is thy freight, 'tis not the Present only,
The Past is also stored in thee,
Thou holdest not the venture of thyself alone, not of the Western
    Continent alone,
Earth's résumé entire floats on thy keel, O ship, is steadied by thy
    spars,
With thee Time voyages in trust, the antecedent nations sink or
    swim with thee,

With all their ancient struggles, martyrs, heroes, epics, wars, thou
    bear'st the other continents,
Theirs, theirs as much as thine, the destination-port triumphant."

Shortly before the Civil War, a great German, exiled from his
native land for his love of freedom, came from his new home among the
pioneers of the Middle West to set forth in Faneuil Hall, the "cradle of
liberty," in Boston, his vision of the young America that was forming in
the West, "the last depository of the hopes of all true friends of
humanity." Speaking of the contrast between the migrations to the
Mississippi Valley and those of the Old World in other centuries,
he said:

> It is now not a barbarous multitude pouncing upon old and
> decrepit empires, not a violent concussion of tribes accom-
> panied by all the horrors of general destruction, but we see the
> vigorous elements—peaceably congregating and mingling to-
> gether on virgin soil—; led together by the irresistible attrac-
> tion of free and broad principles; undertaking to commence a
> new era in the history of the world, without first destroying the
> results of the progress of past periods; undertaking to found a
> cosmopolitan nation without marching over the dead bodies of
> slain millions.

If Carl Schurz had lived to see the outcome of that Germany from
which he was sent as an exile, in the days when Prussian bayonets
dispersed the legislatures and stamped out the beginnings of democratic rule in his former country, could he have better pictured the
contrasts between the Prussian and the American spirit? He went on
to say:

> Thus was founded the *great colony of free humanity*, which
> has not old England alone, but the *world* for its mother country.
> And in the colony of free humanity, whose mother country is
> the world, they established the Republic of equal rights where

the title of manhood is the title to citizenship. My friends, if I had a thousand tongues, and a voice as strong as the thunder of heaven, they would not be sufficient to impress upon your minds forcibly enough the greatness of this idea, the over-shadowing glory of this result. This was the dream of the truest friends of man from the beginning; for this the noblest blood of martyrs has been shed; for this has mankind waded through seas of blood and tears. There it is now; there it stands, the noble fabric in all the splendor of reality.

It is in a solemn and inspiring time, therefore, that we meet to dedicate this building, and the occasion is fitting to the time. We may now see, as never before, the deeper significance, the larger meaning of these pioneers, whose plain lives and homely annals are glorified as a part of the story of the building of a better system of social justice under freedom, a broader, and as we fervently hope, a more enduring foundation for the welfare and progress under individual liberty of the common man, an example of federation, of peaceful adjustments by compromise and concession under a self-governing Republic, where sections replace nations over a Union as large as Europe, where party discussions take the place of warring countries, where the *Pax Americana* furnishes an example for a better world.

As our forefathers, the pioneers, gathered in their neighborhood to raise the log cabin, and sanctified it by the name of home, the dwelling place of pioneer ideals, so we meet to celebrate the raising of this home, this shrine of Minnesota's historic life. It symbolizes the conviction that the past and the future of this people are tied together; that this Historical Society is the keeper of the records of a noteworthy movement in the progress of mankind; that these records are not unmeaning and antiquarian, but even in their details are worthy of preservation for their revelation of the beginnings of society in the midst of a nation caught by the vision of a better future for the world.

Let me repeat the words of Harriet Martineau, who portrayed the American of the thirties:

I regard the American people as a great embryo poet, now moody, now wild, but bringing out results of absolute good sense; restless and wayward in action, but with deep peace at his heart; exulting that he has caught the true aspect of things past and the depth of futurity which lies before him, wherein to create something so magnificent as the world has scarcely begun to dream of. There is the strongest hope of a nation that is capable of being possessed with an idea.

And recall her appeal to the American people to "cherish their high democratic hope, their faith in man. The older they grow the more they must reverence the dreams of their youth."

The dreams of their youth! Here they shall be preserved, and the achievements as well as the aspirations of the men who made the State, the men who built on their foundations, the men with large vision and power of action, the lesser men in the mass, the leaders who served the State and nation with devotion to the cause. Here shall be preserved the record of the men who failed to see the larger vision and worked impatiently with narrow or selfish or class ends, as well as of those who labored with patience and sympathy and mutual concession, with readiness to make adjustments and to subordinate their immediate interests to the larger good and the immediate safety of the nation.

In the archives of such an old institution as that of the Historical Society of Massachusetts, whose treasures run to the beginnings of the Puritan colonization, the students cannot fail to find the evidence that a State Historical Society is a Book of Judgment wherein is made up the record of a people and its leaders. So, as time unfolds, shall be the collections of this Society, the depository of the material that shall preserve the memory of this people. Each section of this widely extended and varied nation has its own peculiar past, its special form of society, its traits and its leaders. It were a pity if any section left its annals solely to the collectors of a remote region, and it were a pity if its collections were not transformed into printed documents and monographic studies which can go to the libraries of all the parts of the

Union and thus enable the student to see the nation as a whole in its past as well as in its present.

This Society finds its special field of activity in a great State of the Middle West, so new, as history reckons time, that its annals are still predominantly those of the pioneers, but so rapidly growing that already the era of the pioneers is a part of the history of the past, capable of being handled objectively, seen in a perspective that is not possible to the observer of the present conditions.

Because of these facts I have taken as the special theme of this address the Middle Western Pioneer Democracy, which I would sketch in some of its outstanding aspects, and chiefly in the generation before the Civil War, for it was from those pioneers that the later colonization to the newer parts of the Mississippi Valley derived much of their traits, and from whom large numbers of them came.

The North Central States as a whole is a region comparable to all of Central Europe. Of these States, a large part of the old Northwest—Ohio, Indiana, Illinois, Michigan and Wisconsin; and their sisters beyond the Mississippi—Missouri, Iowa and Minnesota—were still, in the middle of the nineteenth century, the home of an essentially pioneer society. Within the lifetime of many living men, Wisconsin was called the "Far West," and Minnesota was a land of the Indian and the fur traders, a wilderness of forest and prairie beyond the "edge of cultivation." That portion of this great region which was still in the pioneering period of settlement by 1850 was alone about as extensive as the old thirteen States, or Germany and Austria-Hungary combined. The region was a huge geographic mold for a new society, modeled by nature on the scale of the Great Lakes, the Ohio Valley, the upper Mississippi and the Missouri. Simple and majestic in its vast outlines it was graven into a variety that in its detail also had a largeness of design. From the Great Lakes extended the massive glacial sheet which covered that mighty basin and laid down treasures of soil. Vast forests of pine shrouded its upper zone, breaking into hardwood and the oak openings as they neared the ocean-like expanses of the prairies. Forests again along the Ohio Valley, and be-

yond, to the west, lay the levels of the Great Plains. Within the earth
were unexploited treasures of coal and lead, copper and iron in such
form and quantity as were to revolutionize the industrial processes of
the world. But nature's revelations are progressive, and it was rather
the marvelous adaptation of the soil to the raising of corn and wheat
that drew the pioneers to this land of promise, and made a new era of
colonization. In the unity with variety of this pioneer empire and in its
broad levels we have a promise of its society.

First had come the children of the interior of the South, and with
ax and rifle in hand had cut their clearings in the forest, raised their log
cabins, fought the Indians and by 1830 had pushed their way to the
very edge of the prairies along the Ohio and Missouri Valleys, leaving
unoccupied most of the Basin of the Great Lakes.

These slashers of the forest, these self-sufficing pioneers, raising
the corn and live stock for their own need, living scattered and apart,
had at first small interest in town life or a share in markets. They
were passionately devoted to the ideal of equality, but it was an ideal
which assumed that under free conditions in the midst of unlimited
resources, the homogeneous society of the pioneers *must* result in
equality. What they objected to was arbitrary obstacles, artificial limitations upon the freedom of each member of this frontier folk to work
out his own career without fear or favor. What they instinctively
opposed was the crystallization of differences, the monopolization of
opportunity and the fixing of that monopoly by government or by
social customs. The road must be open. The game must be played
according to the rules. There must be no artificial stifling of equality of
opportunity, no closed doors to the able, no stopping the free game
before it was played to the end. More than that, there was an unformu-
lated, perhaps, but very real feeling, that mere success in the game, by
which the abler men were able to achieve preëminence, gave to the
successful ones no right to look down upon their neighbors, no vested
title to assert superiority as a matter of pride and to the diminution of
the equal right and dignity of the less successful.

If this democracy of Southern pioneers, this Jacksonian democracy, was, as its socialist critics have called it, in reality a democracy of "expectant capitalists," it was not one which expected or acknowledged on the part of the successful ones the right to harden their triumphs into the rule of a privileged class. In short, if it is indeed true that the backwoods democracy was based upon equality of opportunity, it is also true that it resented the conception that opportunity under competition should result in the hopeless inequality, or rule of class. Ever a new clearing must be possible. And because the wilderness seemed so unending, the menace to the enjoyment of this ideal seemed rather to be feared from government, within or without, than from the operations of internal evolution.

From the first, it became evident that these men had means of supplementing their individual activity by informal combinations. One of the things that impressed all early travelers in the United States was the capacity for extra-legal, voluntary association.[1] This was natural enough; in all America we can study the process by which in a new land social customs form and crystallize into law. We can even see how the personal leader becomes the governmental official. This power of the newly arrived pioneers to join together for a common end without the intervention of governmental institutions was one of their marked characteristics. The log rolling, the house-raising, the husking bee, the apple paring, and the squatters' associations whereby they protected themselves against the speculators in securing title to their clearings on the public domain, the camp meeting, the mining camp, the vigilantes, the cattle-raisers' associations, the "gentlemen's agreements," are a few of the indications of this attitude. It is well to emphasize this American trait, because in a modified way it has come to be one of the most characteristic and important features of the United States of today. America does through informal association and understandings on the part of the people many of the things which in the Old World are and can be done only by governmental intervention and compulsion. These associations were in America not due to immemorial custom of tribe or village community. They were extemporized by voluntary action.

The actions of these associations had an authority akin to that of law. They were usually not so much evidences of a disrespect for law and order as the only means by which real law and order were possible in a region where settlement and society had gone in advance of the institutions and instrumentalities of organized society.

Because of these elements of individualistic competition and the power of spontaneous association, pioneers were responsive to leadership. The backwoodsmen knew that under the free opportunities of his life the abler man would reveal himself, and show them the way. By free choice and not by compulsion, by spontaneous impulse, and not by the domination of a caste, they rallied around a cause, they supported an issue. They yielded to the principle of government by agreement, and they hated the doctrine of autocracy even before it gained a name.

They looked forward to the extension of their American principles to the Old World and their keenest apprehensions came from the possibility of the extension of the Old World's system of arbitrary rule, its class wars and rivalries and interventions to the destruction of the free States and democratic institutions which they were building in the forests of America.

If we add to these aspects of early backwoods democracy its spiritual qualities, we shall more easily understand them. These men were emotional. As they wrested their clearing from the woods and from the savages who surrounded them, as they expanded that clearing and saw the beginnings of commonwealths, where only little communities had been, and as they saw these commonwealths touch hands with each other along the great course of the Mississippi River, they became enthusiastically optimistic and confident of the continued expansion of this democracy. They had faith in themselves and their destiny. And that optimistic faith was responsible both for their confidence in their own ability to rule and for the passion for expansion. They looked to the future. "Others appeal to history: an American appeals to prophecy; and with Malthus in one hand and a map of the back country in the other, he boldly defies us to a comparison with

America as she is to be," said a London periodical in 1821. Just because, perhaps, of the usual isolation of their lives, when they came together in associations whether of the camp meeting or of the political gathering, they felt the influence of a common emotion and enthusiasm. Whether Scotch-Irish Presbyterian, Baptist, or Methodist, these people saturated their religion and their politics with feeling. Both the stump and the pulpit were centers of energy, electric cells capable of starting widespreading fires. They *felt* both their religion and their democracy, and were ready to fight for it.

This democracy was one that involved a real feeling of social comradeship among its widespread members. Justice Catron, who came from Arkansas to the Supreme Court in the presidency of Jackson, said: "The people of New Orleans and St. Louis are next neighbors—if we desire to know a man in any quarter of the union we inquire of our next neighbor, who but the other day lived by him." Exaggerated as this is, it nevertheless had a surprising measure of truth for the Middle West as well. For the Mississippi River was the great highway down which groups of pioneers like Abraham Lincoln, on their rafts and flat boats, brought the little neighborhood surplus. After the steamboat came to the western waters the voyages up and down by merchants and by farmers shifting their homes, brought people into contact with each other over wide areas.

This enlarged neighborhood democracy was determined not by a reluctant admission that under the law one man is as good as another; it was based upon "good fellowship," sympathy and understanding. They were of a stock, moreover, which sought new trails and were ready to follow where the trail led, innovators in society as well as finders of new lands.

By 1830 the Southern inundation ebbed and a different tide flowed in from the northeast by way of the Erie Canal and steam navigation on the Great Lakes to occupy the zone unreached by Southern settlement. This new tide spread along the margins of the Great Lakes, found the oak openings and small prairie islands of Southern Michigan and Wisconsin; followed the fertile forested ribbons along the river courses far into the prairie lands; and by the end of the forties began to venture into the margin of the open prairie.

In 1830 the Middle West contained a little over a million and a half people; in 1840, over three and a third millions; in 1850, nearly five and a half millions. Although in 1830 the North Atlantic States numbered between three and four times as many people as the Middle West, yet in those two decades the Middle West made an actual gain of several hundred thousand more than did the old section. Counties in the newer states rose from a few hundred to ten or fifteen thousand people in the space of less than five years. Suddenly, with astonishing rapidity and volume, a new people was forming with varied elements, ideals and institutions drawn from all over this nation and from Europe. They were confronted with the problem of adjusting different stocks, varied customs and habits, to their new home.

In comparison with the Ohio Valley, the peculiarity of the occupation of the northern zone of the Middle West, lay in the fact that the native element was predominantly from the older settlements of the Middle West itself and from New York and New England. But it was from the central and western counties of New York and from the western and northern parts of New England, the rural regions of declining agricultural prosperity, that the bulk of this element came.

Thus the influence of the Middle West stretched into the Northeast, and attracted a farming population already suffering from western competition. The advantage of abundant, fertile, and cheap land, the richer agricultural returns, and especially the opportunities for youth to rise in all the trades and professions, gave strength to this competition. By it New England was profoundly and permanently modified.

This Yankee stock carried with it a habit of community life, in contrast with the individualistic democracy of the Southern element. The colonizing land companies, the town, the school, the church, the feeling of local unity, furnished the evidences of this instinct for communities. This instinct was accompanied by the creation of cities, the production of a surplus for market, the reaching out to connections with the trading centers of the East, the evolution of a more complex and at the same time a more integrated industrial society than that of the Southern pioneer.

But they did not carry with them the unmodified New England institutions and traits. They came at a time and from a people less satisfied with the old order than were their neighbors in the East. They were the young men with initiative, with discontent; the New York element especially was affected by the radicalism of Locofoco democracy which was in itself a protest against the established order.

The winds of the prairies swept away almost at once a mass of old habits and prepossessions. Said one of these pioneers in a letter to friends in the East:

> If you value ease more than money or prosperity, don't come. . . . Hands are too few for the work, houses for the inhabitants, and days for the day's work to be done. . . . Next if you can't stand seeing your old New England ideas, ways of doing, and living and in fact, all of the good old Yankee fashions knocked out of shape and altered, or thrown by as unsuited to the climate, don't be caught out here. But if you can bear grief with a smile, can put up with a scale of accommodations ranging from the soft side of a plank before the fire (and perhaps three in a bed at that) down through the middling and inferior grades; if you are never at a loss for ways to do the most unpracticable things without tools; if you can do all this and some more come on. . . . It is a universal rule here to help one another, each one keeping an eye single to his own business.

They knew that they were leaving many dear associations of the old home, giving up many of the comforts of life, sacrificing things which those who remained thought too vital to civilization to be left.

But they were not mere materialists ready to surrender all that life is worth for immediate gain. They were idealists themselves, sacrificing the ease of the immediate future for the welfare of their children, and convinced of the possibility of helping to bring about a better social order and a freer life. They were social idealists. But they based their ideals on trust in the common man and the readiness to make adjustments, not on the rule of a benevolent despot or a controlling class.

The attraction of this new home reached also into the Old World and gave a new hope and new impulses to the people of Germany, of England, of Ireland, and of Scandinavia. Both economic influences and revolutionary discontent promoted German migration at this time; economic causes brought the larger volume, but the quest for liberty brought the leaders, many of whom were German political exiles. While the latter urged, with varying degrees of emphasis, that their own contribution should be preserved in their new surroundings, and a few visionaries even talked of a German State in the federal system, what was noteworthy was the adjustment of the emigrants of the thirties and forties to Middle Western conditions; the response to the opportunity to create a new type of society in which all gave and all received and no element remained isolated. Society was plastic. In the midst of more or less antagonism between "bowie knife Southerners," "cow-milking Yankee Puritans," "beer-drinking Germans," "wild Irishmen," a process of mutual education, a giving and taking, was at work. In the outcome, in spite of slowness of assimilation where different groups were compact and isolated from the others, and a certain persistence of inherited *morale*, there was the creation of a new type, which was neither the sum of all its elements, nor a complete fusion in a melting pot. They were American pioneers, not outlying fragments of New England, of Germany, or of Norway.

The Germans were most strongly represented in the Missouri Valley, in St. Louis, in Illinois opposite that city, and in the Lake Shore counties of eastern Wisconsin north from Milwaukee. In Cincinnati and Cleveland there were many Germans, while in nearly half the counties of Ohio, the German immigrants and the Pennsylvania Germans held nearly or quite the balance of political power. The Irish came primarily as workers on turnpikes, canals and railroads, and tended to remain along such lines, or to gather in the growing cities. The Scandinavians, of whom the largest proportion were Norwegians, founded their colonies in Northern Illinois, and in Southern Wisconsin about the Fox and the head waters of Rock River, whence in later years they spread into Iowa, Minnesota and North Dakota.

By 1850 about one-sixth of the people of the Middle West were of North Atlantic birth, about one-eighth of Southern birth, and a like fraction of foreign birth, of whom the Germans were twice as numerous as the Irish, and the Scandinavians only slightly more numerous than the Welsh, and fewer than the Scotch. There were only a dozen Scandinavians in Minnesota. The natives of the British Islands, together with the natives of British North America in the Middle West, numbered nearly as many as the natives of German lands. But in 1850 almost three-fifths of the population were natives of the Middle West itself, and over a third of the population lived in Ohio. The cities were especially a mixture of peoples. In the five larger cities of the section natives and foreigners were nearly balanced. In Chicago the Irish, Germans and natives of the North Atlantic States about equaled each other. But in all the other cities, the Germans exceeded the Irish in varying proportions. There were nearly three to one in Milwaukee.

It is not merely that the section was growing rapidly and was made up of various stocks with many different cultures, sectional and European; what is more significant is that these elements did not remain as separate strata underneath an established ruling order, as was the case particularly in New England. All were accepted and intermingling components of a forming society, plastic and absorptive. This characteristic of the section as "a good mixer" became fixed before the large immigrations of the eighties. The foundations of the section were laid firmly in a period when the foreign elements were particularly free and eager to contribute to a new society and to receive an impress from the country which offered them a liberty denied abroad. Significant as is this fact, and influential in the solution of America's present problems, it is no more important than the fact that in the decade before the Civil War, the Southern element in the Middle West had also had nearly two generations of direct association with the Northern, and had finally been engulfed in a tide of Northeastern and Old World settlers.

In this society of pioneers men learned to drop their old national animosities. One of the Immigrant Guides of the fifties urged the newcomers to abandon their racial animosities. "The American laughs at these steerage quarrels," said the author.

Thus the Middle West was teaching the lesson of national cross-fertilization instead of national enmities, the possibility of a newer and richer civilization, not by preserving unmodified or isolated the old component elements, but by breaking down the line-fences, by merging the individual life in the common product—a new product, which held the promise of world brotherhood. If the pioneers divided their allegiance between various parties, Whig, Democrat, Free Soil or Republican, it does not follow that the western Whig was like the eastern Whig. There was an infiltration of a western quality into all of these. The western Whig supported Harrison more because he was a pioneer than because he was a Whig. It saw in him a legitimate successor of Andrew Jackson. The campaign of 1840 was a Middle Western camp meeting on a huge scale. The log cabins, the cider and the coonskins were the symbols of the triumph of Middle Western ideas, and were carried with misgivings by the merchants, the bankers and the manufacturers of the East. In like fashion, the Middle Western wing of the Democratic party was as different from the Southern wing wherein lay its strength, as Douglas was from Calhoun. It had little in common with the slaveholding classes of the South, even while it felt the kinship of the pioneer with the people of the Southern upland stock from which so many Westerners were descended.

In the later forties and early fifties most of the Middle Western States made constitutions. The debates in their conventions and the results embodied in the constitutions themselves tell the story of their political ideals. Of course, they based the franchise on the principle of manhood suffrage. But they also provided for an elective judiciary, for restrictions on the borrowing power of the State, lest it fall under the control of what they feared as the money power, and several of them either provided for the extinguishment of banks of issue, or rigidly restrained them. Some of them exempted the homestead from forced sale for debt; married women's legal rights were prominent topics in the debates of the conventions, and Wisconsin led off by permitting the alien to vote after a year's residence. It welcomed the newcomer to the freedom and to the obligations of American citizenship.

Although this pioneer society was preponderantly an agricultural society it was rapidly learning that agriculture alone was not sufficient for its life. It was developing manufactures, trade, mining, the professions, and becoming conscious that in a progressive modern state it was possible to pass from one industry to another and that all were bound by common ties. But it is significant that in the census of 1850, Ohio, out of a population of two millions, reported only a thousand servants, Iowa only ten in two hundred thousand and Minnesota fifteen in its six thousand.

In the intellectual life of this new democracy there was already the promise of original contributions even in the midst of the engrossing toil and hard life of the pioneer.

The country editor was a leader of his people, not a patent-insides recorder of social functions, but a vigorous and independent thinker and writer. The subscribers to the newspaper published in the section were higher in proportion to population than in the State of New York and not greatly inferior to those of New England, although such eastern papers as the *New York Tribune* had an extensive circulation throughout the Middle West. The agricultural press presupposed in its articles and contributions a level of general intelligence and interest above that of the later farmers of the section, at least before the present day.

Farmer boys walked behind the plow with their book in hand and sometimes forgot to turn at the end of the furrow; even rare boys, who, like the young Howells, "limped barefoot by his father's side with his eyes on the cow and his mind on Cervantes and Shakespeare."

Periodicals flourished and faded like the prairie flowers. Some of Emerson's best poems first appeared in one of these Ohio Valley magazines. But for the most part the literature of the region and the period was imitative or reflective of the common things in a not uncommon way. It is to its children that the Middle West had to look for the expression of its life and its ideals rather than to the busy pioneer who was breaking a prairie farm or building up a new community. Illiteracy was least among the Yankee pioneers and highest among the Southern element. When illiteracy is mapped for 1850 by percentages there appears two distinct zones, the one extending from New England, the other from the South.

The influence of New England men was strong in the Yankee regions of the Middle West. Home missionaries, and representatives of societies for the promotion of education in the West, both in the common school and denominational colleges, scattered themselves throughout the region and left a deep impress in all these States. The conception was firmly fixed in the thirties and forties that the West was the coming power in the Union, that the fate of civilization was in its hands, and therefore rival sects and rival sections strove to influence it to their own types. But the Middle West shaped all these educational contributions according to her own needs and ideals.

The State Universities were for the most part the result of agitation and proposals of men of New England origin; but they became characteristic products of Middle Western society, where the community as a whole, rather than wealthy benefactors, supported these institutions. In the end the community determined their directions in accord with popular ideals. They reached down more deeply into the ranks of the common people than did the New England or Middle State Colleges; they laid more emphasis upon the obviously useful, and became coëducational at an early date. This dominance of the community ideals had dangers for the Universities, which were called to raise ideals and to point new ways, rather than to conform.

Challenging the spaces of the West, struck by the rapidity with which a new society was unfolding under their gaze, it is not strange that the pioneers dealt in the superlative and saw their destiny with optimistic eyes. The meadow lot of the small intervale had become the prairie, stretching farther than their gaze could reach.

All was motion and change. A restlessness was universal. Men moved, in their single life, from Vermont to New York, from New York to Ohio, from Ohio to Wisconsin, from Wisconsin to California, and longed for the Hawaiian Islands. When the bark started from their fence rails, they felt the call to change. They were conscious of the mobility of their society and gloried in it. They broke with the Past and thought to create something finer, more fitting for humanity, more beneficial for the average man than the world had ever seen.

"With the Past we have literally nothing to do," said B. Gratz Brown in a Missouri Fourth of July oration in 1850, "save to dream of it. Its lessons are lost and its tongue is silent. We are ourselves at the head and front of all political experience. Precedents have lost their virtue and all their authority is gone. . . . Experience can profit us only to guard from antequated delusions."

"The yoke of opinion," wrote Channing to a Western friend, speaking of New England, "is a heavy one, often crushing individuality of judgment and action," and he added that the habits, rules, and criticisms under which he had grown up had not left him the freedom and courage which are needed in the style of address best suited to the Western people. Channing no doubt unduly stressed the freedom of the West in this respect. The frontier had its own conventions and prejudices, and New England was breaking its own cake of custom and proclaiming a new liberty at the very time he wrote. But there was truth in the Eastern thought of the West, as a land of intellectual toleration, one which questioned the old order of things and made innovation its very creed.

The West laid emphasis upon the practical and demanded that ideals should be put to work for useful ends; ideals were tested by their direct contributions to the betterment of the average man, rather than by the production of the man of exceptional genius and distinction.

For, in fine this was the goal of the Middle West, the welfare of the average man; not only the man of the South, or of the East, the Yankee, or the Irishman, or the German, but all men in one common fellowship. This was the hope of their youth, of that youth when Abraham Lincoln rose from rail-splitter to country lawyer, from Illinois legislator to congressman and from congressman to President.

It is not strange that in all this flux and freedom and novelty and vast spaces, the pioneer did not sufficiently consider the need of disciplined devotion to the government which he himself created and operated. But the name of Lincoln and the response of the pioneer to the duties of the Civil War—to the sacrifices and the restraints on freedom which it entailed under his presidency, reminds us that they knew how to take part in a common cause, even while they knew that war's conditions were destructive of many of the things for which they worked.

There are two kinds of governmental discipline: that which proceeds from free choice, in the conviction that restraint of individual or class interests is necessary for the common good; and that which is imposed by a dominant class, upon a subjected and helpless people.

The latter is Prussian discipline, the discipline of a harsh machine-like, logical organization, based on the rule of a military autocracy. It assumes that if you do not crush your opponent first, he will crush you. It is the discipline of a nation ruled by its General Staff, assuming war as the normal condition of peoples, and attempting with remorseless logic to extend its operations to the destruction of freedom everywhere. It can only be met by the discipline of a people who use their own government for worthy ends, who preserve individuality and mobility in society and respect the rights of others, who follow the dictates of humanity and fair play, the principles of give and take. The Prussian discipline is the discipline of Thor, the War God, against the discipline of the White Christ.

Pioneer democracy has had to learn lessons by experience: the lesson that government on principles of free democracy can accomplish many things which the men of the middle of the nineteenth century did not realize were even possible. They have had to sacrifice something of their passion for individual unrestraint; they have had to learn that the specially trained man, the man fitted for his calling by education and experience, whether in the field of science or of industry, has a place in government; that the rule of the people is effective and enduring only as it incorporates the trained specialist into the organization of that government, whether as umpire between contending interests or as the efficient instrument in the hands of democracy.

Organized democracy after the era of free land has learned that popular government to be successful must not only be legitimately the choice of the whole people; that the offices of that government must not only be open to all, but that in the fierce struggle of nations in the field of economic competition and in the field of war, the salvation and perpetuity of the republic depend upon recognition of the fact that specialization of the organs of the government, the choice of the fit and the capable for office, is quite as important as the extension of popular control. When we lost our free lands and our isolation from the Old

World, we lost our immunity from the results of mistakes, of waste, of inefficiency, and of inexperience in our government.

But in the present day we are also learning another lesson which was better known to the pioneers than to their immediate successors. We are learning that the distinction arising from devotion to the interests of the commonwealth is a higher distinction than mere success in economic competition. America is now awarding laurels to the men who sacrifice their triumphs in the rivalry of business in order to give their service to the cause of a liberty-loving nation, their wealth and their genius to the success of her ideals. That craving for distinction which once drew men to pile up wealth and exhibit power over the industrial processes of the nation, is now finding a new outlet in the craving for distinction that comes from service to the Union, in satisfaction in the use of great talent for the good of the republic.

And all over the nation, in voluntary organizations for aid to the government, is being shown the pioneer principle of association that was expressed in the "house raising." It is shown in the Red Cross, the Y. M. C. A., the Knights of Columbus, the councils and boards of science, commerce, labor, agriculture; and in all the countless other types, from the association of women in their kitchen who carry out the recommendations of the Food Director and revive the plain living of the pioneer, to the Boy Scouts who are laying the foundations for a self-disciplined and virile generation worthy to follow the trail of the backwoodsmen. It is an inspiring prophecy of the revival of the old pioneer conception of the obligations and opportunities of neighborliness, broadening to a national and even to an international scope. The promise of what that wise and lamented philosopher Josiah Royce called, "the beloved community." In the spirit of the pioneer's "house raising" lies the salvation of the Republic.

This then is the heritage of pioneer experience—a passionate belief that a democracy was possible which should leave the individual a part to play in free society and not make him a cog in a machine operated from above; which trusted in the common man, in his tolerance, his ability to adjust differences with good humor, and to work out an American type from the contributions of all nations—a type for which he would fight against those who challenged it in arms, and for which in time of war he would make sacrifices, even the temporary sacrifice of individual freedom and his life, lest that freedom be lost forever.

NINE

SECTIONS AND NATION

(1922)

W e are apt to think of the United States as we might think of
some one of the nations of the Old World, but the area of
the Union is almost that of all Europe, and this vast country is
gradually becoming aware that its problems and its difficulties
are not altogether unlike those of Europe as a whole.

It may readily be admitted that bigness is not greatness.
But room for population and ample resources for development
are important in the life of all nations. England, France, and
Italy could be placed within the boundaries of the old thirteen
states along the Atlantic Coast, with which this nation began.
The Middle West (the North Central States) could find room
for all the European powers which joined Germany in the
World War in her efforts to conquer Europe.

So considered, the American section takes on a new importance and a new dignity. The various sections of which this
country is composed, are thus seen as potential nations. We

Reprinted by permission from *The Yale Review* 12 (October 1922), copyright
Yale University Press.

are led to wonder why the United States did not in fact become another Europe, by what processes we retain our national unity. The imagination stirs at the possibilities of the future, when these sections shall be fully matured and populated to the extent of the nations of the Old World.

We must also remember that each of the sections of this continental nation—New England, the Middle States, the Southeast, the Southwest, the Middle West, the Great Plains, the Mountain States, the Pacific Coast—has its own special geographical qualities, its own resources and economic capacities, and its own rival interests, partly determined in the days when the geological foundations were laid down.

In some ways, in respect to problems of common action, we are like what a United States of Europe would be. It is true that the differences are not by any manner of means so marked here as in Europe. There are not in the United States the historic memories of so many national wrongs and wars, nor what Gilbert Murray calls the "Satanic spirit" of reliance upon force. There is not here the variety of language and race nor the sharp contrast in cultural types; there has not been the same bitterness of class conflicts; nor the same pressure of economic need, inducing the various regions to seek by arms to acquire the means of subsistence, the control of natural resources. The burden of history does not so weigh upon America. The section does not embody the racial and national feeling of the European state, its impulse to preserve its identity by aggression conceived of as self-defense. But there is, nevertheless, a faint resemblance.

The American section may be likened to the shadowy image of the European nation, to the European state denatured of its toxic qualities. In the relations of European nations with each other, making due allowance for the deep differences, we may find means of understanding some of our own problems. Perhaps even, we may find, in our handling of such problems, suggestions of a better way for Europe.

The geographer Ratzel once remarked, with a characteristic German accent, that "Europe and Australia really have room enough for but one great power." He did not sufficiently consider that the one great power might be like the United States of America—a federative power. Nor is it certain that the leagues of Europe may not grow into a United States of Europe—certainly a more hopeful outlook for liberty and civilization than the triumph of a state like Imperial Germany or Russia.

In a recent book on the *Geography of History*, Brunhes and Vallaux, arguing against the League of Nations, reached the conclusion that Europe must organize in groups of leagues. "In order to form an organism as strong and rich as possible," say these French geographers, "the countries must coöperate in groups to the end that they may include within their federated territories the whole range of natural resources and manufactured products demanded by the growing complexity of social life."

The United States of America has reached a similar result, for its continental spaces, by the peaceful process of settlement of new geographic provinces in the West—a process which in Europe would be called "colonization." We have organized these new lands as territories and then admitted them as equal states in a common Union. We have no regional customs-boundaries to check interstate commerce. We have a system of free trade over an area as large as all Europe. We regulate interstate commerce from a single center, while we recognize separate sectional interests and needs. We legislate instead of going to war.

A leading French statesman, M. Tardieu, said not long ago in the French Chamber of Deputies that "it was immensely difficult for America to understand the psychological state of Europe, its national passions and the moral force of the memories which centuries of bloody struggle had left behind." "But France," he added, "knew these things." Over a century ago a French Minister to the United States said to his government, "An American is the born enemy of all European peoples."

Of course, this is not true. But it is true that an American is the born enemy of the European system of international relationships, and that he does sometimes find it hard to understand the European psychology. No small portion of the American people fled to the New World to escape the European system, and the explanation of our lack of sympathy with the methods and the fundamental assumptions of continental Europe, lies in large measure in the different course which the sections of the Union ran as compared with the nations of Europe. We substituted the system of a sectional union and legislative adjustment, for the settlement by the sword. We learned how to discuss, how to concede, and how to adjust differences, how to combine a loyalty to parties which ran across sectional lines, with loyalty to local interests. Like an elastic band, the common national feeling and party ties draw sections together, but at the same time yield in some measure to sectional interests when these are gravely threatened.

The one tragic exception in America to the unifying influence of parties and a common legislative body lies in the Civil War, when parties did become sectional. But perhaps no more difficult test of peaceful methods of adjustment could arise than that between a slave society and a free society. After that war, peaceful sectional relationships returned, even though an almost solid, but patriotic, South has persisted for over half a century. Nor is it certain that the Civil War was inevitable. Probably the majority of Americans, North as well as South, preferred a different solution and were astonished when secession was followed by war instead of by a reconciliation of differences.

By comparing the relations of the different nations of Europe with each other, we have the means of examining both the European and the American situation and of better understanding the real meaning of what has been in progress and what appears to be likely to influence the development of the United States.

If, for example, we describe the way in which the sections of the Atlantic seaboard have dealt with those of the interior of the United States, in such terms as "colonization," "spheres of influence," "hinterlands," American history takes on a new meaning. The formation of our great zones of population by interstate migration to the West, such as the New York-New England zone, and the Southern zone, extending from the Atlantic across the Mississippi, stands out in a clearer light. When we think of the Missouri Compromise, the Compromise of 1850, the Kansas-Nebraska Act, as steps in the marking off of spheres of influence and the assignment of mandates, we find a new meaning in the rivalry between the slaveholding and nonslaveholding sections of the United States. We see a resemblance to what has gone on in the Old World. If we express sectional contests, in national party conventions and in the federal House and Senate, in such European phrases as "diplomatic congresses," "ententes," "alliances," and attempts at "balance of power," we shall not go altogether wrong in the description of what actually occurs, and we shall find that the rival sections of the United States have played parts not entirely different from those played by European states. But there was a common legislative body, as well as national parties, which brought sections together.

Is it not clear that if Europe could have followed a similar course, substituting for wars and sinister combinations between nations the American device of continental parties and legislation, "woeful Europe," as William Penn called it, would have run a course better suited to the preservation of civilization and the peace of the world? If it be said that such a solution is inconceivable in Europe, we must recall that, in spite of the sharp contrast between the American section and the European nation, there have been diplomatic congresses which attempted to deal with Europe as a whole, there have been great gatherings at The Hague to impose a system of international law, there are European international labor congresses. There is actually the League of Nations which, however imperfect, has in it the possibilities of development.

The results of the Great War have burned deeply into European consciousness the need of some better way of conducting the common enterprise of Europe than by the appeal to the sword. In spite of all the fundamental difficulties which the conferences at Genoa and The

Hague have revealed, we can see in these gatherings the hopeful beginnings of a new age as well as the discouraging persistence of an old order of things. Europe might at least form an assembly, representing the people rather than the diplomats, and empowered to pass resolutions expressive of public opinion. Such recommendations and resolutions might ultimately take the form of law. However this may be, the difficulties which exhibit themselves in Europe, only emphasize the good fortune of the United States in dealing with its similar area. They help us to understand ourselves and our problems.

Bertrand Russell, in a contemporaneous article, insists that the small states of Europe will have to be forced, if necessary, to concede free trade and freedom of intercourse between one another and between neighboring great powers. "Gradually, if Europe is to survive," he says, "it will have to develop a central government controlling its international relations. If it cannot do this, it will become, and will deserve to become, the slave of the United States. . . . The time when the history of the world was made in Europe is past. America and Russia are the great independent powers of the present day." These words are, of course, the utterance of a socialist and internationalist and of a writer who, with a strange European blindness, is alarmed at the prospect of America's becoming the next great imperialistic power and mistress of the world. But they show the contrast between European and American experience.

We in America are in reality a federation of sections rather than of states. State sovereignty was never influential except as a constitutional shield for the section. In political matters the states act in groups rather than as individual members of the Union. They act in sections and are responsive to the respective interests and ideals of these sections. They have their sectional leaders, who, in Congress and in party conventions, voice the attitude of the section and confer and compromise their differences, or form sectional combinations to achieve a national policy and position. Party policy and congressional legislation emerge from a process of sectional contests and sectional bargainings. Legislation is almost never the result of purely national or purely sectional considerations. It is the result of sectional adjustments to meet national needs. For the most part, such adjustments take place in the formative stages of bills, in the committee rooms, and in the process of framing the measures by amendments. It is in these stages that the bill is most easily affected by sectional interests. The vote on the third reading of the bill affords opportunity for dissent; but after the completion of the measure, party discipline and party loyalty assert themselves and, in spite of discontent, usually furnish the necessary votes to pass the measure.

But even final votes in the Congress of the United States, both in the Senate and the House, upon important matters are, as President Lowell has demonstrated, far less frequently by parties than is ordinarily supposed. If we proceed a step further and, instead of taking account of congressional majorities by totals and reckoning the votes by party affiliation, we arrange those votes by sections and place the result on a map of the United States, we shall be astonished at how much is concealed by the mere alphabetical or party record. Under the drawing pen, as vote after vote by congressional districts is recorded on the map, they gradually arrange themselves to show the outlines of contending sections. The areas of great geographic provinces are revealed by the map of votes.

Of course, in the maps it will often be shown that some single party dominates a whole section, as so often occurs in the case of New England or the South. But again and again, in the construction of bills and in elections, party ties are broken, and the Republicans, for example, divide into sectional wings, composed of a conservative New England and Middle State area, a divided and mediating Old Northwest (lying between the Great Lakes and the Ohio River), and a radical trans-Mississippi Middle West, voting in exact opposition to the Northeast and sometimes in alliance with the Democratic South.

From colonial days to the Civil War, the conscious and avowed policies of the leading statesmen rested on the necessity of considering the conflicting interests of the various sections and sectional wings and adjusting them by bargains, compromises, and arrangements for balance of power in congressional legislation. It is, however, impossible here even to sketch the evidences of the persistent sectionalism in party contests and congressional legislation in American history. The more the reader will probe into the distribution of votes and the utterances of statesmen and editors, the more he will see that sectionalism was the dominant influence in shaping our political history upon all important measures—not the sectionalism of North and South alone, but a much more complex thing, a sectionalism also of East and West, and of East North Central and West North Central states, shifting as economic and social conditions changed, but persistently different from the East.

Since the Civil War, although by the march of settlement to the West new sections have been added, all the important political contests have revealed the same interplay of section with section. The sectional wings of the Republican party in the seventies exhibited a New England ultraconservative; a Middle Atlantic transitional and divided; a North Central for free silver. In the later eighties the East North Central division divided and finally joined the North Atlantic States against free silver, but swung to the side of the West North Central group on the question of terminating the Silver Purchase Act. It was a mediating section with a balance of power, but responsive to party discipline.

Problems of trust regulation, free silver, banking, tariff, and devices to secure popular government have led to sectional contests. Roosevelt's "square deal" held the Eastern and Western wings of the Republicans together for a time, but when President Taft after hesitation turned to the conservative Eastern wing, insurgency followed, and the Middle West became, in his words, "enemy country." The Western programme of primary elections, popular election of United States senators, initiative, referendum, recall—all the devices for direct popular participation in government—resulted in a party rebellion which broke the power of the speakership and overthrew the rule of the elder statesmen in the Senate. All these are familiar examples of the new forces. They found their strength in the Middle West and Pacific Coast, and finally made a split in the Republican party, resulting in the formation of the Progressives under Roosevelt. It is idle to think of these events in terms of rival leaders like La Follette, Cummins, Roosevelt, and Aldrich; Bryan, Cleveland, Hill, and Parker. Such leaders really led, and some of them deeply influenced the strategy and tactics of the fighting; but their power to lead was based upon the rival sectional interests. It was not a "fight of the captains." It cannot be explained in terms of personality alone, nor even primarily.

Economic changes and the results of the Civil War had decreased the importance of the state in the nation and turned all interests toward the federal government. Some fifteen years ago, one of the most distinguished of American publicists, Elihu Root, warned the states that "our whole life was crystallizing about national centers." State sovereignty, upon which the political philosopher John Taylor had once relied to avoid the collision of geographical interests, proved a broken reed. Congress was, in fact, becoming almost unconsciously "an assembly of geographical envoys," but an assembly which operated under American conceptions of the need of compromise.

Mr. Root spoke at a time when Roosevelt's strenuous assertion of national power was at its height. Little seemed to intervene between individuals and the stark power of the nation, unless it were in that twilight zone, between state and federal governments, wherein the trusts flourished. National legislation has steadily diminished the area of this "no man's land." The Great War increased the energy and scope of the federal government. But today it may fairly be asked whether all these forces of centralization of power in Washington have promoted national unity and consolidation, or on the other hand have increased sectional expression.

As the states have declined, sectional self-consciousness has risen. All those factors which were relied on to destroy sectionalism, such as the development of means of transportation, expanding domestic commerce, increase of population, have in Europe been among the most important of the forces to bring about national rivalries. If this is the result in Europe, it is certainly not clear that the opposite result must follow in the United States.

Although political sectionalism is still a term of reproach, implying unfairness and a disregard of national interests, the section reproved is seldom conscious that its action is adverse to the common good. We are so large and diversified a nation that it is almost impossible to see the situation except through sectional spectacles. The section either conceives of itself as an aggrieved and oppressed minority, suffering from the injustice of the other sections of the nation, or it thinks of its own culture, its economic policies, and well-being as best for all the nation. It thinks, in other words, of the nation in terms of itself. "I love thy rocks and rills, thy woods and templed hills," runs our American anthem. It was written by a New Englander and its scene is that of New England, not of the snow-capped mountains, the far stretches of Great Plains, or Arid America. We think sectionally and do not fully understand one another.

Underneath the party sectionalism there is, of course, a sectionalism of material interests—of business, manufacturing, mining, agriculture, transportation. To illustrate this economic sectionalism, I may point out that, of the capital invested in manufactures in the United States, nearly one-half is in the North Atlantic division, composed of New England and the Middle States; while on the other hand the great bulk of the wheat and corn, cattle and swine—the food supply for labor and the great cities—comes from the North Central States of the upper Mississippi Valley. Over half the federal income and profits tax in 1920 was paid by the North Atlantic section of the United States, which has less than one-third the population of the Union, though the appropriation of these revenues was made for the nation considered as a unit. Obviously these differences between sections in economic interests mean also differences in political interests.

Significant facts appear in the relations between sectional material interests and sectional forms of society. The group of states which has the highest ratio of automobiles to population is the region of the great wheat states west of the Mississippi—the area of the Republican wing of the "Farmers' *Bloc*." This indicates that there is in that section a more general diffusion of prosperity. The sections which have the lowest ratio are the South and the Middle States of the Atlantic seaboard—the regions, respectively, of the negro and of the great industries. The American conscription statistics in the World War show that the regions which had the best record for physical fitness were those of the West North Central and the Mountain sections, while the lowest is again the industrial Northeast. On the other hand, a map of the reading habit, as shown by the number of books in circulation proportioned to population, reveals that the old Federalist section—New England, New York, and New Jersey— has a distinct preëminence. The statistics in the American *Who's Who* for 1916–17 show that over half of those who achieved the necessary distinction to be included in that volume, lived in the Northeastern section of the United States, and that nearly the same number were born there. In other words, while preëminence in physical fitness and the more even distribution of wealth belong to the agricultural West, more men of talent and a larger concentration of great wealth are to be found in the Northeast. Recent inquiries show that there is a sectionalism of "wet" and "dry" areas, in public opinion on the Volstead Act. The most emphatic support of Prohibition comes from the West North Central and the South Central states—the area of the Farmers' *Bloc*.

There is a sectionalism of culture. School-teachers, historians, scientists, church associations, meet increasingly in sectional gatherings. This is in part due to the high railroad fares; but it is also due to a real consciousness of sectional solidarity. We are all aware that Kansas is not New York; nor South Carolina, New Hampshire. We have in mind a certain quality when we speak of the South, or New England, or the

Pacific Coast, or the Middle West—there is in each a special flavor, social, psychological, literary, even religious.

Popular speech, likewise, reveals our sectionalism, not only in matters of pronunciation, idioms, and so on, but also in the mental attitude that underlies the expressions. When we hear that "no man in the wrong can stand up against the fellow that's in the right and keeps on a-comin'," we know that we aren't in New England, in spite of the moral flavor, and we suspect that we may be in Texas. When told that "high class swine are unknown and impossible among a low class people," that the hog of a certain state "in his sphere typifies the good, the true, and the beautiful . . . like the State that lends him as a solace to humanity," or that still another state produces the "most perfect cow that ever was by sea or land," we have little difficulty in getting our sectional bearings. It is not necessary to examine the Agricultural Atlas, for we recognize a Middle Western spiritual as well as material attitude. When we read, "We don't have to pray for rain out here, we open the irrigation ditch and stop worrying about Providence; we don't have to ask for health, we got it when we bought our railroad ticket," it is not alone the reference to the irrigation ditch that carries our thought to the exhilarating high altitudes of the Far West—the land of optimism, determination, and exaggeration. One doesn't weigh words, or cultivate restraint and the niceties, when nature is big and rough and lavish.

No one can make a sectional list of the men and women who have achieved distinction in literature, and fail to see that, whether in prose or poetry, fiction or essay, there is a special sectional quality in each, a reflection of the region's common interests and soul. Our American literature is not a single thing. It is a choral song of many sections.

We may better understand how far sectional consciousness has gone in the United States if, by way of example, we consider one of the most avowedly sectional portions of the Union—namely, New England. Her restraint, her respect for established order, for vested rights and steady habits, are traditional. As many of her discontented and disturbing elements left the section and migrated to the West, and as the interests of manufacturing and capitalism increased in sectional importance, this inheritance passed easily into an economic conservatism. Even now, when two-thirds of her population is either foreign-born or descended from one or both parents foreign-born, the fundamental economic attitude of New England is still unchanged.

Historically respectful of the rights of property, this section has been, and is, the stronghold against attacks upon banking interests, "sound money," and the protective tariff. It opposed the federal income tax, and is alarmed over national appropriations for roads, bills for national educational control, and similar measures which take from the section more than they return to it. To New England this seems like draining the wealthier region of its property in order to spend it in distant and less prosperous lands—like expropriation under the plea of national unity. There is a striking analogy between its attitude in this respect and the views of the ante-bellum South as voiced by Calhoun.

Particular reasons' exist for New England's sectional discontent and alarm. She finds that the protective tariff is so shaped by Western and Southern agricultural interests that it increases the cost of the raw material of her manufacture and the food for her labor population. Dependent upon transportation for the food, the fuel, and the raw material which she uses but does not produce in her own midst, and also dependent upon transportation for access to her markets, she is concerned over the differential railroad rates of the Interstate Commerce Commission which work to the advantage of Philadelphia, Baltimore, and the Southern ports. In the grand strategy of railroad wars, she has reason to apprehend the transfer of control over her own lines, to New York, even to fear that her roads will go into bankruptcy. She is discussing the question of unifying and controlling the railroads of her section. Attempting to build up the port of Boston, New England is more than reluctant to see the federal government undertake the deep waterway from the Great

Lakes by the St. Lawrence to the sea—a measure pressed by the North Central States. The Mayor of Boston, with a Celtic lack of restraint, recently protested that this "would obliterate New England absolutely." Evidently he forgot that Boston is not a place.

By her well-united group of twelve senators, and with the large number of votes cast in the House by New York and parts of Pennsylvania and New Jersey acting in concert with her, New England has not only had in the past a direct influence upon legislation but a preponderating position in the councils of the Republican party. As the Middle West grew in strength, this power finally brought about a reaction. A prominent congressman broke out in 1908 with the interesting suggestion that "if New England could be ceded to Canada, the legislative difficulties of this country would be cut in half." "Let us not forget," remarked a leading Boston newspaper in 1912, "that the influence long exercised by New England in both Houses of Congress, to the great advantage of this section, has resulted in powerful combinations against us in business as well as in politics." The Boston editors denounced what they called a "Southern-Western alliance against the industrial Northeast." The Western sections in their turn demanded larger popular participation in government. Western insurgency and progressivism broke the traditional control of the Republican organization and divided the party. The victory of the Democrats under President Wilson transferred the ascendency in Congress to the South, "where once," said a Boston editor regretfully, "it belonged to New England."

Under the stress of these events and the more recent combination of the agricultural South and West, New England is becoming a little pessimistic and self-conscious. It is taking measures for more effective sectional organization. Under the heading, "All New England, the Six States Should Act as a Unit on the Issues Which Concern their Similar Interests," the *Boston Transcript* last spring voiced this conception of sectional organization, saying: "The New England States have different governments and are separate and distinct political organizations, but they are bound together by geographic, historic, political, and industrial interests. What helps one New England State in the shape of legislation originating in Washington, helps all New England States. What injures one New England State in the shape of legislation originating at Washington, will hurt all New England States." Recently the Governor of Massachusetts said to the Vermont Press Association: "Other parts of the country regard New England as a unit and treat it accordingly. We being all one stock [!], should regard ourselves in the same light and act as a body, work towards one end." Various Boston editors endorsed the Governor's view, one of them saying that "while certain artificial limitations exist between the New England States, there are no real barriers between them; essentially they are one." Senator Lodge advanced a step farther, looking to a combination of North Atlantic states—a Northeastern *Bloc* to counteract the Farmers' *Bloc*. "The great empire State of New York," he said, "has almost identically the same interests as New England. Well, New York has forty-three members of Congress while New England has thirty-two members of Congress and twelve Senators." He added that they would make a formidable *"bloc,"* if put together. The suggestion recalls the ultra-Federalist proposals in the days of Jefferson and Madison.

Responding to these ideas, New England has developed a semi-governmental machinery for the section by means of conferences of the governors of the New England States, to consider matters reaching from railroad regulation and rates to the fuel supply and the milk question. A New England States Council, "the voice of the section," has been organized, made up of mercantile, manufacturing, financial, transportation, and agricultural (but not labor) organizations, which send delegates or reply to questionnaires from the different cities or states of the section. New England's congressional delegations consult and dine together in Washington in order to foster common action. A New England Bureau at the seat of government is a further development. From all these things it would not be a long step to the creation of a common legislative assembly and executive for the section as a whole.

I have dwelt upon the situation in New England because it shows so clearly the tendency of the time to a sectional organization of interests, to sectional feeling, and to sectional action. But New England is by no means alone. The South has long been known (somewhat inaccurately) as the "Solid South," dominated by the Democratic party, as New England is usually by the Republican party. Naturally, when the Democratic party comes into power, its leadership falls to the South, just as, when the Republican party comes into power, its leadership is in the North and particularly, in the past at least, in the Northeast. The Middle West has also a sectionalism of its own, changing as conditions change. But on the whole its eastern half reflects its diverse economic and social interests and origins, and constitutes a divided buffer region holding the balance of power—an umpire between sections.

Leaders are reluctant to think in sectional terms. President Wilson was in origin a Southern man, proud of the political talent of the South and anxious to reveal it to the nation; but he reprobated sectionalism as such, saying in a speech in Indianapolis in 1916: "Any man who revives the issue of sectionalism in this country, is unworthy of the government of the nation; he shows himself a provincial; he shows that he himself does not know the various sections of his own country; he shows that he has shut his heart up in a little province and that those who do not see the special interests of that province are to him sectional, while he alone is national. That is the depth of unpatriotic feeling."

This is good doctrine, to be taken to heart by all Americans. But if, in Mr. Wilson's phrase, we "uncover realities," we are obliged to face the fact that sections are among these realities. Adjustments are in fact made, not between individuals in the nation, nor between states, but between sections. The whole period of Mr. Wilson's presidency emphasizes this fact, for the tariff was shaped by Southern and Western interests to the discontent of Northeastern manufacturing interests, just as the reverse had occurred when the Northeast was in power. The central-bank plan of the Northeast was replaced by the regional-bank reserve system which gives a sectional organization to credit; and before President Wilson left the White House, a plan was under way for regional administration and regional consolidation of the railroad systems. He found, moreover, that as President he was obliged to take note of the fact that the Republican agricultural West was in distinct opposition to that degree of preparedness which he supported as the World War developed. It furnished the bulk of the votes in favor of the McLemore resolution abandoning American rights on the high seas, and against the declaration of war. He had to use his party leadership to the full in order to procure the adhesion of a hesitant South to his national programme. Mr. Wilson's policy took account of the need of convincing reluctant sections, while North Atlantic leaders, in particular, were impatient and would have him proceed as though that section was itself the nation.

President Harding, in his turn, about a year ago voiced his belief that "state lines have well-nigh ceased to have more than geographical significance." "We have had," he said, "the test of disunion, the triumph of reunion, and now the end of sectionalism." But his wish was father to his thought. He illustrated the tendency of all administrations, from whatever sections they derive their power, to deny or to decry as unpatriotic any sectional dissent from the national measures of the party in power. In a few months after this funeral sermon over sectionalism, President Harding found it necessary to urge that "there is vastly greater security, immensely more of the national point of view, much larger and prompter accomplishment, where our divisions are along party lines in the broader and loftier sense, than to divide geographically or according to pursuits or personal following." The occasion for this utterance, in spirit so like that of Mr. Wilson, was the organization of the Agricultural *Bloc* in Congress, made up of Western Republicans and Southern Democrats, to secure legislation favorable to their interests. Again and again this sectional combination rejected his recommendations as the head of the Republican party and imposed its own programme in spite of the organization centered in the Northeast. The revolting Middle West conceives of the Northeast as selfishly sectional, and it thinks of the South and West, combined, as representing the really national interests. New England, on the other hand, denounces the Agricultural *Bloc* as sectional.

Last year the *Chicago Tribune* published an editorial under the title, "A Square Deal in Congress for the Middle West." This influential newspaper alleged that the Middle West had not enjoyed this square deal in the past and demanded that the section's congressmen, whom it significantly called "our Middle Western agents," should act with more effectiveness for the promotion of the interests of the section as a whole. "We have been paying long enough to enhance the prosperity of the coasts to our own disadvantage," cried the editor.

Middle Western political revolts usually occur in periods of agricultural depression, and in such times temporary third parties have formed, with their strength in the discontented sections. It is not necessary to enumerate the many illustrations of this, from the days of the Grangers, the Populists, the Insurgents, to the Progressives, the Non-Partisan League, the Farm Bureau Federation, the Farmers' *Bloc*, and the contemporary opposition by senators from the North Central States to high protection in the textile schedules of the tariff. All of them are successive stages of the protest of the agricultural sections against the industrial North Atlantic States. They are also reflections of different social conditions and ideals.

What is the logic of all this? Does it mean the ultimate political organization of the different groups of states into sectional units for representation and administration—the formal recognition of a new federation, a replacement of the feeble states by powerful sections, each with its special economic interest? Does it mean that in the last analysis men shape their political action according to their material advantage?

This last question is not radically different from the question of the interpretation of history in general. No single factor is determinative. Men are not absolutely dictated to by climate, geography, soils, or economic interests. The influence of the stock from which they sprang, the inherited ideals, the spiritual factors, often triumph over the material interests. There is also the influence of personality. Men do follow leaders, and sometimes into paths inconsistent with the section's material interests. But in the long run the statesman must speak the language of his people on fundamentals, both of interests and ideals. Not seldom the ideals grow out of the interests. It is the statesman's duty and his great opportunity to lift his section to a higher and broader, a more far-seeing, conception of its interests as a part of the Union, to induce his section to accept the compromises and adjustments which he arranges with the leaders of other sections in the spirit of reconciliation of interests in the nation as a whole. He must be at once the section's spokesman, its negotiator, and its enlightened guide, loyal to the nation as a whole.

At the same time that we realize the danger of provincialism and sectional selfishness, we must also recognize that the sections serve as restraints upon a deadly uniformity. They are breakwaters against overwhelming surges of national emotion. They are fields for experiment in the growth of different types of society, political institutions, and ideals. They constitute an impelling force for progress along the diagonal of contending varieties; they issue a challenge to each section to prove the virtue of its own culture; and they cross-fertilize each other. They promote that reasonable competition and coöperation which is the way of a richer life. A national vision must take account of the existence of these varied sections; otherwise the national vision will be only a sectional mirage.

As the case stands, sections still, as in the past, reflect the distances and the differences of the American continent. Improvements in communication, such as the automobile, the telephone, radio, and moving pictures, have diminished localism rather than sectionalism. Class conflict and sectional conflict often coincide. The triumph of Bolshevism or of capitalism would still leave a contest of sections. But in countless ways the power of the section is conditioned largely upon its moderation. Every section is in unstable equilibrium; public opinion is often closely divided and responds to national ideals.

For, underneath all, there is a common historical inheritance, a common set of institutions, a common law, and a common language. There is an American spirit. There are American ideals. We are members of one body, though it is a varied body. It is inconceivable that we should follow the evil path of Europe and place our reliance upon triumphant force. We shall not become cynical, and convinced that sections, like European nations, must dominate their neighbors and strike first and hardest. However profound the economic changes, we shall not give up our American ideals and our hopes for man, which had their origin in our own pioneering experience, in favor of any mechanical solution offered by doctrinaires educated in Old World grievances. Rather, we shall find strength to build from our past a nobler structure, in which each section will find its place as a fit room in a worthy house. We shall courageously maintain the American system expressed by nation-wide parties, acting under sectional and class compromises. We shall continue to present to our sister continent of Europe the underlying ideas of America as a better way of solving difficulties. We shall point to the *Pax Americana*, and seek the path of peace on earth to men of good will.

TEN

THE SIGNIFICANCE
OF THE SECTION IN
AMERICAN HISTORY

(1925)

A generation ago I published in the *Proceedings* of this Society a paper, which I had read at the summer meeting of the
American Historical Association, on "The Significance of
the Frontier in American History." The Superintendent of the
Census had just announced that a frontier line could no longer
be traced, and had declared: "In the discussion of its extent, its
westward movement, etc., it cannot therefore any longer have
a place in the census reports."

The significance in American history of the advance of the
frontier and of its disappearance is now generally recognized.
This evening I wish to consider with you another fundamental
factor in American history—namely, the Section. Arising
from the facts of physical geography and the regional settlement of different peoples and types of society on the Atlantic
Coast, there was a sectionalism from the beginning. But soon

Reprinted by permission from *Wisconsin Magazine of History* 8 (March 1925).

this became involved and modified by the fact that these societies were expanding into the interior, following the frontier, and that their sectionalism took special forms in the presence of the growing West. Today we are substantially a settled nation without the overwhelming influence that accompanied the westward spread of population. Urban concentration, chiefly in the East, has reversed the movement to a considerable extent. We are more like Europe, and our sections are becoming more and more the American version of the European nation.

First let us consider the influence of the frontier and the West upon American sections. Until our own day, as I urged in that paper, the United States was always beginning over on its outer edge as it advanced into the wilderness. Therefore, the United States was both a developed and a primitive society. The West was a migrating region, a stage of society rather than a place. Each region reached in the process of expansion from the coast had its frontier experience, was for a time "the West," and when the frontier passed on to new regions, it left behind, in the older areas, memories, traditions, an inherited attitude toward life, that persisted long after the frontier had passed by. But while the influence of the frontier permeated East as well as West, by survival of the pioneer psychology and by the reaction of the Western ideals and life upon the East, it was in the newer regions, in the area called the West at any given time, that frontier traits and conceptions were most in evidence. This "West" was more than "the frontier" of popular speech. It included also the more populous transitional zone adjacent, which was still influenced by pioneer traditions and where economic society had more in common with the newer than with the older regions.

This "West," wherever found at different years, thought of itself and of the nation in different ways from those of the East. It needed capital; it was a debtor region, while the East had the capital and was a creditor section. The West was rural, agricultural, while the East was becoming more and more urban and industrial. Living under conditions where the family was the self-sufficing economic unit, where the complications of more densely settled society did not exist, without accumulated inherited wealth, the frontier regions stressed the rights of man, while the statesmen who voiced the interests of the East stressed the rights of property.

The West believed in the rule of the majority, in what John Randolph, the representative of the Virginia tidewater aristocracy, called "King Numbers." The East feared an unchecked democracy, which might overturn minority rights, destroy established institutions, and attack vested interests. The buoyant, optimistic, and sometimes reckless and extravagant spirit of innovation was the very life of the West. In the East innovation was a term of reproach. It always "stalked" like an evil spirit. The East represented accumulated experience, the traditions of the family living generation after generation in a single location and under a similar environment, as President Thwing, of Western Reserve University, has aptly put it. But out in the newer West, through most of its history, men lived in at least two or three states in the course of their migrations. Of the hundred and twenty-four members of the first Wisconsin constitutional convention in 1846, the average was three states for each member. Four had moved eight times. Sixteen had lived in five or more different states, or foreign countries and states; six had lived in seven or more.

The West demanded cheap or free lands on which to base a democratic farming population. The ruling interests in the East feared that such a policy would decrease land values at home and diminish the value of lands which its capitalists had purchased for speculation in the interior. It feared that cheap lands in the West would draw Eastern farmers into the wilderness; would break down the bonds of regular society; would prevent effective control of the discontented; would drain the labor supply away from the growing industrial towns, and thus raise wages.

The West opened a refuge from the rule of established classes, from the subordination of youth to age, from the sway of established and revered institutions. Writing in 1694, when the frontier lay at the borders of Boston Bay, the Reverend Cotton Mather asked: "Do our *Old* People any of them *Go Out* from the Institutions of God, swarming into New Settlements where they and their Untaught Families are like *to Perish for Lack of Vision?*" To their cost, he said, such men have "got unto the *Wrong side of the Hedge*" and "the Angel of the Lord becomes their enemy."

No doubt all this makes too sharply contrasted a picture. But from the beginning East and West have shown a sectional attitude. The interior of the colonies on the Atlantic was disrespectful of the coast, and the coast looked down upon the upland folk. The "men of the Western World" when they crossed the Alleghenies became self-conscious and even rebellious against the rule of the East. In the thirties the tidewater aristocracy was conquered by the Jacksonian Democracy of the interior.

And so one could go on through the story of the antimonopolists, the Grangers, the Populists, the Insurgents, the Progressives, the Farmers' *Bloc*, and the La Follette movement, to illustrate the persistence of the sectionalism of the West, or of considerable parts of it, against the East.

Perhaps Eastern apprehension was never more clearly stated than by Gouverneur Morris, of Pennsylvania, in the Constitutional Convention of 1787. "The busy haunts of men, not the remote wilderness," said he, are "the proper school of political talents. If the western people get the power into their hands they will ruin the Atlantic interests. The back members are always averse to the best measures." He would so fix the ratio of representation that the number of representatives from the Atlantic States should always be larger than the number from the Western States. This, he argued, would not be unjust "as the Western settlers would previously know the conditions on which they were to possess their lands." So influential was his argument that the convention struck out the provision in the draft which guaranteed equality with the old states to the states thereafter to be admitted to the Union.

But on the motion that the representatives from new states should not exceed those from the Old Thirteen, the affirmative vote was cast by Massachusetts, Connecticut, Delaware, and Maryland; Pennsylvania was divided; and the motion was defeated by the votes of the Southern States plus New Jersey.

To the average American, to most American historians, and to most of the writers of our school textbooks (if one can trust the indexes to their books), the word *section* applies only to the struggle of South against North on the questions of slavery, state sovereignty, and, eventually, disunion.

But the Civil War was only the most drastic and most tragic of sectional manifestations, and in no small degree the form which it took depended upon the fact that rival societies, free and slave, were marching side by side into the unoccupied lands of the West, each attempting to dominate the back country, the hinterland, working out agreements from time to time, something like the diplomatic treaties of European nations, defining spheres of influence, and awarding mandates, such as in the Missouri Compromise, the Compromise of 1850, and the Kansas-Nebraska Act. Each Atlantic section was, in truth, engaged in a struggle for power; and power was to be gained by drawing upon the growing West. In the Virginia ratification convention of 1787 William Grayson, by no means the most radical of the members, said: "I look upon this as a contest for empire. . . . If the Mississippi be shut up, emigrations will be stopped entirely. There will be no new states formed on the Western Waters. . . . This contest of the Mississippi involves the great national contest; that is whether one part of this continent shall govern the other. The Northern States have the majority and will endeavor to retain it." Similar conceptions abound in the utterances of North Atlantic statesmen. "It has been said," declared Morris in 1787, "that North Carolina, South Carolina and Georgia only, will in a little time have a majority of the people of America. They must in that case include the great interior country and everything is to be apprehended from their getting power into their hands."

If time permitted, it would be possible to illustrate by such utterances all through our history to very recent times how the Eastern
sections regarded the West, with its advancing frontier, as the raw
material for power. To New England, until her own children began to
occupy the prairies ("reserved by God," as her pioneers declared, "for
a pious and industrious people"), this aspect of the West threatened to
enable the South perpetually to rule the nation. The first great migration, the most extensive in the area covered, flowed into the interior
from the Southern upland. Some of the extreme leaders of the New
England Federalists did not so much desire to break away from the
South as to deprive that section of the three-fifths representation for
its slaves, and either to permit the Western states to leave the Union
or to see them won by England. Then the Old Thirteen could be united
under conditions which would check the expansion of the South and
would leave New England in control.

Writing in 1786 Rufus King, of New York, later senator and minister to England, while admitting that it was impolitic at the time wholly
to give up the Western settlers, declared that very few men who had
examined the subject would refuse their assent "to the opinion that
every Citizen of the Atlantic States, who emigrates to the westward of
the Alleghany is a total loss to our confederacy."

"Nature," he said, "has severed the two countries by a vast and
extensive chain of mountains, interest and convenience will keep them
separate, and the feeble policy of our disjointed Government will not
be able to unite them. For these reasons I have ever been opposed to
encouragements of western emigrants. The States situated on the
Atlantic are not sufficiently populous, and losing our men is losing our
greatest source of wealth."

Of course the immediate complaint in New England and New York
was against the South itself, its Jeffersonian principles (so obnoxious
to New England Puritanism), its slavery, its pro-French sympathies.
But all these gained much of their force by the conviction that the
West was a reservoir from which the South would continue to draw its

power. Among the proposals of the Hartford Convention was that no new state should be admitted into the Union without the concurrence of two-thirds of both houses of Congress. Had this proposed amendment been made, the New England States with two other states in the Senate could have blocked the West from future statehood. The report warned the old states against "an overwhelming Western influence" and predicted that "finally the Western States, multiplied in numbers and augmented in population will control the interests of the whole." Nathan Dane, after whom Dane County in this state is named, furnished the argument for this proposed amendment by his elaborate tabulations and schedules. He pointed out that in the commercial states capital was invested in commerce, and in the slaveholding states in Western lands. When "Kentucky, Ohio and Tennessee were raised up by this interest & admitted into the Union, then the balance was, materially, affected. The non-commercial states pressed the admission of Louisiana and turned the balance against the Northeast." "It clearly follows," he reasoned, "that if a bare majority in Congress can admit new States into the union (all interior ones as they must be) at pleasure, in these immense Western regions, the balance of the union as once fairly contemplated, must soon be destroyed."

But Jackson defeated the British at New Orleans. The Mississippi Valley remained within the Union, Louisiana's interests became affiliated with the commercial states in many ways, and New England people poured so rapidly into the West that New England found in the northern half of the Valley the basis for a new alliance and new power as disturbing to the slaveholding South as the Southern and Western connection had been to New England.

By the middle of the century the South was alarmed at the Western power much in the way that New England had been. "I have very great fears," wrote Justice Campbell, later of the federal Supreme Court, from Mobile to Calhoun in 1847, "that the existing territories of the United States will prove too much for our government. The wild and turbulent conduct of the members upon the Oregon question and

their rapacity and greediness in all matters connected with the appropriation of the revenue induces great doubt of the propriety of intro-
ducing new States in the Union so fast as we do." Of the legislators
from the Western states he said: "Their notions are freer, their impulses stronger, their wills less restrained. I do not wish to increase
the number till the New States already admitted to the Union become
civilized."

On the other hand, it must be clearly borne in mind that as the
West grew in power of population and in numbers of new senators, it
resented the conception that it was merely an emanation from a rival
North and South; that it was the dependency of one or another of the
Eastern sections; that it was to be so limited and controlled as to
maintain an equilibrium in the Senate between North and South. It
took the attitude of a section itself.

From the beginning the men who went West looked to the future
when the people beyond the Alleghenies should rule the nation. Dr.
Manasseh Cutler, the active promoter of the Ohio Company of Associates, which made the first considerable permanent settlement in the
Old Northwest Territory, wrote in 1787 a *Description of Ohio*. Though
himself the minister at Ipswich, in the heart of that stronghold of
conservatism, the "Essex Junto," he declared that on the Ohio would
be "the seat of empire" for the whole Union. Within twenty years, he
predicted, there would be more people on the western side of the
Allegheny watershed than in the East, and he congratulated these
people that "in order to begin right there will be no wrong habits to
combat and no inveterate systems to overturn—there will be no
rubbish to remove before you lay the foundations." Evidently it did
not take long to produce the Western point of view!

In the Senate in 1837 Benton, of Missouri, scorned the proposals of
Calhoun regarding the disposition of the public domain, and boasted
that after the census of 1840 had shown the weight of the West it would
be so highly bid for that it would write its own bill. Perhaps the debate
over the Compromise of 1850 brings out the self-assertive Western

attitude in these years most clearly. Calhoun had argued that the equilibrium between North and South was being destroyed by the increase in free states made out of the western territories. But Stephen A. Douglas, of Illinois, spoke for the West when he attacked the Southern statesman for the error of thinking of the West as property of the older sections. "What share had the South in the territories," he asked, "or the North, or any other geographical division unknown to the Constitution? I answer none—none at all." And Douglas calculated that if its right to self-determination were admitted, the West would form at least seventeen new free states, and that therefore the theory of equilibrium was a hopeless one.

It was not only the slavery struggle that revealed the Eastern conception of the West as merely the field of contest for power between the rival Atlantic sections, and the West's counter assertion of its own substantive rights. The same thing was shown in many different fields. For example, rival Eastern cities and states, the centers of power in their respective sections, engaged in contests for the commercial control of the Mississippi Valley by transportation lines. The contests between rival European powers for the control of the Bagdad railway, the thrust of Germany toward the rich hinterlands made up of the Balkans and India, and the project of "Central Europe" in the history of the World War, have a resemblance to these American sectional contests for the still more valuable hinterland of the Mississippi Valley. American sections did not go to war over their trade and transportation interests. Nevertheless, they recognized that there were such interests. A Southern writer in *DeBow's Review* in 1847 declared:

A contest has been going on between the North and South not limited to slavery or no slavery—to abolition or no abolition, nor to the politics of either whigs or democrats as such, but a contest for the wealth and commerce of the great valley of the Mississippi—a contest tendered by our Northern brethren, whether the growing commerce of the great West shall be thrown upon New Orleans or given to the Atlantic cities.

Shortly after this, in 1851, the *Western Journal* of St. Louis published articles lamenting that "the Western States are subjected to the relation of Provinces of the East" and that New Orleans was giving way to New York as their commercial city. Since (so the argument ran) exports can never build up a commercial city, the mouth of the Mississippi must be so improved that imports would enter the Valley by way of New Orleans. "Then," said the writer, "a line of cities will arise on the banks of the Mississippi that will far eclipse those on the Atlantic coast."

The middle of the century saw an extension of this sectional contest for economic power derived from the growing West; but it was the railroad trunk lines rather than the canals that occupied the foreground. The goal became the ports of the Pacific. The Memphis convention of 1845 and the Chicago convention of 1847 illustrate how interior cities were now repeating the rivalry for Western trade which had earlier been seen on the Atlantic Coast. The contests between New Orleans, Memphis, St. Louis, and Chicago influenced the Kansas-Nebraska Act, and the later strategy of the struggle for position between the Pacific railroads.

Throughout our history, then, there has been this sectionalism of West and East, and this Eastern conception of the West as recruiting ground merely for the rival Atlantic Coast sections. Nation-wide parties have had their Eastern and Western wings, often differing radically, and yet able by party loyalty and by adjustments and sacrifices to hold together. Such a struggle as the slavery contest can only be understood by bearing in mind that it was not merely a contest of North against South, but that its form and its causes were fundamentally shaped by the dynamic factor of expanding sections, of a West to be won.

This migratory sectionalism has not always been obvious, but it was none the less real and important. Year after year new Wests had been formed. Wildernesses equal in area to the greater European nations had been turned into farms in single decades.

But now the era of the frontier advance has ended. The vast public domain, so far as it is suited to agriculture, is taken up. The competent experts of the Department of Agriculture now tell us that "the nation reached and passed the apogee of agricultural land supply in proportion to population about 1890, and that we have entered a period which will necessarily be marked by a continually increasing scarcity of land." The price of lands has risen as the supply of free lands declined. Iowa farm lands mounted from an average of thirty dollars per acre in 1890 to over two hundred dollars in 1920.

Shortly after 1890, men began to speak less confidently of the inexhaustible forest supply. The reclamation act early in the twentieth century began a new era in governmental conservation and governmental economic activity. The Conservation Congress met in 1908, three centuries after the Jamestown settlers sank their axes into the edge of the American forest. The purpose of the congress was to consider the menace of forest exhaustion, the waste of soil fertility and of mineral resources, the reclamation of the deserts, the drainage of the swamps. Now we are told by high authority that we shall feel the pinch of timber shortage in less than fifteen years. The free lands are no longer free; the boundless resources are no longer boundless. Already the urban population exceeds the rural population of the United States.

But this does not mean that the Eastern industrial type of urban life will necessarily spread across the whole nation, for food must come from somewhere, and the same expert authorities that predict that within about fifty years the United States itself will be unable to feed its population by its home supply, also conclude that the deficient food supply will not be available from outside the nation, because the same phenomenon of the encroachment of population upon food is in evidence throughout the world. Already Europe as a whole depends upon importation for its food supply. Its large population in proportion to its area and resources cannot be made the basis for estimates of what is possible in the United States, for Europe's large population was made possible by these imports from the United States as well as from other nations.

If the prediction be true, or if anything like it be true, then there must remain in the United States large rural farming interests and sections. The natural advantages of certain regions for farming, or for forestry, or for pasturage will arrest the tendency of the Eastern industrial type of society to flow across the continent and thus to produce a consolidated, homogeneous nation free from sections. At the same time that the nation settles down to the conditions of an occupied land, there will be emphasized the sectional differences arising from unlike geographic regions.

To President Coolidge, as a speech of his in November last shows, the prospect is of a nation importing its supplies of food and resources, facing "the problem of maintaining a prosperous, self-reliant, confident agriculture in a country preponderantly commercial and industrial." Whether our destiny is to become a nation in which agriculture is subordinate, or one in which it is an equal partner with urban industrial interests, it seems clear that there will be sectional expression of the differences between these interests; for in certain geographic provinces agriculture will be entirely subordinate to manufacture, as in others such industry will be insignificant as compared with farming.

Unlike such countries as France and Germany, the United States has the problem of the clash of economic interests closely associated with regional geography on a huge scale. Over areas equal to all France or to all Germany, either the agricultural or the manufacturing types are here in decided ascendency. Economic interests are sectionalized. The sections occupied by a rural population are of course far inferior in numbers of voters to the sections of urban industrial life. The map is deceptive in this respect, for Greater New York City, which would be a point on the map, has almost as many people as live in all the vast spaces of the Mountain and Pacific States. The population of the New England States and the Middle States of the North Atlantic division is over thirty millions, while the combined population of Wisconsin, Minnesota, North and South Dakota, Montana, Wyoming, Idaho, Washington, and Oregon is less than ten millions. On the map these states take an imposing space, but owing to physical geography a large portion will always remain sparsely settled. Nevertheless, New England and the Middle States together have only eighteen senators, while the states of the section which I have just named have also eighteen senators. New York State alone has a larger population than this northwestern zone of states; but this wealthy and populous state has only two senators as against the eighteen senators of the other region.

On a map constructed so as to give to each state a space proportioned to its population, or to its income tax, instead of to its dimensions in square miles, the Western lands would shrink in their map space in a startling fashion. But in the Senate is exhibited the outcome of the tendencies which statesmen like Gouverneur Morris saw so clearly—namely, the great power of the newer states by their equal representation in the Senate and their ability to take property by taxation from the wealthier section and to distribute it according to numbers, or even according to deficiencies, throughout the Union as a unit. Obviously, there is here the certainty of a sectional clash of interests not unlike those which led to Calhoun's South Carolina Exposition.

Sectionalism will hereafter be shaped by such new forces. We have become a nation comparable to all Europe in area, with settled geographic provinces which equal great European nations. We are in this sense an empire, a federation of sections, a union of potential nations. It is well to look at the result of our leap to power since the ending of the frontier, in order to appreciate our problems arising from size and varied sections.

We raise three-fourths of the world's corn, over a third of its swine, over half its cotton, and over one-fifth its wheat. Out of the virgin wilderness we have built such industrial power that we now produce two-thirds of the pig iron of the world, over twice the steel tonnage of England, Germany, and France combined. We mine nearly half the world's coal. We have fully half the gold coin and bullion of the world, and in 1920 our national wealth exceeded the combined wealth of the United Kingdom, France, and Germany. In the World War President Wilson gave the word that sent two million Americans across the seas to turn the scale in that titanic conflict. We are forced to think of ourselves continentally and to compare ourselves with all Europe. Why, with so vast a territory, with so many geographic provinces, equal in area, in natural resources, and in natural variety to the lands of the great nations of Europe, did we not become another Europe? What tendencies have we developed that resembled those of Europe in the course of our history? Are there tendencies toward the transformation of our great sections into types similar to European nations?

It was evident at the outset of a study of the frontier movement that the American people were not passing into a monotonously uniform space. Rather, even in the colonial period, they were entering successive different geographic provinces; they were pouring their plastic pioneer life into geographic moulds. They would modify these moulds, they would have progressive revelations of the capacities of the geographic provinces which they won and settled and developed; but even the task of dealing constructively with the different regions would work its effects upon their traits.

Not a uniform surface, but a kind of checkerboard of differing environments, lay before them in their settlement. There would be the interplay of the migrating stocks and the new geographic provinces. The outcome would be a combination of the two factors, land and people, the creation of differing societies in the different sections. European nations were discovered, conquered, colonized, and developed so far back in history that the process of nation-making is obscure. Not so with section-making in the United States. The process has gone on almost under our own observation. But by the bondage to the modern map, as John Fiske put it, much American history has been obscured. Our constitutional forms, in contrast with the realities, provide for a federation of states. Our historians have dealt chiefly with local history, state history, national history, and but little with sectional history. Our students of government have been more aware of the legal relations of states and nation than with the actual groupings of states into sections, and with the actions of these sections beneath the political surface. State sovereignty, for example, has in fact never been a vital issue except when a whole section stood behind the challenging state. This is what gave the protest reality.

One of the most interesting features of recent geographical studies is the emphasis placed upon regional geography and human geography. Europe has given more attention to such studies in human geography than has the United States. Perhaps this is because European nations have been forced to consider the geographical aspects of the self-determination of nations and the rearrangement of the map by the treaty which seemed to close the World War. Perhaps in the hard realities of that war the military staffs and the scientists who had to deal with the problem of supplies of food and of raw material were compelled to give attention to the subject. But even before and after this war, the increasing pressure of population upon the means of life compelled in Europe the study of the natural regions, their resources and peoples, and their relations to each other. Now the conditions which I have been attempting to make clear in the United States are forcing us to face the same problem. We, like European nations, are approaching a saturation of population.

That sectionalism which is based on geographical regions has been in evidence from the early colonial period, but it has been obscured and modified by the influence of the unoccupied West. The states have been declining and are likely to continue to diminish in importance in our politics; but the groups of states called sections are likely to become more significant as the state declines. A study of votes in the federal

House and Senate from the beginning of our national history reveals the fact that party voting has more often broken down than maintained itself, on fundamental issues; that when these votes are mapped or tabulated by the congressional districts or states from which those who cast them came, instead of by alphabetical arrangement, a persistent sectional pattern emerges.

There has been in the earlier periods the sharp clash between New England and the South, with the Middle States divided and unstable, constituting a buffer zone and often holding the balance of power. Then, as population spread westward, the greater parties were composed of sectional wings. Normally, in the Republican party there came to be a fairly solid conservative New England, a mixed and uncertain Middle Region, and a more radical North Central wing, ready in the shaping of legislation to join the Democrats in a kind of sectional *bloc* (even before the days of the *bloc*) to oppose the conservative and dominant Eastern wing. As time went on, the East North Central States came into closer connection with the Eastern wing, and in the West North Central lay the areas of radical dissent and of third-party movements. Legislation was determined less by party than by sectional voting. Bills were shaped for final passage by compromises between wings or by alliances between sections. The maps of presidential elections showing majorities by counties look like maps of North against South; but there was always a concealed East and West which temporarily laid aside their differences.

I think it not too much to say that in party conventions as well as in Congress the outcome of deliberations bears a striking resemblance to treaties between sections, suggestive of treaties between European nations in diplomatic congresses. But over an area equal to all Europe we found it possible to legislate, and we tempered asperities and avoided wars by a process of sectional give-and-take. Whether we shall continue to preserve our national, our intersectional, party organization in the sharper sectional conflicts of interest that are likely to accompany the settling down of population, the completer revelation of the influence of physical geography remains to be seen.

As an illustration of the newer forms of sectionalism, take the movement for the Great Lakes–St. Lawrence deep waterway. Middle Western leaders are arguing that there is "in the heart of the continent a large area beyond the radius of logical rail haul for the movement of bulk commodities to either seacoast." "Nature," runs the argument, "which has indicated the extent of the area which sends its surplus to the Atlantic seaboard and to the Gulf and to the Pacific ports, has provided the American continent with one potential seacoast not yet utilized. Upon the map of economic divides indicated by geography— the Atlantic seaboard, the Gulf territory, and the Pacific slope—there is, as it were, an economic desert a thousand miles east and west, five hundred miles north and south beyond the radius of logical rail haul to either coast." The desire to give an outlet to what is called this "land-locked commerce to the coast," leads to the demand for "a fourth economic divide based upon the Great Lakes as linked with the ocean, giving to the coast of the Great Lakes access to marine commerce" and permitting the erection of each rail system upon the sea base.

When ex-Senator Townsend, of Michigan, was running for reelection, a Detroit daily reported: "The East is opposed to him because of his leadership in the waterways movement, but the entire West from Ohio to Idaho is looking hopefully and earnestly to Michigan to give him the largest majority he has ever received. The east and the west will be 'listening in' election night—the east hoping for a reduced Townsend vote, the west hoping fervently that his vote will be a knockout blow to the eastern opposition to the St. Lawrence waterway."

I quote this to take the opportunity to point out that sweeping statements like these exaggerate the sectional feeling. As a matter of fact, of course, very few Eastern voters knew much about Townsend, and, East and West, most of the radio fans were listening in to the vaudeville or the football game or the real prize fight.

But while Duluth writers press the importance of what they call this "frustrated seaway," New York writers protest that the outlet should be through an enlarged Erie Canal if there is to be such a water route at all, and it is argued that the projected St. Lawrence route would be "Our Dardanelles," liable to be closed against the West by Canadian or British government whenever disagreements invited this mode of coercion. In New England, meantime, there are fears that Boston would be injured as a port, besides the loss of her advantages by sea-borne commerce to the Pacific Coast. A few years ago Mayor Curley, of Boston, indignantly declared that such a waterway "would obliterate New England absolutely."

I read, the other day, editorials in the *Chicago Tribune* which made the decision of the Supreme Court against the claim of the sanitary district to divert water from Lake Michigan, without the permission of the Secretary of War, the occasion for this language: "It is time for Chicago, Illinois, and the entire Mississippi Valley to rise in revolt against a tyranny which now threatens its very existence.... This is neither a conquered country nor a colony but an integral part of a nation, and as such entitled to the same consideration afforded to New England and New York." The editorial goes on to demand action to prevent the houses of Congress from organizing, etc. In another editorial of that issue, under the caption "The West is West, but the East is London," it is said: "It is natural that the East should turn to London for London policy is Atlantic policy"; and the editor speaks of "London and its provinces in Montreal, Boston, New York and Washington."

No doubt this language is not to be taken with entire seriousness, but it is vigorous enough. It proposes revolt, and paralysis of government; and it, in effect, reads a rather substantial "chunk" of America out of the Union. Allowing for New England's restraint in speech, mildly similar utterances can be found in the press of that section whenever its interests seem threatened by West or South. When Senator John Taylor, of Virginia, informed Jefferson that the Northeast felt that union with the South was doomed to fail, that philosophic statesman replied in words that are worthy of extended quotation as illustrating both a tolerant spirit and an amusing impression of New England.

"It is true that we are completely under the saddle of Massachusetts and Connecticut and that they ride us very hard, cruelly insulting our feelings, as well as exhausting our strength and substance. Their natural friends, the three other eastern states, join them from a sort of family pride, and they have the art to divide certain other parts of the Union so as to make use of them to govern the whole." But, "seeing," said Jefferson, "that an association of men who will not quarrel with one another is a thing which never existed ... seeing we must have somebody to quarrel with, I had rather keep our New England associates for that purpose than to see our bickerings transferred to others. They are circumscribed within such narrow bounds, and their population is so full, that their numbers will ever be in the minority, and they are marked, like the Jews, with such perversity of character, as to constitute from that circumstance the natural division of our parties." It will be observed that although he does not extol New England he does not read her out of the Union. The significant fact is that sectional self-consciousness and sensitiveness is likely to be increased as time goes on and crystallized sections feel the full influence of their geographic peculiarities, their special interests, and their developed ideals, in a closed and static nation.

There is a sense in which sectionalism is inevitable and desirable. There is and always has been a sectional geography in America based fundamentally upon geographic regions. There is a geography of political habit, a geography of opinion, of material interests, of racial stocks, of physical fitness, of social traits, of literature, of the distribution of men of ability, even of religious denominations. Professor Josiah Royce defined a "province" or section, in the sense in which I am using the word, as "any one part of a national domain which is geographically and socially sufficiently unified to have a true consciousness of its own ideals and customs and to possess a sense of its distinction from other parts of the country." It was the opinion of this eminent philosopher that the world needs now more than ever before the vigorous development of a highly organized provincial life to serve as a check upon mob psychology on a national scale, and to furnish that variety which is essential to vital growth and originality. With this I agree. But I wish also to urge here, as I have elsewhere, that there is always the danger that the province or section shall think of itself naïvely as the nation, that New England shall think that America is merely New England writ large, or the Middle West shall think that America is really the Middle West writ large, and then proceed to denounce the sections that do not perceive the accuracy of this view as wicked or ignorant and un-American. This kind of nationalism is a sectional mirage, but it is common, and has been common to all the sections, in their unconscious attitude if not in clear expression. It involves the assumption of a superiority of culture, of *Kultur*, to which good morals require that the nation as a whole must yield.

We must frankly face the fact that in this vast and heterogeneous nation, this sister of all Europe, regional geography is a fundamental fact; that the American peace has been achieved by restraining sectional selfishness and assertiveness and by coming to agreements rather than to reciprocal denunciation or to blows.

In the past we have held our sections together, partly because while the undeveloped West was open there was a safety valve, a region for hopeful restoration; partly because there were national political parties, calling out national party allegiance and loyalty over all sections and at the same time yielding somewhat under stress to sectional demands. Party was like an elastic band.

But there would often have been serious danger, such as showed itself when parties became definitely sectionalized just before the Civil War, had it not been the fact that popular party majorities over most of the sections are much closer than is usually supposed. The party held its tenure of power by a narrow margin and must use its power temperately or risk defeat. It must conciliate sectional differences within itself.

Not only the narrowness of normal party majorities, county by county over the nation, but also the existence, within each of the large sections, of smaller sections or regions which did not agree with the views of their section as a whole, constituted a check both upon party despotism and upon sectional arrogance and exploitation of other sections.

In every state of the Union there are geographic regions, chiefly, but not exclusively, those determined by the ancient forces of geology, which divide the state into the lesser sections. These subsections within the states often cross state lines and connect with like areas in neighboring states and even in different sections of the larger type. Many states have now been made the subject of monographic studies of their internal sections shown in party politics, in economic interests, in social types, in cultural matters such as education, literature, and religion. I have prepared such maps of the United States for the year 1850. For example, the map by counties showing the distribution of white illiteracy so closely resembles the map of the physiographic regions that the one might almost be taken for the other. Much the same is true for the map of farm values by counties. I have also mapped the Whig and Democratic counties in the presidential elections from 1836 to 1852 and combined them in a map, which shows that certain regions, certain groups of counties, were almost always Whig and others normally Democratic through all these years. Then I have had the photographer superimpose these maps one upon another. As a result it is shown that the rough, the poorer lands, the illiterate counties were for the most part the Democratic counties, while the fertile basins—like the richer wheat areas of the Old Northwest; the limestone islands about Lexington, Kentucky, and Nashville, Tennessee; the Black Belt of the Gulf States, the center of the cotton and slavery interests, the abode of the wealthy and educated great slave-holding planters—were Whig. The Whigs tended to be strong in the areas of the greater rivers and commercial centers and routes, and in the counties with the better record in the matter of illiteracy.

Now I am not saying that Democracy and illiteracy and poor soils are necessarily connected. One of the interesting results of the study is to show that there were exceptions that prevent any such exclusively physical explanations. In North Carolina, for example, very notable Whig areas were in the most illiterate, rough, mountainous counties of that state, where the poor whites were antagonistic to the wealthy slaveholding Democratic planters of the eastern counties. Certain regions, like western New York and the Western Reserve of Ohio, show not so much the influence of physical geography as of the fact that they were colonized by New Englanders and carried on the interest in vested rights which distinguished the Puritan stock.

In short, the studies show that generalizations which make physical geography or economic interests alone the compelling explanation of political groupings are mistaken. There are also the factors of ideals and psychology, the inherited intellectual habits, derived from the stock from which the voters sprang. Sometimes these ideals carry the voters into lines that contradict their economic interests. But as a rule there has been such a connection of the stock, the geographic conditions, the economic interests, and the conceptions of right and wrong, that all have played upon each other to the same end.

Next I wish to emphasize the fact that these regional subdivisions are persistent. Often they remain politically the same for several generations. Probably the mass of voters inherit their party and their political ideas. Habit rather than reasoning is the fundamental factor in determining political affiliation of the mass of voters, and there is a geography, a habitat, of political habit.

There is the same geography of culture, though I am not able in the time that remains to develop this. For example, in a recent map of short-story areas (of what the author calls local-color areas) almost exactly the same regions are shown as appear on the maps which I have mentioned.

There is, then a sectionalism of the regions within the larger divisions, a sectionalism of minority areas, sometimes protesting against the policies of the larger section in which they lie and finding more in common with similar regions outside of this section. Herein lies a limitation upon the larger section in case it attempts a drastic and subversive policy toward other sections. As Professor Holcombe has pointed out, in this kind of nation, in this vast congeries of sections, voters cannot hope to have a choice between parties any one of which will stand for all the measures which they oppose. The most they can reasonably hope for, he thinks, "is the formation of a party, resting upon a combination of sectional interests which are capable of coöperation in national politics without too much jealousy and friction, and including that particular interest with which they are themselves most closely associated. No sectional interest is strong enough, alone and unaided, to control the federal government, and no major party can be formed with a fair prospect of domination in national politics which does not contain more or less incongruous elements."

With this I agree, and indeed have long been on record to this effect. It emphasizes the need for tolerance, for coöperation, for mutual sacrifices by the leaders of the various sections. Statesmanship in this nation consists, not only in representing the special interests of the leader's own section, but in finding a formula that will bring the different regions together in a common policy. The greatest statesmen have always had this goal before them. If there were time I should like to quote the striking confirmation of this in writings of even such men as John Quincy Adams, Van Buren, and Calhoun, who are ordinarily thought of as rather definitely sectional. Each formulated plans for concessions to the various sections whereby a national pattern could emerge.

The significance of the section in American history is that it is the faint image of a European nation and that we need to reëxamine our history in the light of this fact. Our politics and our society have been shaped by sectional complexity and interplay not unlike what goes on between European nations. The greater sections are the result of the joint influence of the geologists' physiographic provinces and the colonizing stocks that entered them. The result is found in popular speech in which New England, the Middle States, the South, the Middle West, etc., are as common names as Massachusetts or Wisconsin. The Census divisions are more definite and official designations. Of course, the boundary lines are not definite and fixed. Neither are those of European nations. These larger sections have taken their characteristic and peculiar attitudes in American civilization in general.

We have furnished to Europe the example of a continental federation of sections over an area equal to Europe itself, and by substituting discussion and concession and compromised legislation for force, we have shown the possibility of international political parties, international legislative bodies, and international peace. Our party system and our variety in regional geography have helped to preserve the American peace. By having our combination of sections represented in a national legislative body, by possessing what may be called a League of Sections, comparable to a League of Nations, if it included political parties and a legislative body, we have enabled these minority sections to defend their interests and yet avoid the use of force.

The thing to be avoided, if the lessons of history are followed, is the insistence upon the particular interests and ideals of the section in which we live, without sympathetic comprehension of the ideals, the interests, and the rights of other sections. We must shape our national action to the fact of a vast and varied Union of unlike sections.

THE SIGNIFICANCE OF THE FRONTIER IN AMERICAN HISTORIOGRAPHY

A GUIDE TO FURTHER READING

In the 1990s, a century after Frederick Jackson Turner first delivered "The Significance of the Frontier in American History," western history is in the news once more. The cover story in a leading national news magazine announced that historians had now concluded that the American West was not "some rough-hewn egalitarian democracy, where every man had a piece of land and the promise of prosperity, but a world quickly dominated by big money and big government"; not a land "where the sodbuster might dwell in sweet harmony with nature, but a nearly unmitigated environmental catastrophe"; not a society of close-knit pioneer families, but one in which men, women, and children were "torn apart by the great desert emptiness of the West." These revisions, the article stated, led to an inevitable conclusion: "The Turnerian view of the West is falling apart these days."[1]

This is news? In a world of dizzying intellectual fashion changes—from modernism to postmodernism to claims of an end of history itself—it may come as something of a surprise that it has taken so long for historians of the American West to overturn the interpretation of a century-old conference paper. The report of Turner's fall from grace strikes me as a headline from the past.

Yet many of today's most prominent "new western historians" believe the field remains "stuck in a Turnerian rut." In the words of Donald Worster, the author of *Under Western Skies: Nature and History in the American West* (1992), "Turner presides over western history like a Holy Ghost." At meetings of the Western History Association, he remarks, "heads still bowed dutifully at the name of Frederick Jackson Turner, and a few still crossed themselves in reverence." Sentiments like these have roused the few remaining Turnerians. Martin Ridge, coauthor with the late Ray Allen Billington of the classic Turnerian textbook, *Westward Expansion: A History of the American Frontier* (1949; 5th ed., 1982) dares historians like Worster to "explain what is new about their work other than their personal assumptions and value judgments." Arguing that they have little to offer as a replacement for Turner's interpretation, Ridge fires back that they "may find that it is exceedingly difficult to bury his ghost." Less temperate is Gerald D. Nash, professor of history at the University of New Mexico, who slams the new western historians for their "profound pessimism about the American Westering experience," and compares their arguments to the "*modus operandi* of Nazi Fascists and Communist academicians in their heyday." Yes, the arguments over western history sometimes get ill-tempered.[2]

For an overview of the debate that has continued since Turner delivered his paper, the best book to turn to is Nash's *Creating the West: Historical Interpretations, 1890–1990* (1991). He shows that critics first began attacking Turner's views in earnest in the 1920s, when an important component of post–World War I intellectual radicalism took the form of a kind of inverted frontier thesis, invoking the western past to account for many of the negative aspects of American civilization. The frontier, John Dewey declared in 1922, was most notable for its "depressing effect upon the free life of inquiry and criticism." Other scholars began to question what one of them called "the shibboleth of the frontier" in American historiography, picking away at Turner's fuzzy definitions, his internal inconsistency, his sometimes faulty logic. Charles Beard, with an economic determinist thesis of his own to promote, blasted "orthodox historians" for dwelling on the frontier thesis to the exclusion of nearly all other interpretations; "the tabu is almost perfect," he remarked. "The American Historical Association officially is as regular as Louis XVI's court scribes."[3]

In the last years of Turner's life, and following his death in 1932, critics pummeled his work unmercifully, and numerous studies appeared with alternate readings of his historical evidence. The geographer Isaiah Bowman argued that Turner's idea of a vanished frontier was simply wrong, and in an article in the prestigious *American Historical Review*, Paul Wallace Gates demonstrated that, in effect, there had never really been any "free land." Democratic institutions had been imported from the East, asserted Louis B. Wright; Fred A. Shannon disputed the claim that the West had acted as a safety valve for urban discontent; and folklorist Mody C. Boatright took on and demolished Turner's "myth of frontier individualism." Finally, in 1942, George Wilson Pierson of Yale University performed a kind of intellectual postmortem on the frontier thesis. Reviewing these criticisms, and scathingly dissecting Turner's own prose, Pierson concluded: "In what it proposes, the frontier hypothesis needs painstaking revision. By what it fails to mention, the theory disqualifies itself as an adequate guide to American development."[4]

Of more positive significance was the emergence in the 1930s of a number of alternate frameworks for western history. In a presidential address to the American Historical Association, Herbert Eugene Bolton of the University of California at Berkeley, who pioneered the study of the "Spanish Borderlands" of the United States, called for a multinational and multiethnic history of the North American West. Bernard DeVoto, a son of the western desert living on the shores of Massachusetts Bay, spawned a school of "colonial" western history when he angrily charged that the West had always been a "plundered province" of the East. In Kansas, meanwhile, James C. Malin began the first serious work on western social and environmental history, while in Texas Walter Prescott Webb argued for the West as an arid region. After World War II Carey McWilliams inaugurated the history of the Mexican-American people, and Joseph Kinsey Howard of Montana wrote an epic narrative of the mixed-ancestry Métis people of the northern plains, reminding us of another of the continent's expanding peoples. Professor Earl Pomeroy of the University of Oregon insisted that the westerner was "fundamentally imitator rather than innovator," and Henry Nash Smith of Berkeley investigated the sources of the American myth of the West, including the deep background of the frontier thesis itself. There are insightful intellectual portraits of some of these historians who shaped western historiography in Richard Etulain's excellent collection, *Writing Western History: Essays on Major Western Historians* (1991). Their approaches were all new, had very little to do with the frontier thesis, and within a quarter century of Turner's death had inspired several shelves of good, non-Turnerian western history. "Such is the force of the anti-, un-, and non-Turnerian groups," William N. Davis concluded after considering the results of a poll of historians in 1964, "that it would appear only a matter of time until they attain majority status."[5]

That time has come. For a stimulating overview of the new arguments, turn to Patricia Nelson Limerick's *Legacy of Conquest: The Unbroken Past of the American West* (1987), and for her new western history manifesto see *Trails: Toward a New Western History* (1991), which she edited with Clyde A. Milner II and Charles E. Rankin. Limerick fits the participants in the current debate over western history into categories of "old" and "new." This sometimes requires considerable tailoring, for some old ideas, she admits, turn out to be "new." The frontier thesis was the cornerstone of the "old western history," but then Turner himself argued for rethinking the past in light of the present, which made him "new" as well; Walter Prescott Webb was, says Limerick, "decidedly New in his emphasis on the West's limited water and decidedly Old in his patronizing treatment of Indians and Hispanics"; and so on. Are we likewise to dismiss some new ideas as "old"? The rhetoric of "new" and "old" seems simply a way of distinguishing between arguments one does and doesn't like.[6]

According to Donald Worster, western history has been remade by a "younger generation, shaken by the experience of Vietnam and other national disgraces," although he qualifies this by adding, "I do not mean to say that this is the sole achievement of scholars under the age of fifty." Indeed, while there has been an outpouring of significant new historical work on the American West in the past twenty years, the publications first articulating the themes now identified with the "new western history" were in fact written by historians of a previous generation who were at work long before I, and most of my contemporaries, had entered graduate school. In the 1950s Jack D. Forbes challenged historians to reimagine the frontier from the perspective of Indian people, and A. Irving Hallowell, one of the first to combine history and ethnography, discussed the impact of American Indians on American culture. In the early 1960s historians such as David M. Potter and Roger Daniels began to consider how the experience of women and ethnic minorities might challenge the frontier thesis, while Richard Maxwell Brown and Wilbur Jacobs argued for a new history of western violence and environmental change. In 1973 Robert V. Hine distilled a great deal of this new work in a stimulating new interpretive history of the American West.[7]

Failing to give full recognition to these pathbreaking studies violates a cardinal rule of history: close attention to antecedents. Whether they realize it or not, today's western historians build on the contributions of their "anti-, un-, or non-Turnerian" predecessors. Alternate approaches to the history of the American West have existed among historians since the reconsideration of the frontier thesis began in earnest, and contrasting interpretations have less to do with "generations" than with social theory, moral values, and the angle and breadth of historical vision.

Perhaps Turner's most significant contribution was his historical vision. The Turnerians composed what might be called imperialist chronicles—success stories that, as Turner once put it, told of "the advance of the pioneer into the wastes of the continent." For a century now, the belief that "westering" defines our unique national heritage, and that it amounted to the purest expression of American idealism, has been what the late historian Warren Susman called "the official American ideology." It has been played out in a fascinating interchange of ideas and images among movies, popular history, and political rhetoric. The original master of ceremonies for this discourse, of course, was the showman William Cody, or "Buffalo Bill," whose Wild West barnstormed America and the world for more than thirty years, turning western style and action, and a particular idyll about American destiny, into one of the most bankable commodities in show business.[8]

In a way, what Turner did when he first codified his theory of the importance of the western past was provide intellectual legitimization for Cody's images. As Theodore Roosevelt wrote in an admiring letter to the young Wisconsin professor, "I think you have struck some first-class ideas, and put into definite shape a good deal of thought that has been floating around rather loosely." According to Turner's thesis, westward expansion was the very marrow of the American experience, the crucible in which an individualistic character was formed in a confrontation between "savagery and civilization." The movement westward secured political and social democracy by the availability of

free land, and fueled economic growth with successive frontier bo-
nanzas. Roosevelt himself employed Cody's floridity and Turner's
ideas in several popular books such as *The Winning of the West* (1889–
96), and he was one of the first modern politicians to demonstrate the
political utility of western images, borrowing the name of his cavalry
regiment during the Spanish-American War, for example, from the
"Congress of Rough Riders," which was an act in Cody's show.[9]

Following the recipe perfected by Cody, early silent westerns
combined scenes and narratives drawn from western pulp fiction with
authentic details of costume and scenery, creating a mythic storyscape
that has remained essentially unchanged. The streets and storefronts
of William H. Hart's silent film *Hell's Hinges* (1916) could be the same
western town featured in George Steven's *Shane* (1953) or Clint East-
wood's *Unforgiven* (1992). Richard Slotkin's *Gunfighter Nation: The
Myth of the Frontier in Twentieth-Century America* (1992), the final
volume of his monumental trilogy on frontier imagery in American
culture, details this history. Slotkin emphasizes the western genre's
ideological embrace of violence as "an essential and necessary part of
the process through which American society was established and
through which its democratic values are defended and enforced."
Westerns typically conclude in a singular act of violence that, Slotkin argues, recapitulates America's violent frontier past and offers a
justification for the use of righteous violence in the contemporary
world. Metaphors of western violence—showdowns, hired guns, last
stands—permeated American politics in the twentieth century.
"Would a Wyatt Earp stop at the 38th Parallel in Korea when the
rustlers were escaping with his herd?" wrote a political commentator
in the 1950s. "Would a Marshal Dillon refuse to allow his deputies to
use shotguns for their own defense because of the terrible nature of
the weapon itself? Ha!"[10]

The important role that the history of the West has played in the
"official ideology" of modern America underlines the importance of a
new historical vision that speaks to the needs of our own time. In her

contribution to *Under an Open Sky: Rethinking America's Western Past* (1992), a collection of essays in honor of western historian Howard R. Lamar of Yale University, Sarah Deutsch calls for "a new narrative form more appropriate to a pluralistic concept of history." In that same collection, George Miles observes that in rethinking the Indian past over several decades, historians have tended to depict Indians and whites in antithetical terms, making it difficult "to imagine an approach in which Indian history can be incorporated into the mainstream of American historiography." But because both groups contributed to the making of the West, he argues, historians interested in a common narrative need to become more attentive to interchange rather than conflict. Jay Gitlin suggests the necessity of analyzing the contrasts between the frontiers created by different European colonial powers in North America. "The Spanish Empire evolved as an amalgam of people and places, and Native American communities had standing in that heterogeneous polity," while the French, with their isolated communities and their reliance on the fur trade, "had no choice but to recognize the sovereignty of Indian tribal communities and observe the boundaries of legal jurisdiction." Looking elsewhere besides the British-Indian frontier reveals a rich history of consort as well as conflict.[11]

Historians of western women are also building on prior scholarship. Peggy Pascoe carefully acknowledges the contribution of the first wave of western women's history, while noting its rather narrow preoccupation with "westering," a Turnerian view if there ever was one. "Now that it is impossible to believe that there is only one cultural theme in American history," she writes, "we're struggling to figure out how to write a history that does justice to them all." She argues for a focus on western women who were "intercultural brokers, mediators between two or more very different cultural groups," pointing to the work of Sylvia Van Kirk on women in fur trade society and of Sarah Deutsch on gender and ethnicity in the Southwest. I would add Pascoe's own examination of the relationships of Anglo-American women reformers to Omaha Indian women, polygamous Mormon wives, and Chinese prostitutes.[12]

Another theme commanding considerable attention these days is the history of the urban and twentieth-century West, something the Turnerians ignored because of their focus on the closing of the rural continental frontier at the end of the last century. Here, too, today's western historians can look to a legacy of challenge to Turnerian views. During the 1890s, as the frontier thesis began to work its way into the historical imagination of this country, Adna F. Weber produced the first statistical study of the growth of American cities, showing that the West "was more heavily urban" than any other region except the Northeast. Noting the urban-rural dynamic at the heart of western settlement and development, he pointed out that "a Mississippi Valley empire rising suddenly into being without its Chicago and smaller centres of distribution is almost inconceivable." American western historians rediscovered the urban dimension in the postwar period, making it possible, as Carey McWilliams argued in 1949, to see "the West from a new point of view: from its centers, not its fringes; from the places where its interests are articulated, not where they are most dispersed." Weber's and McWilliam's suggestions have been fully realized with the publication of William Cronon's *Nature's Metropolis: Chicago and the Great West* (1991).[13]

Focusing on the urban-rural connection breaks the distinction between "old West" and "new West," with a divide at the "closing" of the frontier in 1890. When Patricia Limerick rightly insists on the continuity of western history across the centuries to the present she is repeating a call issued by western historians from James Malin to John Caughey, who twenty years ago urged his colleagues to end their "self-imposed imprisonment in the early and antique West." But problems of periodization remain. As Michael P. Malone argues in *Trails: Toward a New Western History*, Turner may have misidentified the wrenching changes of the 1890s as a final closing of the frontier, but he was surely correct in identifying the period as one of major transition in the relationship of the West to the nation, just as the expansionist 1840s had been an earlier watershed decade. A consensus has also developed among today's western historians that another such transition occurred during the period from 1933 to 1945, when massive federal infusions of capital transformed the region into an economic and cultural pacesetter for the rest of the nation. Gerald Nash makes this argument most forcefully in his influential books on the twentieth century West.[14]

Bernard DeVoto was among the first to recognize that World War II had transformed the West. "New Deal measures, war installations, and war industries have given the West a far greater and more widely distributed prosperity than it has ever had before," he wrote in 1946; "the ancient Western dream of an advanced industrial economy . . . is brighter than it has ever been before." But while the war certainly transformed southern California and other urban centers, the western interior remained a hinterland controlled by metropolitan elites. "Most western men and women may still be paying economic tribute today," writes Michael E. McGerr in *Under an Open Sky*, "but now they are paying more of it to other westerners."[15]

Turner portrayed the West as the region of self-reliance, but in his new survey of western history, *"It's Your Misfortune and None of My Own": A New History of the American West* (1991), Richard White arrestingly argues that "more than any other region" the West "has been historically a dependency of the federal government." Before the Civil War, Washington's power was subordinate to the states. Only in the territorial West, therefore, was the federal government really able to flex its muscles. The Bureau of Indian Affairs, the Land Office, and the Interior Department were primarily western agencies; the Army's principal mission was supervising Indian removal and waging the war of territorial conquest against Mexico. The West, in one of White's most memorable phrases, was "the kindergarten of the American state."

views become evident, for example, in the ways the two handle the problem of "suitcase farmers," the westerners who commute between their rural acres and their residences in town. Worster argues that such a pattern encourages "an exploitative relationship with the earth." Stegner suggests that the suitcase farmer's adaptation is "as natural as the mobility of the buffalo," an example of how "as we have gone about modifying the western landscape, it has been at work modifying us." Differences like these are owed to fundamental assumptions. Worster condemns the ethical perspective that "has made man the measure of all things." I hear the warning about anthropocentrism issuing from the environmentalists, but I find myself in agreement with Stegner, who writes wisely, "I know no way to look at the world, settled or wild, except through my own human eyes. I know that it wasn't created especially for my use, but I am the only instrument that I have access to by which I can enjoy the world and try to understand it."[20]

But Worster is fair enough to reflect on some of the limitations of his approach. "We do need a better story than the one we've been telling about the West," he writes, "if nothing else than to save us from gloom and excessive pessimism." In the end, he suggests a historical study that seems to move closer to Malin's concerns: "We need a new past, one with the struggle for adaptation as its main narrative, one that regards successful adaptation as a kind of heroism too."[21]

Perhaps the theme that sparks the most debate today is the old Turnerian matter of West and frontier considered as place and process. Worster counts himself among those arguing strongly for place, for a regional approach. He adheres to Webb's declaration that "the heart of the West is a desert, unqualified and absolute." "I know in my bones," writes Worster, "that Webb was right." All the West, of course, is not desert, but aridity has played a shaping role on the region as a whole. Consider, for instance, the role of river engineering in the Pacific

Northwest, or the impact of water-hungry southern California on the water-rich northern portion of the state. In Webb's phrase, the American West is an oasis civilization, but developers have often created those oases by diverting water from somewhere else. Other traits help define the region: the extraordinary control over land and resources exercised by the federal government, the continuing dependency on extractive industries with a resulting boom-and-bust economy, and the largest populations of Hispanics, Indians, and Asians in the country. In addition, as Michael P. Malone points out, "a major part of the region's shared cultural heritage lies in the drama and recency of the frontier's passing." To objections that such traits fail to add up to a coherent regional identity, Limerick responds sensibly that "judged by equally stern standards, very few regions—and fewer nations—would qualify as genuine units of society or units of study."[22]

Problems arise not so much from the loose regional boundaries of today's West, but from the contingency of the term *West* itself. Moving back through the American past, it refers to ever more eastward regions of the continent: to Arkansas, Missouri, and Iowa before the Civil War, when Americans considered the West of today to be "the Far West"; to the Old Northwest and Old Southwest territories at the end of the eighteenth century; to Kentucky and Tennessee during the American Revolution. Turner used the phrase "the Great West" to encompass them all. But the new western regionalists have no patience with such historically mobile definitions. "If 'the West' is sometimes in Massachusetts, sometimes in Florida, sometimes in Kentucky, sometimes in Illinois, sometimes in California, sometimes in Colorado," says Limerick, "then what on earth is a 'western American historian?' "[23]

Another group of western historians answers by arguing for a revised concept of the frontier—by no means does regionalism command a consensus these days. Indeed, say the editors of *Under an Open Sky*, the paradox of process and place is "the central problem" of western history. "The West may be the region lying somewhere beyond the Mississippi River, but it is also the experience of going there." In this view, western history is the study of "the Great West," with special attention to the "last" West in the vast and arid trans-Mississippi region, an approach that obviously owes a great deal to Turner. "We share his belief that a comparative study of parallel regional changes—'frontier processes'—has much to offer," they write, for "without it, regional history loses much of its broader significance." Where their model differs from Turner's is in the nature of those processes, which they characterize as a series of open-ended transformations carrying no imperial implications about progress.[24]

What I find most inspiring about Turner's work is his engagement in the issues of his time. Clearly, one of the dangers of present-minded history can be its insensitivity to a consideration of the past on its own terms. Turner's concern with the big issues of his day energized his history, but his use of the word *frontier* itself illustrates just such an absence of historicism. For him the American frontier was the "outer margin" of white settlement, and his work leaves the impression that it had always been so defined. But *frontier* enjoyed three centuries of usage before Turner, with a range of meanings far richer than he allowed. The observation of a reporter in 1825, for example, that the American frontier "was literally alive with a floating population," suggests that the density of settlement had relatively little to do with earlier definitions. Indeed, before the second half of the nineteenth century, Americans understood frontiers to be borderlands between peoples or nations. Across the western border of the nation lay Indian country, lands inhabited by independent peoples with their own sovereignty and their own homelands. The frontier was the region of encounter in between, an area of contest but also of consort between cultures. As John T. Juricek of Emory University pointed out a number of years ago in a brilliant article on the American usage of *frontier*, it was only the practical elimination of Indian country as a political force that made possible Turner's erasure of the traditional transactional meanings.[25]

The colonization of North America created a multidimensional world inhabited by Indians and settlers of varied ethnic backgrounds, as well as people of mixed ancestry, the offspring of this messy colonial process. The merger of peoples and cultures—what in Mexico was known as *mestizaje*, in New France as *métissage*—has characterized the history of the frontiers of all of North America. The notion of the frontier as "a territory or zone of interpenetration between two previously distinct societies," was first fully articulated by Howard Lamar and Leonard Thompson in their influential collection *The Frontier in History: North America and Southern Africa Compared* (1981). Since then historians of the American West have rediscovered what Richard White calls the "common world" of natives and colonists. From the villages of the Southwest to the towns of the Mississippi and Ohio Valleys, from the outposts of the Hudson's Bay Company to the forts of the Russians on the Pacific, "it was impossible to find a social world in which Indians did not play intimate and essential roles," White writes. "Indians might be abused and oppressed, but Indians mattered." Among the new and exciting works that explore the common world, Ramón Gutiérrez writes of the complex Spanish-Indian relationships of New Mexico, Janet Lecompte of the marriages *à la façon du pays* between fur trappers and Indian women in the southern Rockies, Daniel Unser of the "network of cross-cultural interaction" that characterized the lower Mississippi Valley in the eighteenth century.[26]

In the belief that the term *frontier* is compromised by the years of Turnerian usage, White is careful not to use it in *"It's Your Misfortune."* In *Legacy of Conquest*, Patricia Limerick dismisses it as an "unsubtle concept for a subtle world." But David J. Weber, whose *The Spanish Frontier in North America* (1992) has quickly become the standard historical work on the borderlands, argues that "abandoning the idea of the frontier and making the West as *place* the center" threatens to drain away "the drama of life on the *edges* where people and places meet." The frontier, writes historian Stephen Aron, was the intersection where peoples came together—to trade, to fight, to procreate, to preach contrary conceptions of the good life, to restore old worlds, and to make sense of new worlds. . . . As everyone knows, intersections can be dangerous places, especially for historians who enter without first looking in all directions. With proper precautions, however, intersections make the most interesting history.

The word *frontier* is not about to go away, for it will always hold a privileged place in the American cultural lexicon. By refusing to contest its meaning with our new understanding of the past, historians simply concede its use to others who continue to believe in, or perhaps long for, imperialist chronicles.[27]

Turner studied the frontier not merely because it was his special area of interest, but foremost because he believed its history could illuminate the broader story of America. The power of the frontier thesis derived from its commitment to the study of what it has meant to be American. That is part of the Turnerian view we would do well to preserve. But the Turnerian interpretation of western expansion read back into the past both the assurance and the arrogance of the victors in a centuries-long campaign of conquest. Turner made that victory seem inevitable, but the history of the American West now being written serves to remind us that there was nothing smooth about it at all—that the victory of one people was usually at the expense of another. The deeper history of the frontier that now opens to us is rich with the stories of the diverse peoples who tried to find a place in the American West. It offers cautionary tales as well as ones of inspiration. Just as Turner's frontier thesis responded to his perception of the needs of the America of a century ago, so this new history of the frontier speaks to the issues and struggles of our own time.

N O T E S

Introduction

1. William Appleman Williams, "The Frontier Thesis and American Foreign Policy," in *History as a Way of Learning* (New York, 1973), 142; William N. Davis quoted in Gerald D. Nash, *Creating the West: Historical Interpretations, 1890–1990* (Albuquerque, 1991), 74.

2. Ray Allen Billington, *Frederick Jackson Turner: Historian, Scholar, Teacher* (New York, 1973), 126, and *The Genesis of the Frontier Thesis: A Study in Historical Creativity* (San Marino, Calif., 1971), 172.

3. Wilbur R. Jacobs, *The Historical World of Frederick Jackson Turner: With Selections from his Correspondence* (New Haven, 1968), 154–55; Billington, *Turner*, 196.

4. Jacobs, *Historical World*, 136–37.

5. Frank J. Popper and Deborah E. Popper, "Yo, Pioneers! Guess What? The Western Frontier Is Coming Back Strong," *Washington Post*, September 5, 1993.

6. Jacobs, *Historical World*, 161.

7. Fish quoted in William Appleman Williams, *The Roots of the Modern American Empire: A Study of the Growth and Shaping of Social Consciousness in a Marketplace Society* (New York, 1969), 360; Wilson and Rockefeller quoted in Williams, "The Frontier Thesis and American Foreign Policy," 148–49, 155; Roosevelt quoted in Richard Slotkin, *Gunfighter Nation: The Myth of the Frontier in Twentieth-Century America* (New York, 1992), 106.

8. Slotkin, *Gunfighter Nation*, 58–59.

9. Richard Hofstader, *The Progressive Historians: Turner, Beard, Parrington* (New York, 1969), 110–11; William Appelman Williams, *Empire as a Way of Life* (New York, 1980).

1. The Significance of History (1891)

1. James E. Thorold Rogers, *The Economic Interpretation of History* (New York, 1889).

2. The Significance of the Frontier in American History (1893)

1. "Abridgment of Debates of Congress," v, p. 706.

2. Bancroft (1860 ed.), iii, pp. 344, 345, citing Logan MSS.; [Mitchell] "Contest in America," etc. (1752), p. 237.

3. Kercheval, "History of the Valley"; Bernheim, "German Settlements in the Carolinas"; Winsor, "Narrative and Critical History of America," v, p. 304; Colonial Records of North Carolina, iv, p. xx; Weston, "Documents Connected with the History of South Carolina," p. 82; Ellis and Evans, "History of Lancaster County, Pa.," chs. iii, xxvi.

4. Parkman, "Pontiac," ii; Griffis, "Sir William Johnson," p. 6; Simms's "Frontiersmen of New York."

5. Monette, "Mississippi Valley," i, p. 311.

6. Wis. Hist. Cols., xi, p. 50; Hinsdale, "Old Northwest," p. 121; Burke, "Oration on Conciliation," Works (1872 ed.), i, p. 473.

7. Roosevelt, "Winning of the West," and citations there given; Cutler's "Life of Cutler."

8. Scribner's Statistical Atlas, xxxviii, pl. 13; McMaster, "Hist. of People of U.S.," i, pp. 4, 60, 61; Imlay and Filson, "Western Territory of America" (London, 1793); Rochefoucault-Liancourt, "Travels Through the United States of North America" (London, 1799); Michaux's "Journal," in *Proceedings, American Philosophical Society*, xxvi, No. 129; Forman, "Narrative of a Journey Down the Ohio and Mississippi in 1780–'90" (Cincinnati, 1888); Bartram, "Travels Through North Carolina," etc. (London, 1792); Pope, "Tour Through the Southern and Western Territories," etc. (Richmond, 1792); Weld, "Travels Through the States of North America" (London, 1799); Baily, "Journal of a Tour in the Unsettled States of North America, 1796–'97" (London, 1856); Pennsylvania Magazine of History, July, 1886; Winsor, "Narrative and Critical History of America," vii, pp. 491, 492, citations.

9. Scribner's Statistical Atlas, xxxix.

10. Turner, "Character and Influence of the Indian Trade in Wisconsin" (Johns Hopkins University Studies, Series ix), pp. 61 ff.

11. Monette, "History of the Mississippi Valley," ii; Flint, "Travels and Residence in Mississippi," Flint, "Geography and History of the Western States," "Abridgment of Debates of Congress," vii, pp. 397, 398, 404; Holmes, "Account of the U.S."; Kingdom, "America and the British Colonies" (London, 1820); Grund, "Americans," ii, chs. i, iii, vi (although writing in 1836, he treats of conditions that grew out of western advance from the era of 1820 to that time); Peck, "Guide for Emigrants" (Boston, 1831); Darby, "Emigrants' Guide to Western and Southwestern States and Territories"; Dana, "Geographical Sketches in the Western Country"; Kinzie, "Waubun"; Keating, "Narrative of Long's Expedition"; Schoolcraft, "Discovery of the Sources of the Mississippi River," "Travels in the Central Portions of the Mississippi Valley," and "Lead Mines of the Missouri"; Andreas, "History of Illinois," i, 86–99; Hurlbut,

"Chicago Antiquities"; McKenney, "Tour to the Lakes"; Thomas, "Travels Through the Western Country," etc. (Auburn, N.Y., 1819).

12. Darby, "Emigrants' Guide," pp. 272 ff; Benton, "Abridgment of Debates," vii, p. 397.

13. De Bow's *Review*, iv, p. 254; xvii, p. 428.

14. Grund, "Americans," ii, p. 8.

15. Peck, "New Guide to the West" (Cincinnati, 1848), ch. iv; Parkman, "Oregon Trail"; Hall, "The West" (Cincinnati, 1848); Pierce, "Incidents of Western Travel"; Murray, "Travels in North America"; Lloyd, "Steamboat Directory" (Cincinnati, 1856); "Forty Days in a Western Hotel" (Chicago), in *Putnam's Magazine*, December, 1894; Mackay, "The Western World," ii, ch. ii, iii; Meeker, "Life in the West"; Bogen, "German in America" (Boston, 1851); Olmstead, "Texas Journey"; Greeley, "Recollections of a Busy Life"; Schouler, "History of the United States," v, 261–267; Peyton, "Over the Alleghanies and Across the Prairies" (London, 1870); Loughborough, "The Pacific Telegraph and Railway" (St. Louis, 1849); Whitney, "Project for a Railroad to the Pacific" (New York, 1849); Peyton, "Suggestions on Railroad Communication with the Pacific, and the Trade of China and the Indian Islands"; Benton, "Highway to the Pacific" (a speech delivered in the U.S. Senate, December 16, 1850).

16. A writer in *The Home Missionary* (1850), p. 239, reporting Wisconsin conditions, exclaims: "Think of this, people of the enlightened East. What an example, to come from the very frontier of civilization!" But one of the missionaries writes: "In a few years Wisconsin will no longer be considered as the West, or as an outpost of civilization, any more than Western New York, or the Western Reserve."

17. Bancroft (H. H.), "History of California, History of Oregon, and Popular Tribunals"; Shinn, "Mining Camps."

18. See the suggestive paper by Prof. Jesse Macy, "The Institutional Beginnings of a Western State."

19. Shinn, "Mining Camps."

20. Compare Thorpe, in *Annals American Academy of Political and Social Science*, September, 1891; Bryce, "American Commonwealth" (1888), ii, p. 689.

21. Loria, Analisi della Proprieta Capitalista, ii, p. 15.

22. Compare "Observations on the North American Land Company," London, 1796, pp. xv, 144; Logan, "History of Upper South Carolina," i, pp. 149–151; Turner, "Character and Influence of Indian Trade in Wisconsin," p. 18; Peck, "New Guide for Emigrants" (Boston, 1837), ch. iv; "Compendium Eleventh Census," i, p. xl.

23. See *post*, for illustrations of the political accompaniments of changed industrial conditions.

24. But Lewis and Clark were the first to explore the route from the Missouri to the Columbia.

25. "Narrative and Critical History of America," viii, p. 10; Sparks' "Washington Works," ix, pp. 303, 327; Logan, "History of Upper South Carolina," i; McDonald, "Life of Kenton," p. 72; Cong. Record, xxiii, p. 57.

26. On the effect of the fur trade in opening the routes of migration, see the author's "Character and Influence of the Indian Trade in Wisconsin."

27. Lodge, "English Colonies," p. 152 and citations; Logan, "Hist. of Upper South Carolina," i, p. 151.

28. Flint, "Recollections," p. 9.

29. See Monette, "Mississippi Valley," i, p. 344.

30. Coues, "Lewis and Clark's Expedition," i, pp. 2, 253–259; Benton, in Cong. Record, xxiii, p. 57.

31. Hehn, *Das Salz* (Berlin, 1873).

32. Col. Records of N.C., v, p. 3.

33. Findley, "History of the Insurrection in the Four Western Counties of Pennsylvania in the Year 1794" (Philadelphia, 1796), p. 35.

34. Hale, "Daniel Boone" (pamphlet).

35. Compare Baily, "Tour in the Unsettled Parts of North America" (London, 1856), pp. 217–219, where a similar analysis is made for 1796. See also Collot, "Journey in North America" (Paris, 1826), p. 109; "Observations on the North American Land Company" (London, 1796), pp. xv, 144; Logan, "History of Upper South Carolina."

36. "Spotswood Papers," in Collections of Virginia Historical Society, i, ii.

37. [Burke], "European Settlements" (1765 ed.), ii, p. 200.

38. Everest, in "Wisconsin Historical Collections," xii, pp. 7 ff.

39. Weston, "Documents connected with History of South Carolina," p. 61.

40. See, for example, the speech of Clay, in the House of Representatives, January 30, 1824.

41. See the admirable monograph by Prof. H. B. Adams, "Maryland's Influence on the Land Cessions"; and also President Welling, in Papers American Historical Association, iii, p. 411.

42. Adams' Memoirs, ix, pp. 247, 248.

43. Author's article in The Ægis (Madison, Wis.), November 4, 1892.

44. Compare Roosevelt, "Thomas Benton," ch. i.

45. Political Science Quarterly, ii, p. 457. Compare Sumner, "Alexander Hamilton," chs. ii–vii.

46. Compare Wilson, "Division and Reunion," pp. 15, 24.

47. On the relation of frontier conditions to Revolutionary taxation, see Sumner, "Alexander Hamilton," ch. iii.

48. I have refrained from dwelling on the lawless characteristics of the frontier, because they are sufficiently well known. The gambler and desperado, the regulators of the Carolinas and the vigilantes of California, are types of that line of scum that the waves of advancing civilization bore before them, and of the growth of spontaneous organs of authority where legal authority was absent. Compare Barrows, "United States of Yesterday and To-

morrow"; Shinn, "Mining Camps"; and Bancroft, "Popular Tribunals." The humor, bravery, and rude strength, as well as the vices of the frontier in its worst aspect, have left traces on American character, language, and literature, not soon to be effaced.

49. Debates in the Constitutional Convention, 1829–1830.

50. [McCrady] Eminent and Representative Men of the Carolinas, i, p. 43; Calhoun's Works, i, pp. 401–406.

51. Speech in the Senate, March 1, 1825; Register of Debates, i, 721.

52. Plea for the West (Cincinnati, 1835), pp. 11 ff.

53. Colonial travelers agree in remarking on the phlegmatic characteristics of the colonists. It has frequently been asked how such a people could have developed that strained nervous energy now characteristic of them. Compare Sumner, "Alexander Hamilton," p. 98, and Adams, "History of the United States," i, p. 60; ix, pp. 240, 241. The transition appears to become marked at the close of the War of 1812, a period when interest centered upon the development of the West, and the West was noted for restless energy. Grund, "Americans," ii, ch. i.

3. The Problem of the West (1896)

1. Charles Eliot Norton.

2. The present States of Ohio, Indiana, Illinois, Michigan, and Wisconsin.

3. Written in the year of Mr. Bryan's first presidential campaign.

5. Pioneer Ideals and the State University (1910)

1. Printed from an earlier version; since published in his "Songs from Books," p. 93, under the title, "The Voortrekker." Even fuller of insight into the idealistic side of the frontier is his "Explorer," in "Collected Verse," p. 19.

2. Written in 1910.

6. Social Forces in American History (1910)

1. Van Hise, "Conservation of Natural Resources," pp. 23, 24.

2. *Atlantic Monthly*, December 1908, vii, p. 745.

3. I have outlined this subject in various essays, including the article on "Sectionalism" in McLaughlin and Hart, "Cyclopedia of Government."

4. It is not impossible that they may ultimately replace the State as the significant administrative and legislative units. There are strong evidences of this tendency, such as the organization of the Federal Reserve districts, and proposals for railroad administration by regions.

5. See R. G. Wellington, "Public Lands, 1820–1840"; G. M. Stephenson, "Public Lands, 1841–1862"; J. Ise, "Forest Policy."

6. Professor J. B. Clark, in Commons, ed., "Documentary History of American Industrial Society," I. 43–44.

8. Middle Western Pioneer Democracy (1918)

1. See De Tocqueville's interesting appreciation of this American phenomenon.

Afterword

1. Miriam Horn, "How the West Was Really Won," *U.S. News & World Report*, May 21, 1990.

2. Donald Worster quoted in T. R. Reid, "Shootout in Academia over History of U.S. West," *Washington Post*, October 10, 1989; Donald Worster, *Under Western Skies: Nature and History in the American West* (New York, 1992), 8; Martin Ridge, "Frederick Jackson Turner and His Ghost: The Writing of Western History," *Proceedings of the American Antiquarian Society* n.s. 101 (1991): 76; Ray Allen Billington and Martin Ridge, *Westward Expansion: A History of the American Frontier* (New York, 1949; 5th ed., 1982); Gerald D.

Nash, "Point of View: One Hundred Years of Western History," *Journal of the West* 32 (January 1993): 4.

3. Dewey and Beard quoted in Nash, *Creating the West*, 22, 24.

4. John C. Almack, "The Shibboleth of the Frontier," *Historical Outlook* 16 (May 1925): 197–202; Paul Wallace Gates, "The Homestead Law in an Incongruous Land System," *American Historical Review* 41 (1936): 652–81; Isaiah Bowman, *The Pioneer Fringe* (New York, 1931); Louis B. Wright, "American Democracy and the Frontier," *Yale Review* 22 (1930): 349–65; Fred A. Shannon, "The Homestead Act and Labor Surplus," *American Historical Review* 41 (1936): 637–51; Mody C. Boatright, "The Myth of Frontier Individualism," *Southwestern Social Science Quarterly* 22 (1941): 14–32; George Wilson Pierson, "The Frontier and American Institutions: A Criticism of the Frontier Theory," *New England Quarterly* 16 (June 1942): 224–255.

5. Herbert Eugene Bolton, "The Epic of Greater America," *American Historical Review* 38 (1933): 448–74; Walter Prescott Webb, "The American West: Perpetual Mirage," *Harper's* 214 (May 1957): 25–31; James C. Malin, "The Turnover of Farm Population in Kansas," *Kansas Historical Quarterly* 4 (1935): 339–72, and "The Adaptation of the Agricultural System to Sub-Humid Environment," *Agricultural History* 10 (1936): 118–41; Carey McWilliams, "Introduction," in *Rocky Mountain Cities*, ed. Ray B. West (New York, 1949); Henry Nash Smith, *Virgin Land: The American West as Symbol and Myth* (Cambridge, Mass., 1950); Joseph Kinsey Howard, *Strange Empire: Louis Riel and the Métis People* (New York, 1952); Earl Pomeroy, "Towards a Reorientation of Western History: Continuity and Environment," *Mississippi Valley Historical Review* 41 (1955): 579–600; Bernard DeVoto, "The West: A Plundered Province," *Harper's* 169 (August 1934): 355–64. See the essays by Donald E. Worster on Bolton, Elliott West on Webb, Allan Bogue on Malin, Michael P. Malone on Pomeroy, and Lee Clark Mitchell on Smith in *Writing Western History: Essays on Major Western Historians*, ed. Richard W. Etulain (Albuquerque, 1991). William N. Davis quoted in Nash, *Creating the West*, 74.

6. Patricia Nelson Limerick, "The Trails to Santa Fe: The Unleashing of the Western Public Intellectual," in *Trails: Toward a New Western History*, ed.

Patricia Nelson Limerick, Clyde A. Milner II, and Charles E. Rankin (Lawrence, Kan., 1991), 61.

7. Worster, *Under Western Skies*, 11–12; A. Irving Hallowell, "The Backwash of the Frontier: The Impact of the Indian on American Culture," in *The Frontier in Perspective*, ed. Walker D. Wyman and Clifton B. Kroeber (Madison, 1957); Jack D. Forbes, "The Indian in the West: A Challenge for Historians," *Arizona and the West* 1 (1959): 206–15, and "Frontiers in American History," *Journal of the West* 1 (1962): 63–73; David M. Potter, "American Women and the American Character," [first published 1962] reprinted in *History and American Society: Essays of David M. Potter*, ed. Don E. Fehrenbacher (New York, 1973); Roger Daniels, "Westerners from the East: Oriental Immigrants Reappraised," *Pacific Historical Review* 35 (1966): 373–83; Richard Maxwell Brown, "Historical Patterns of Violence in America," in *Violence in America: Historical and Comparative Perspectives*, ed. Hugh Davis Graham and Ted Robert Gurr (New York, 1969); Wilbur Jacobs, "British Colonial Attitudes and Policies towards the Indian in the American Colonies," in *Attitudes of Colonial Powers toward the American Indian*, ed. Howard Peckham and Charles Gibson (Salt Lake City, 1969), and "The Great Despoliation: Environmental Themes in American History," *Pacific Historical Review* 47 (1978): 1–26; Robert V. Hine, *The American West: An Interpretive History* (Boston, 1973; 2nd ed., 1984).

8. Turner quoted in Theodore Roosevelt, *The Winning of the West: Selections*, ed. Harvey Wish (New York, 1962), xxi; Warren I. Susman, "History and the American Intellectual: The Uses of a Usable Past," in *Culture as History: The Transformation of American Society in the Twentieth Century* (New York, 1984).

9. Roosevelt quoted in Lee Benson, "The Historical Background of Turner's Frontier Essay," *Agricultural History* 25 (1951): 80.

10. Slotkin, *Gunfighter Nation*, 352; David Shea Teeple in *The American Mercury* (1958), quoted in J. Fred MacDonald, *Who Shot the Sheriff? The Rise and Fall of the Television Western* (New York, 1987), 109.

11. Sarah Deutsch, "Landscape of Enclaves: Race Relations in the West, 1865–1990"; George Miles, "To Hear an Old Voice: Rediscovering Native Americans

in American History"; and Jay Gitlin, "On the Boundaries of Empire: Connecting the West to Its Imperial Past," all in *Under an Open Sky: Rethinking America's Western Past*, ed. William Cronon, George Miles, and Jay Gitlin (New York, 1992), 112, 54, 75.

12. Peggy Pascoe, "Western Women at the Cultural Crossroads," in *Trails: Toward a New Western History*, 56, 55; Sylvia Van Kirk, *"Many Tender Ties": Women in Fur Trade Society in Western Canada* (1980; reprinted Norman, Okla., 1983); Sarah Deutsch, *No Separate Refuge: Culture, Class, and Gender on an Anglo-Hispanic Frontier in the American Southwest* (New York, 1987); Peggy Pascoe, *Relations of Rescue: The Search for Female Moral Authority in the American West, 1874–1939* (New York, 1990).

13. Weber and McWilliams quoted in Nash, *Creating the West*, 160–61, 176; William Cronon, *Nature's Metropolis: Chicago and the Great West* (New York, 1991).

14. Caughey quoted in Nash, *Creating the West*, 97; Patricia Nelson Limerick, "What on Earth Is the New Western History," and Michael P. Malone, "Beyond the Last Frontier: Toward a New Approach to Western American History," in *Trails: Toward a New Western History*, 86, 158; Gerald Nash, *The American West Transformed: The Impact of the Second World War* (Bloomington, Ind., 1985), and *World War II and the West: Reshaping the Economy* (Lincoln, Nebr., 1990).

15. DeVoto quoted in Nash, *Creating the West*, 116, 118–19; Michael E. McGerr, "Is There a Twentieth-Century West?" in *Under an Open Sky*, 244; also see DeVoto, "The West: A Plundered Province," and "The Anxious West," *Harper's* 193 (December 1946); Walter Prescott Webb, *Divided We Stand: The Crisis of a Frontierless Democracy* (New York, 1937); and Joseph Kinsey Howard, *Montana: High, Wide, and Handsome* (New Haven, 1943).

16. Richard White, *"It's Your Misfortune and None of My Own": A New History of the American West* (Norman, Okla., 1991), 57, 155.

17. Worster, *Under Western Skies*, 15.

18. Worster, *Under Western Skies*, 94–95; Richard White, *Land Use, Environment, and Social Change: The Shaping of Island County, Washington* (Seattle, 1980); Cronon, *Nature's Metropolis*; for a selection of Malin's work see James C. Malin, *History and Ecology: Studies of the Grassland*, ed. Robert P. Swierenga (Lincoln, Nebr., 1984).

19. Worster, *Under Western Skies*, 15, 77; Richard White, "Trashing the Trails," in *Trails: Toward a New Western History*, 32.

20. Worster, *Under Western Skies*, 15–16; Wallace Stegner, *Where the Bluebird Sings to the Lemonade Springs: Living and Writing in the West* (New York, 1992), 52.

21. Worster, *Under Western Skies*, 253.

22. Webb quoted in McGerr, "Is There a Twentieth-Century West?" 246; Worster, *Under Western Skies*, 24; Malone, "Beyond the Last Frontier," 150; Limerick, "Trails to Santa Fe," 70.

23. Limerick, "Making the Most of Words: Verbal Activity and Western America," in *Under an Open Sky*, 168.

24. William Cronon, George Miles, and Jay Gitlin, "Becoming West: Toward a New Meaning for Western History," in *Under an Open Sky*, 26, 6.

25. John T. Juricek, "American Usage of the Word 'Frontier' from Colonial Times to Frederick Jackson Turner," *Proceedings of the American Philosophical Society* 110 (1966): 10–34, quote on 16.

26. Howard Lamar and Leonard Thompson, "Comparative Frontier History," in *The Frontier in History: North America and Southern Africa Compared*, ed. Lamar and Thompson (New Haven, 1981), 7; White, "*It's Your Misfortune*," 85; Ramón Gutiérrez, *When Jesus Came, The Corn Mothers Went Away: Marriage, Sexuality, and Power in New Mexico, 1500–1846* (Stanford, 1991); Janet Lecompte, *Pueblo, Hardscrabble, Greenhorn: The Upper Arkansas, 1832–1856* (Norman, Okla., 1978); Daniel H. Unser, Jr., *Indians, Settlers, & Slaves in a Frontier Exchange Economy: The Lower Mississippi Valley Before 1783* (Chapel Hill, 1992).

27. Limerick, *Legacy of Conquest*, 25; Weber comment in *"The Legacy of Conquest*, by Patricia Nelson Limerick: A Panel of Appraisal," *Western Historical Quarterly* 20 (1989): 317; David J. Weber, *The Spanish Frontier in North America* (New Haven, 1992); Stephen Aron, "Lessons in Conquest: Towards a Greater Western History," *Pacific Historical Review* 63 (1994).